Gree.. Economics Reader

27/03/2011

Photo : Miriam Kennet.

Green Economics: a new way of looking at the world.
Provisioning for all people everywhere, nature, the planet and its
systems as beneficiaries, not throw away inputs to the conventional
economics machine.

Edited by Miriam Kennet

The Green Economics Institute

2012

ISBN 978 -907543-02-9

Green Economics Reader

The Green Economics Institute: 2010, 2011, and 2012
Registered Office: 6 Strachey Close, Tidmarsh, Reading RG8 8EP
greeneconomicsinstitute@yahoo.com
Selection and editorial matter 2011 and 2012 Miriam Kennet
Typeset by Miriam Kennet
Printed and bound in Great Britain by
Marston Book Services Limited, Didcot

www.greeneconomics.org.uk
greeneconomicsinstitute@yahoo.com

A catalogue record for this book is available from the British Library
ISBN: 978-1-907543-02-9

Preface

Miriam Kennet

Green Economics Institute

greeneconomics.org.uk
greeneconomicsinstitute@yahoo.com

This book is a collection of essays, speeches and articles from The Green Economics Institute (GEI) whose work has given rise to the global movement known as Green Economics and the Green Economy. It was the aim and the achievement of The Green Economics Institute to turn the vision of a few campagners and innovators into a massive global movement for change and one which has beeen taken up by almost all global transnational institutions and almost all governments. In addition it has developed into an accepted and robust new acadmemic discipine which people of all levels of society, from paupers to princes are proud to espouse in public and which has its own academic journal, its own magazine and its own books.. This innovation came from the work of The Green Economics Institute and its network of members and its core team of visionaries and innovators, and is probably the only beacon of hope regularly mentioned for the world economy as a cure for the current instability and downturns. Green Economics is now firmly a global movement for change in the third millennium.

The new discipline of Green Economics is an entirely new and exciting discipline or school of economics which is based on a completely new assessment of the problems, options and solutions available to society to deal with the challenges of the ever more rapidly changing complex, fragile, and vulnerable physical and social environments. It is the one ray of hope for dealing with the related crises- of climate, biodiversity loss, species extinction and the global economic downturn and aiming to preventing poverty and gender imbalance.

Green economics reclaims economics from the preserve of purely quantitative measurement, graphs, statistical data and the assumption of "homo economicus" to create a complex, interdisciplinary, holistic, long term, social science which is informed by qualitative and quantitative data from natural science. Its long-termism describes the evolution of societies within archaeological and palaeontological time frames, which provides a better setting and better tools for understanding such problems as climate change than are offered by current conventions and short term business cycles. Economics is reclaimed as an independent science from business administration studies.

Green Economics is concerned with establishing definitions of an overall well- being and happiness for all people everywhere and the planet and earth systems, rather than deriving simplistic quantitative statistics. The purpose of economics is redefined, positive and normative statements are clearly differentiated and a distinction is made between destruction on the one hand, calculated and hidden as economic "growth" and true growth and abundance of natural resources for people and nature on the other hand.

Green Economics is reworking the philosophy behind economic theory, adding more recent philosophical discourses and ideas of "difference". It builds on its enlightenment roots, adding feminism, postmodernism, and ideas about institutions and scientific investigations. It adds back the social and ethical element to decision making, while acknowledging the pivotal role of women and nature in real wealth creation. Green Economics opposes the simplistic undifferentiated growth imperative and many of the uncritical technical and social methods of economic propositions currently dominating economics but which are implicated in Global Environmental Change (GEC) and poverty. History, time, social and environmental justice are all incorporated back into the discourse to develop a truly "real" social and natural science, together with new learning from environmental science and philosophy.

Key ideas include provisioning for all people everywhere, other species, nature, the planet and its systems, and always considering that everyone and everything on the planet has economics needs, impacts and responsibilities. All decision making and activities are based on the complex mesh of social and environmental justice. Green Economics is the economics of doing and the economics of sharing with everyone and everything on the planet. Humans can't survive on their own – we need each other and we need other species. A Green Economics perspective no longer uses other things on the planet as throw away inputs or resources to the economy but as beneficiaries of the economics of sharing and of economics transactions. This is a unique and innovative stance in economics!

This book is the first collected volume to bring these core ideas to the general reader and to provide an insight into its development, theory and features.

The Green Economics Institute

Photo: Introduction to Green Economics Course at Oxford University:
by Bogusia Igielska

The Green Economics Institute has worked to create a
discipline or school of Economics called "Green Economics" and also to
reform mainstream economics itself into a well-defined goals-based
discipline which provides practical answers to existing and future
problems by incorporating all relevant aspects, knowledge and complex
interactions into a truly holistic understanding of the relevant issues. It
uses complexity, holism, pluralism and interdisciplinary working in
order to widen the scope of economics, adding the science from the
green aspects, and the social ideas from economics discourses. This
new scope for the first time avoids partial explanations or solutions and
also biased and partial perspectives of power elites. According to
economics professor, Jack Reardon from the USA (2007) The Institute
has been very successful in creating a robust academic basis for this
new idea.

The Institute began to influence the methodology of
mainstream economics, according to Professor Tony Lawson of
Cambridge University's Economics Department (2007). It uses trans-
disciplinary and interdisciplinary methods so that it can factor in the
complexity of nature into economics. It seeks to provide all people
everywhere, non human species, the planet and earth systems with a
decent level of well-being based on practical and theoretical
approaches targeting both methodology and knowledge and based a

comprehensive reform of the current economic mainstream. It can, for example, comfortably incorporate glacial issues, climate change and volcanic, seismic and earth sciences into its explanations and thus in this, and many other ways, it is far more complete and reflects reality much more closely than its predecessors on which it builds. The current narrow conventional economic approach using purposely designed methods, is challenged to bring areas and concepts into its scope which have been until now   neglected. Existing outdated or inappropriate propositions and solutions are examined and revised to provide a realistic and more comprehensive understanding of the subject.

The Green Economics Institute argues for economic development based on economic access and decision making for all, including respect for cultural diversity and normative freedom. It does this by bringing together all the interested parties, who want to help in developing this progressive discipline, by inviting them to its events, and conferences and by means of such activities as writing books and publications and using its research, its campaigns and its lobbying and its speeches and lecturing all over the world.

The Green Economics Institute created the first green academic journal *International Journal of Green Economics* with publishers Inderscience and the first green book series *Green and Sustainable Growth, Green Economics and Sustainable Development* with its publishers Gower Management Publishers and Ashgate Academic Press as well as the first Green International College teaching Green Economics.   Our new book series, deals with *Philosophy for the 20th and 21st Century and methodology, realism and critical realism, truth and data.*

In 2011 we have created two more Green Economics Books series, *The Green Economics Reader Series* and the *Green Economics Handbook Series.*

The Green Economics Institute has its own delegation to the Kyoto Protocol, to the RIO + 20 Earth Summit and it was recommend by the UK government as a reviewer on the IPCC. Members of the Green Economics Institute have lectured or worked at Surrey University, the Schumacher College, The University of Bolzano, the Tyrollean Cabinet, via Skype in Thessaloniki, FYRO Macedonia, Turkey, the National Government School in the UK with top Cabinet Officials, at University in Cambridge and Oxford, Transition Towns, Oslo Norway, Liverpool University, Lancaster University, Abuja, Nigeria and Gondar, Ethiopia and attended conferences in many places including Cancun Mexico and Riga, Latvia and appeared on TV and radio in Italy and Tallin in Estonia and the UK and Bangladesh amongst many others and received invitations from President Putin in Russia, the Government and the government and several universities in China and from governments and Princes in several Gulf States as well as parts of the United Nations and the International Labour Organisation!

The consolidation of that spread has led in 2012 to the RIO + 20 Earth Summit being held on Green Economy: Rethinking Growth. As a result of the incredible spread of the ideas of the Institute, the CEO of the Green Economics Institute has just been named in 2011 as one of 100 of the Most Powerful Unseen Women Leaders on the planet who make change, by an NGO in London.

This Reader Book brings these ideas for the first time to a broader group of readers, students, policy makers, academics and campaigners in this ground breaking volume.

The Green Economics Institute Directors
Miriam Kennet UK, Volker Heinemann UK, Germany,and Michelle S. Gale d' Oliviera UK, USA, Brazil
The Green Economics Institute, 6 Strachey Close, Tidmarsh, Reading, RG8 8EP   greeneconomicsinstitute@yahoo.com
www.greeneconomics.org.uk
greeneconomicsinstitute@yahoo.com

Contents

Photographs

Front Cover photo by Miriam Kennet 2011.
Back Cover photo by Frederique at the European Parliament
All other photos by Miriam Kennet, except where stated below
Other photos by Paul Kennet, Kristina Jocuite, Bogusia Igielska
Additionally :
a) Unknown photographer from sustainable development course
Venice for REC Hungary 2009 at Venice International University
b)Tree Hugging in Berlin: 2008 Young Greens in Berlin on a Green
Economics Institute Training Course with The Green Economics
Institute and The Green European Foundation. Photo Iida
Kalmanlehto from Finland.
c) Photo of Youth in Action Certificates: Reading 2011 photo by
Makedonka Petrova American University of FYRO Macedonia

List of Contributors

David Amos
David Amos is a member of St. Peter's College, Oxford University, where he was regarded as the brightest student in his year. He was a consultant at the Green Economics Institute before joining the fast track government economics service. He worked as associate editor of the *International Journal of Green Economics*, and deputy editor of *The Green Economist*. He also holds a Bachelor of Arts degree in Economics & Management from Oxford University. He has previously worked with People & Planet, a UK student campaigning network, on government climate change policy. His research interests include Green Economics, the economics of climate change and the interrelation of development aid and climate change.

Ben Armstrong-Haworth
A researcher in Management at Cass Business School, City University London. Originally preferring the natural and physical sciences at school and sixth form, his undergraduate studies at Birkbeck College, University of London, moved into the social sciences and gained a first class BA (Hons) Management in 2005. This was followed by an MSc Innovation Management & Technology Policy, gained with distinction in 2008, also from Birkbeck College. The core of Ben's research interest is innovation in the low carbon stationary power industry. The focus of his PhD is *The Emergence of Partnering as Part of Innovation*, in which case studies of fuel cell technology firms active in the UK and Germany are being developed to understand how these firms have used partnerships to take their technology from the laboratory to market. His MSc dissertation which looked at *The Increase of Electricity Generation from Renewable Energy Sources in the UK* received an award from the National Endowment for Science, Technology and the Arts. Ben also has broader interests in energy generation, energy economics, means of moderating greenhouse gas emissions and climate change economics. Ben was a student of Miriam Kennet

Sophie Billington
An economist and econometrician at Bristol University. Her main areas of interest are developmental economics and econometrics. Sophie is interested in applied econometrics, econometric theory and the wide ranging and changing approaches to modelling economic problems. She has been instrumental in methodology debates in Green Economics.

Katie Black
A chemist from Leeds University in 2010 and specialises in innovative low-carbon solutions including new solutions for carbon capture and storage. She represented the Green Economics Institute at the COP16 climate change conference in Cancun 2010 taking part in the discussions which led to the agreement and has experience of Africa and of running our low-carbon cycling tour round South-East Asia. She worked at the Green Economics Institute.

Dr Susan Canney

Dr canney has worked on a variety of nature conservation projects in Africa, Asia and Europe (living for several years in Niger and Tanzania) and as a research officer for Sir Crispin Tickell at the Green College Centre for Environmental Policy & Understanding.

With MAs in Natural Sciences, Landscape Design, and Environmental Policy, and a Doctorate for understanding the drivers behind changing human land use and its impact on a protected area in Tanzania, her current research activities are centred on the use of spatial techniques for understanding human impact on ecosystems and wildlife. This understanding is used to find sustainable solutions in order to manage human-wildlife conflict; plan and implement conservation strategy; and develop participatory approaches to conservation management. Current projects include assuring a future for a unique population of elephants in the sub-Sahara of Mali as Project Leader of the WILD Foundation's Mali Elephant Project.

Based in Oxford University's Zoology Department, she teaches global ecology and is particularly interested in the shift in scientific perspective presented by systemic approaches such as Lovelock's Gaia Theory; and in exploring the implications of this shift for society, its institutions, as well as for the individual's experience of Nature. She is the Secretary and a Co-founder of the Earth System Science Special Interest Group of the Geological Society of London, and of the Gaia Network. She teaches on the issues surrounding the notion of valuing nature for the Green Economics Institute and is a member of their Biodiversity Group. She was tutor to Miriam Kennet at Oxford University.

Eleni Courea
Lives in Cyprus but is of Greek, English, Scottish and Indian background. She brings a young scholar's perspective to questions of the importance of geography to green economics. She has participated

it several conferences around the world, including World Individual Public Speaker and Debating Championships in Brisbane, Australia (2011) and The Hague International Model United Nations in the Netherlan*ds (2011). She also organised organised the Youth Voice Conference in Cyprus (2011).* She was the Editor of the *Handbook of Green Economics.*

Henry Cox

Henry Cox Dug for Victory and was in the Home Guard while a schoolboy. Paid work as an Engineer started on analogue, vacuum valve electronics: radio while a conscript in the Army, then 8 years on airborne radar with 9 months in Australia. Changing to digital transistor systems applied to the control of most types of infrastructure, with 7 months in NE India and various short visits to plant. From the Green Gathering of 1983 he has been 'retired' from paid work and now has 70 years experience of gardening, of growing plants on land productively.

Siti Nadiah Ahmad Fuad
A Research Officer at Malaysian Institute of Economics Research (MIER). With a B. Sc (Statistics) from Universiti Teknologi MARA (UiTM), Malaysia. She has been serving MIER for 2 years. She researches in Economic Impact studies for the Government.

Michelle S. Gale de Oliveira
Director of the Green Economics Institute, UK. She studied at International Relations Department at Richmond, the American International University in London (RAIUL), and was SOAS, London University and lives in the remote rainforest in Brazil. She has edited the Green Economics Institute's members' magazine, *The Green Economist,* and was a deputy editor for the International Journal of Green Economics. Her writing has been featured in *Europe's World,* one of the foremost European policy magazines. She lectures and speaks on Environmental and Social Justice, Gender Equity, and International Development from a Green Economics perspective. She is founder/ chair of the Gender Equity Forum. She organised a Green Economics conference on women's unequal pay and poverty in Reading, UK, and lectured on green economics in Berlin, Germany, at retreats in Glastonbury, UK, and and the American University in FYRO Macedeonia. She is a regular speaker at international conferences, and was on the Green Economics Institute's Delegation to Copenhagen COP15 Kyoto Conference and headed up its delegation to Cancun Mexico COP16 Kyoto Conference and represented the GEI at the

United Nations in New York at the launch of the AOSIS Association of Small Island States campaign for 1.5 degrees limit to global warming.

Aija Graudina

Doctor of Economic sciences, she works as an Associate Professor of BA School of Business and Finance (Latvia). Specialization: insurance and reinsurance industry, insurance economy. She is a member of the International Insurance Society (iis) and the Latvian Association of Economics.

Volker Heinemann

An economist who studied at the Universities of Goettingen, Kiel and Nottingham. He is a specialist in international and developing economics, monetary economics and macroeconomic theory and policy. He is author of the book "Die Oekonomie der Zukunft," "The Economy of the Future," a book outlining a green structure for a contemporary economy that accepts the pressing changes that are needed to outdated current economic thinking. He is co-founder and Director and CFO of the Green Economics Institute, a member of the Institute of Chartered Accountants in England and Wales, trained at PWC and other major Institutions and is a Deputy Editor of the International Journal of Green Economics. He is a popular radio and TV speaker in Europe and a former Die Gruenen Councillor.

Meredith Hunter MLA

Meredith is the Leader of the ACT Greens and the Chair of the Climate Change Environment and Water Committee. Prior to entering parliament she was the Non-Executive Director of the ACTION Board, Chair of the Joint Community Government Reference Group, the Youth Homelessness Working Group and the Anti-Poverty ACT Facilitating Group; a board member of ACT Shelter, National Shelter and the Australian Youth Affairs Coalition. She is also an Adjunct Professional Associate, Youth Work, at University of Canberra.

Manan Jain, PGPM student, IIM Shillong

Manan Jain is currently pursuing PGPM from Indian Institute of Management, Shillong. He has worked in Green IT with Hewlett Packard. He has presented innovative green ideas in the annual worldwide technical conference of Hewlett Packard. His professional interests include proposing and bringing newer green technologies to market in order to bring a more sustainable development in the business sector and in society.

Norfaryanti Kamaruddin
A Research Officer at Techno Economics and Policy Laboratory, Institute of Tropical Forestry and Forest Products, Universiti Putra Malaysia (UPM). It has been five years serving UPM as a researcher. Graduated in M.Sc (Agribusiness) in 2004, she has interests in the field of green economics. Being young and enthusiastic, she has involved in various projects specifically in developing kenaf and bio composite industry in Malaysia.

Miriam Kennet
 An economist, environmental scientist and member of Mansfield College, Oxford University, the Environmental Change Institute, Oxford University and the Oxford Union and IPCC. She co-edited "Green Economics, beyond Supply and Demand to Meeting People's Needs", and author of over 100 articles on green economics and stakeholder theory, corporate social responsibility and economics transformation, green jobs, geo engineering and women's unequal pay and poverty, climate change, poverty prevention and biodiversity economics. CEO, director and co-founder of the Green Economics Institute, a member of the Chartered Institute of Purchasing and Supply (MCIPS) and the founder/ editor of the International Journal of Green Economics and The Green Economist, she is a regular trainer, speaker, lecturer and adviser to governments, including the National Government School in the UK. She lectures and speaks on the international stage and many universities around the world and has appeared on radio and TV in many countries, most recently Estonia and Spain, Italy,Belgium and the UK and as well as running a very lively international interns college and regular influential,international green economics conferences and has her own delegation to the Kyoto Process. A UK government recommended reviewer for the IPCC and is reviewer and writer for the International Labour Organisation. She is on the Assembly of the Green European Foundation and on the steering group of the European Network of Political Foundations.

Dr. Natalie West Kharkongor, Assistant Professor, IIM Shillong,India

Dr. Natalie, an Assistant Professor of Economics at IIM Shillong, received the Broad Outlook Learner Teacher Award from the Prime Minister, Dr. Manmohan Singh in 2004. She also received the Rashtriya Gaurav Award with Certificate of Excellence in 2011 in New Delhi. She has presented and published a number of papers. She was the Joint Secretary of North Eastern Economic Association and the Vice President of Meghalaya Economic Association.

Rakesh Kumar

A vice president in Gartner Research, where he specializes in enterprise infrastructure and operations strategies. With more than 23 years of international experience, Kumar is a recognized leader in data center architectures, infrastructure, high availability and operational processes. Kumar is also leading the research in data center power and cooling issues and is an established international authority in environmental and "green" IT strategies. He has worked with the European Union and various governments around the world on energy-related technology issues. Kumar has spent considerable time in India working with many companies and government departments. He is one of the world's foremost experts on the development of core IT infrastructure in India. Kumar joined Gartner in April 2005 with the acquisition of Meta Group, where he was senior vice president and co-research director (EMEA). In this position, apart from his core research areas, he drove changes in the European research organization and was instrumental in delivering Meta Group's leading Operations Excellence transformation program. Before Meta Group, Kumar was EMEA marketing manager for HP's commercial Unix and NT business. He has also held various positions with IBM in software development, sales and consultancy management. Kumar is a part qualified Chartered Accountant, having trained with KPMG.

Bente Teelgard Madeira

Worked in Development Education since 1987 working on issues such as AIDS & Racism, Debt cancellation,the MAI, GATS & EPA's. She was a trustee of Women's Environmental Networkfor 9 years. She is Reading's Fair-trade Townco-ordinator and set up an 'If Women Counted" group as a result of Marilyn Waring's economic analysis.I have spoken as part of the Eco-feminist Network at conferences atInnsbruck University on Water, Women against GATS & Privatisation of the National Health Service in Cologne.

Clive Lord

A founder member of the English and Welsh Greens in 1973, He served as a Probation officer for 30 years, retiring in 1994. Clive's books are, 'A Citizens' Income - a Foundation for a Sustainable World' published in 2003, and *Green Economics and Citizens Income* in November 2011. The foundation of the greens when the only then existing party based on ecological principles was the New Zealand Values Party, He foresaw developments and obstacles to attaining global sustainability which still thwart progress. He was a Probation Officer, he believes he has some crucial ideas to contribute which are essential for survivability.

Isayvani Naicker
A Geographer at the University of Cambridge, looking at the interaction of science and policy in society, focused on a case study of biodiversity conservation in South Africa. Her previous degrees include a Master of Science (Geology) from the University of Cape Town in South Africa and Master of Science (Philosophy of Social Science) from the London School of Economics and Political Science in he UK. She has work experience in the environmental and sustainable development field in Africa.

Professor Dr **Alejandra Caporale Madi**

She is a Professor and researcher at the Instituto de Economia, State University of Campinas, Brazil. She is the author of Monetary Policy in Brazil: a Post-Keynesian interpretation and her recent publications include: Corporate social responsibility: credit and banking inclusion in Brazil and. Financialization, Employability and their Impacts on the Bank Workers' Union Movement in Brazil (1994-2004).

Max Marioni
A graduate of International Relations at Royal Holloway researching environmental degradation and conflict in the Horn of Africa. He has previously worked at the Institute for Cultural Diplomacy in Germany, where he was Director of Media and Communications and editor of Cultural Diplomacy News, and in the past he has studied at the Green Economics Institute, and European Studies at the University of Reading and at the University of Düsseldorf (Germany).

Maret Merisaar Doctor of Biology and recent MP in the Estonian National Parliament, she is a specialist in Baltic Sea biodiversity.

Mahelet Alemayehu Mekonnen
An Ethiopian economist interested in economics and political science who studied Richmond The American University in London. She heads up our Africa team and is editor of our special issue of our academic journal on Africa and our forthcoming book about Africa. She is economics advisor for the management team. She is a firm believer in education and believes in tackling one of the most important problems we are facing in the global world, particularly the issue of climate change and inequality towards women. Her work relates to examining large projects and questions of sustainability – and development.

Chidi Magnus Onahue
A Development Economist/Research Fellow with the African Institute for Applied Economics, Enugu, Nigeria. He served as a National Expert in the United Nations Industrial Organization UNIDO)/ Institute of African Studies, Oxford University, UK, survey of the manufacturing sector in Nigeria in 2004. Member, Climate Change Roundtable, Nigeria's Federal Ministry of Environment. He is the Executive Director, Green Economics Nigeria.

Mohd. Shahwahid Othman
Professor and Doctorate in Forest Resource Management and Policy. He is an expert in the field of Forestry Economics and Evaluation Economics. He is a Deputy Dean (Research and Innovation) in the Faculty of Economics and Management, University Putra Malaysia.

Ahmad Fauzi Puasa
The Malaysian Institute of Economics Research (MIER) as Deputy Director (Research). His areas of expertise are Forestry Economics and Agroforestry Management. Before he joined MIER, he served Forest Research Institute Malaysia (FRIM). He has a PhD in the field of Forestry Economics.

Miriam Prasse
A member of The Green Economics Institute's Intern's College and was a speaker at our annual conference at Oxford University, starting the trend for young people at school to have a voice in the formulation of Green Economics at the highest level. She is based in Munich in Germany.

Sandra Ries
Editor and writer, she was an award winning representative of her country of Denmark at the International Young Climate talks in Poland. She has a special interest in Development and International Relations and has spent her life equally in Denmark and New Zealand giving her unusual insight into two cultures on different sides of the world.

Grit Silberstein

An Economist trained at the University of Göttingen in Germany. Born in Germany and raised in Ecuador she considers both countries as home. In 2010 she has been working at the Green Economics Institute advising on Economic Issues. She is researching in International Economics at the University of Göttingen in Germany, specializing in development economics and at Nottingham University in the UK. Her interests include matters of sustainable development in European development aid and the European Union. She also works with Galextur in the Galapagos Islands promoting biodiversity.

Dr. Enrico Tezza

A senior training specialist and has a background in social research and evaluation studies. After a career in the Italian Ministry of Labour and local public institutions, he joined the International Labour Organisation in Turin in 1992. He is labour market advisor for the Green Economics Institute. Subjects covered vary from training policy to employment and active labour market measures. His current focus interest is on social dialogue for green jobs. His main publication was Evaluating Social Programmes: the relevance of relationships and his latest publications include Dialogue for Responsible Restructuring and Green Labour Market for Transitions.

Dr Jeffrey Turk Phd

A doctorate in particle physics from Yale University and after working as a physicist at the European Laboratory for Particle Physics (CERN) gaining an MA in transition economics at the Central European University in Budapest and then a DPhil in contemporary European Studies from the University of Sussex and a research fellow at the Scientific Research Centre of the Slovenian Academy of Sciences and Arts, where he researches realist biography and European Policy. He ran a research conference at the University of Leuwen on critical realist narrative biographical methods. He has produced many articles on Green Economics and methodological innovation.

Dr.Wei Lu

Associate Professor and Assistant Dean at School of Management, University of Science and Technology of China (USTC). Active in teaching, research and consulting, he has been involved in many international projects including the renewable energy business development training in China, sponsored by the W. Alton Jones Foundation and the Cleaner Production Survey in China sponsored by UNESCO and mainstreaming climate change and CDM in the Chinese Financing Sector sponsored by the Global Opportunity Fund. He co-authored the book: Greening Chinese Business: Barriers, Trends and Opportunities for Environmental Management, Greenleaf Publishing.

Wenjun Wang

Financial Engineer at USTC and qualified in Mathemporatioatics from Anhui University, China in 2005. She has participated in several projects, including Mainstreaming Climate Change and CDM in the Chinese Financing Sector, sponsored by the Global Opportunity Fund and a bi-country survey on college student entrepreneurship in China and the USA. She also co-authored Millington's book *Entrepreneurship and Venture Capital.*

Dr. Song Weiming is a professor of forest economics in School of Economics and Management, Beijing Forestry University. At present, he is president of the university, and has published many papers and books on forest economics, and more than 5 state awards of China have been earned from 1990 to 2010.

Dr. Zhang Ying is a professor of natural resources economics in School of Economics and Management, Beijing Forestry University. He gained a PhD in 1999, and studied as a post-doc. in Korea University in 2000. In 2007-2008, he was a Fulbright visiting professor in Yale University. His major is forest economics, and over 110 papers and 19 books by sole author and co-authors have been published in this field and 4 state awards of China have been earned from 1999 to 2010.

Chapter 1 Introduction To Green Economics

1.1 A Global Movement for Change

Miriam Kennet

Green Economics has become one of the most contemporary global movements for change. In the age of austerity it has taken over from the round of stimulus packages, as governments all over the world attempt to claw back from the crippling debt and porous infrastructure that has been created by 60 year orgy of post war drunken resource use and exhaustion.

The world economy and the world's ecosystem services are experiencing what can only be described as the aftermath of an enormous hangover of over consumption, waste and over spending on a devastating scale, which has put human civilisation and the economy into the "intensive care" ward. Suddenly, frugality is the name of the game, saving and only spending on essentials is how people are managing their lives and their government budgets in most developed countries. In the UK David Cameron's "Big Society" is a thinly disguised attempt to disband almost every cost of welfare, education, health care and any costs of government and push it back to the private sector and profiteering by large companies in a major ideological shift.

What is so sad is that this huge 60 year party was only attended by people in the first world - and mainly by white middle class men in the west. The rest weren't invited; they were there to provide the waiters, the inputs to the party, the raw materials, resources and staffing! The frills and the entertainment. Now everyone has to pay for this party and to clean up the mess. The conducive climate for human civilisation has been damaged, the plentiful biodiversity like butterflies and bees, not to mention healthy fish stocks have been irreparably depleted and squandered and the seas are polluted and have major dead zones incompatible with life itself. Lamarck warned 200 years ago that man would continue to expand until he had totally damaged the planet and then would destroy himself!

We need as a species to stop and take stock – the party is over, if we don't stop drinking from the fountain of waste and exploitation of nature and eco systems we may well have had our day and be joining the rapid extinction of species.

As the Head of the Environment Agency in Europe has said, there is nothing that says we ourselves are immune from this process! So we need to watch out and do something about it quickly. Hence the age of green economics, not the age of spending on green consumption or green wash, or even the green stimulus. Green economics has never meant green stimulus. Green economics is about living within our means and paying for what we use as we go, NOT leaving the clean-up for the next generation!

We need to clean up and put our house in order. We often say oikonomics is about managing the estate or managing our household. That household is the earth and all its resources, all of us humans, all living things and all the planet's systems. We have unbalanced the climate, the sea plankton which regulate it, the earth systems have been unleashed, the glaciers are melting, the north pole is navigable suddenly and the seismic character of the earth with volcanoes and earthquakes has been set in motion.

Green economics is the one system which factors all this in. It works by preventing poverty and inequality and does NOT start from a premise of as one intern said to me once "I am here to get rich quick". Green economics is about putting the house in order. In this case it's about clearing up, not before our parents get home and see the stains on the carpet and cigarette burns on the curtains, but about clearing up the house before we hand it on to our children – before they notice what a total mess we have made and start to bitterly resent us for what we have done and the depleted resources we have left for them!

Suddenly we are all faced with the complete loss of the illusion, as it was all an illusion, that modern economics had conquered all and was all powerful to lift the "bottom billon out of poverty" by means of more GDP growth, more expansion, spending in the economy and ever more resource use, especially oil and fossil fuel, using up most of the provisions laid down for 1000s of years and squandered in one or two generations.

The age of plenty is over. If we want a future, it must be the age of green economics which teaches us firstly how to share with each other. The people who never shared in this bonanza are now in some cases better placed to lead us out of the mess.

The USA, with an average carbon footprint of 25 tonnes a person, is in no position to lead the rest of the world, currently bickering with the UK over who caused the worst oil spill in history, finishing off whatever fish stocks were left in the ocean. India and Africa, with very low carbon footprints of less than 2 tonnes each per person, are gaining ground.

What we have found is that while the developed world is arguing over who spilt the wine, in parts of Africa, not only do they not have the wine, but they are actually still using stone-age implements. We found agriculture was being done with wooden tools, wooden ploughs, no anvil, no bronze-age innovations, people without shoes, let alone fashion items, and small children tending the animals in the fields with an average life expectancy of around 30 to 40 years!

The age of plenty passed them by completely, with 65% of them still unable to read and write, high female mortality and a complete failure to implement the Millennium Development Goals. If we call ourselves civilised, we cannot allow this situation. We need to consider what we have done and we need to take action to change it. Over use, hogging and squandering of our resources is no longer fashionable and is no longer a desired outcome of our economics system.

Green economists have worked hard to create an economics which is now fit and ready to lead the world forward. Our journey now has come a long way. We have been told that we have indeed created a new discipline in economics, Green economics, which is ready to take its place amongst economics theory, discipline and practise.

"Green economics is NOT just about the environment, green is about efficiency in economics". It was about reclaiming economics and provisioning for the needs of everyone and everything on the planet, other species, nature, the planet and its systems. It is therefore a progressive discipline, and about ensuring that economics is used for progression, not regression. Green economics is therefore about doing and about SHARING, sharing with each other, the rest of humanity, and about sharing the planet with other species and with the planet's systems. If we don't want to unleash multiple earthquakes and volcanoes we need to maintain a suitable climate and temperature range around 14 degrees. Everything has an impact and every system has feeder input requirements. We have responsibilities to all these systems and to each other.

That time has come. We need to get a grip and manage better. However this year one thing that has become completely clear is that if we thought we had tamed nature and that our economics system was "in charge- and had conquered nature" this was a total fallacy, as nature has shown. Just one volcano in the northern hemisphere was enough to ground all aeroplanes for days on end and to disrupt the economy severely.

The Green Economics concept is as complex as it is timely. It is inclusive in all senses valuing not great wealth or riches, but diversity, sustainability, caring sharing and sensitivity for all of life on earth including our own and those of others.

Photo: The Economics of the systems of the Planet: Volcano Dawn 2010. This year the question arose: If we fiddle with the climate, will it lead to more seismic activity globally? Miriam Kennet 2010

It is time to end the party, it is time to share, everyone should have access to proper drinking water as a minimum. We should not rest until that job has been done. It is not that difficult to do, we just need to notice. To notice each other, the whole human family and to notice the biodiversity and the little things that bring us happiness. These are going to be the pleasures of the 21st century- NOT the arrival of a new Porsche in the household.

This chapter was first published in the Proceedings of The Green Economics Institute 5th Annual Conference at Oxford University July 2010.

Photo. Tree Hugging in Berlin: Young Greens in Berlin on a Green Economics Institute Training Course with The Green Economics Institute and The Young Greens and the Green European Foundation. Photo. Iida Kalmanlehto Finland

1.2 A Short Introduction to Green Economics

Miriam Kennet

The Green Economics Institute (GEI) is developing a new discipline of economics based on a reassessment of a world undergoing social and environmental change. Green Economics returns to the fundamentals, basing economics on oikia, which is Greek for household or estate management. Indeed, the Earth is the household on which we all depend. Our goal is to challenge the narrow scope of mainstream economics using holistic and interdisciplinary explanations, instruments and tools.

The Green Economics Institute is an independent, international networking body. We specifically work on campaigns for promoting green business, for alleviating and preventing poverty, for supply chain fairness openness and equity, and for the reform and integration of the academic and intellectual philosophy of economics in line with ecological reality.

Green Economics reclaims economics from purely quantitative measurement and the assumptions of a "homo economicus" perspective. In this way, it is an entirely new approach, standing in sharp contrast to the reductionist mathematics and assumptions of mainstream research. Its long-term outlook reflects the evolution of societies within paleontological time frames, which provides better tools for understanding problems such as climate change than current conventions and short term business cycles. Economics is thus a science independent of business administration studies.

It is also concerned with establishing definitions of an overall well-being for all—humans, other species and the planet—rather than deriving simplistic quantitative statistics. A distinction is made between hidden destruction, what we currently call economic "growth," and our definitions of true growth, which is an abundance of natural resources and growth in and of nature.

Green is commonly misunderstood to be solely focused on the environment. Actually, a "green" perspective situates economics within the Earth as a given and looks outward from that starting point. It builds on top of ecological economics, which focuses on democratic accountability for the sake of the environment. Green Economics develops these themes further in order to achieve simultaneous social and environmental justice, as they are inseparable parts of a whole.

The bridge to social justice is an acknowledgement that the poor suffer more from environmental degradation. Therefore, Green Economics looks for solutions that simultaneously address poverty, climate change and biodiversity within an equitable framework. The impulse first arose from the global ethic of 1960s culture. It was Rachel Carson's 1962 book, Silent Spring, that first raised awareness of the debilitating effects of our economic growth: the output of our economic production was depleting biodiversity.

Green Economics research focuses on developing the tools and methods that are required to master today's economic problems in society. For example, we are currently examining how the creation of scarcity came to mean the creation of value, as this idea contradicts the finite resources of the earth. We are assessing the adoption of an economics of abundance rather than scarcity. Green Economics looks at how growth can be practical but not unlimited and how theories of growth have led to current economic aims of high mass consumption.

We need to ensure our economic theories capture "even the poorest and most wretched in our society as well as the most powerful". Because conventional economics evolved in the nineteenth century, under a different set of circumstances, and is still constructed to meet those past needs, it is unsuitable to solve today's problems. Green Economics, in utilizing holistic and modern scientific perspectives, is ideally positioned to inform mainstream requirements for economics, rather than simply being a niche addition to the discourse.

In November 2007, the Green Economics Institute took part in a think tank at the United Kingdom's Schumacher College, which gathered eminent writers and thinkers in the field of holistic economics. We worked on a basic and foundational aspect of microeconomics—that of individual preferences of the rational economic man. We discussed the idea of "mutuality" in values and whether we could incorporate this into a concept of "mutual economic preferences." Our economic values therefore should have a sense of reverence for the physical world and should create a sense of connectivity between us and the natural world.

As humans, we require some connectedness in our lives and we need to put it back into our economics principles.

Ghandi once said that "Economics without values is like churning sand to make butter." We need a concept of "enoughness," contentedness, sufficiency, and coherence. We need to acknowledge our biological roots. We need agriculture to feed people rather than an agribusiness. We need fulfilment in our work and we need to share resources fairly. Therefore, we need to re-orientate ourselves and our economics, manoeuvring it back onto its rightful course to a better "life-world" result. Green Economics sees the failure of mainstream economics in our modern world, where one-fifth of humans still live in poverty and there is a pending environmental crisis.

This article originally appeared in the Harvard College Economics Review, Vol II, Issue I.

Photo: REC official Photographer.The Green Economics Institute in Venice teaching Sustainable Development to Balkan government officials with REC Hungary.

1.3 An academic discipline offering a progressive take on the current problems confronting humanity.

Miriam Kennet

Green Economics was formally approved as an academic mode of study in December 2011 when Birmingham City University in the Uk approved the first ever taught masters mode in Green Economics at its academic board meeting. Its strapline is Provisioning for the benefit of all people everywhere, other species, nature, the planet and its systems. The economics of abundance, of sharing and the economics of doing to create social and environmental justice. This is underpinned by the concepts of environmental and social justice in all its work and it has a strong innovative ethos of inclusion for everyone including those who dont have a voice and those who get drowned out by the more powerful. Its role models are more diverse and often include people with special needs and other difficulties. This is especially true as humanity is facing unpredented problems today and only those who have had to face life changing adversity probably have the internal strength, insight and resources to rise about the day to day and to reflect on what needs to be done and how to achieve a positive outcome. It is not enough just to spread doom and gloom, the Green Economics perspective is one of hope and action and to create a vision of the future that can and is leading the way both for the economy and also for a reworking of some basic philosophical assumptions.

This new "Green Economics" school of thought took shape. It set out to explore its aims, its roots and philosophical underpinning. It originally critiqued mainstream economics from a Green Economics perspective, proposing where it needed reform. It argued that Green Economics brings to economics the core drivers of ecology, equity, social and environmental justice.

The development and contribution of these ideas are now mapped through its sister disciplines such as welfare economics, feminist economics, eco-feminism, eco-socialism, environmental economics, and ecological economics and updates them to lower growth economics, lower carbon economics and more appropriate scales of both new types of efficiency such as reuse, reduce, recycle repair, larger scale where it is needed for example in combating cross border pollution and contamination, fighting corruption, and also an element of localism in food production and in fuel reduction and in economics.

Green Economics examines reality by means of multidisciplinary, complex, holistic, and very long-term methods as well as taking into account the political and social aspects. The range provides an opportunity to frame economics within both the natural sciences, (which main stream economists have been striving to achieve with limited success), and also the within the social sciences. It reorients modelling approaches so they are congruent with natural science processes, and it embraces the context of more verbal narrative. The range particularly brings political economy, moral sentiments, and ethics back within its borders.

The aim of Green Economics was at the time to create a new discipline which works for the benefit of all people everywhere, for the planet, nature, other species,the planet and its systems Green Economics integrates ideas and theories which also are designed to help to end the systemic and institutional causes of inequity and poverty as well as solving climate change and preventing further runaway warming and stopping biodiversity loss and mass extinction of species.

What was simply taking an inclusive approach, promoting fairness, equity, participation, freedom and democracy with social and environmental justice at its core has now evolved to a full blown discipline which can be described as progressive at its core with all that that entails and one if its main rationales. However, sadly within the green movement this is contested -as it has changed and at least in Anglo Saxon countries it is more characterised by steady state economics masquerading as xenophobic steady state population stances. Where once the movement championed inclusion and all comers and fought for those injustices to end, it has become a shadow of its former self in terms of a beacon of hope for the oppressed and disadvantaged.

However Green Economics has become something rather different and is now a wide ecclectic and global movement with a very strong movement for progressive global change which has probably affected every single country and government on earth with a strong feminist message, a strong equality and access and a strong inclusion message, in addition to a message of preserving the bundle of resources on earth for the future and for future generations. The climate has changed in terms of more fear and more worry about the Age of Austerity and where love thy neighbour is being rejected in those very countries which seemed to lead the 60s revolutions for peace and love. Green Economics advocates strongly for the good of the whole community but remembers the individual especially where the voice is weak or unheard. Rather than simply working for individuals (and their preferences) or the requirements of powerful private corporations, it is instead developing a new mix of needs and rights which will ensure genuine very long term sustainability, survivability, well being and happiness for all people everywhere, always within the limits and comfort of nature.

Green Economics and its methodology

We first posited that civilisation may not survive this upheaval and cavalier attitude and now this has become a mainstream idea. At the time it was regarded as an odd supposition. Now it is almost universally acknowledged that we need to act to care for the foundations of our society and our world.

"Civilisation" and mainstream economics are post-ice age phenomena. Climate instability is predicted to create unprecedented conditions more hostile to society as we have constructed it and the very survival of our society or our species starts to become uncertain. Mainstream economics tends to limit its focus to short term concerns. Green Economics, with its precautionary principle, works to prevent foreseeable, adverse effects on people and nature, and factors in the widest possible range of costs (regardless of the origin). Green Economics is able to do this also because it is inherently more aligned with the natural sciences and many of its practitioners are trained in natural sciences and archaeology as well as economics. As a consequence of adopting a very long-term view of events, intergenerational equity and the rights of future generations are integral. Not surprisingly, Green Economics strongly advocates the need for each generation to leave behind an adequate bundle of resources and a habitable planet. Mainstream economics is still too bound up with concerns of price, profit, economic growth and the perspective of the owners of production versus the workers as "other" and therefore entirely fails to grasp this new reality.

Green Economics methodology also brings new perspectives to conventional economics tools, in terms of both time and space. This new context enables it to reveal, disentangle, and unravel the power relationships and vested interests in the new global market place. The logic of Green Economics advocates local production for local needs, and reusing, reducing, repairing and possibly recycling rather than global expansion of corporations. Thus wisdom and holism are re-introduced into economic problem solving. It also re- incorporates political economy and the moral and transformational aspects of the economics of Adam Smith (1776), while offering new solutions to "managing the commons", which has been often restricted to game theoretical models and exercises based on the prisoner's dilemma or voting issues.

Photo Miriam Kennet. The world is warming and some micro climates are already impacting the economy. Here melting glaciers in the European Alps near Bolzano impact power supplies for industry and business.

1.4 The ten key values of Green Economics

Miriam Kennet, Jeff Turk and Michelle S. Gale de Oliveira

The ten key values of the Green Economics Institute have been defined as follows:

1.   Green economics aims to provision for the needs of all people everywhere, other species, nature, the planet and its systems, all as beneficiaries of economics transactions, not as throw away imputs.

2.   This is all underpinned by social and environmental justice, tolerance, no prejudice and creating quality of life for everyone including future generations and all the current generations, including older and younger people.

3. Ensuring and respecting other species and their rights. Ending the current mass extinction of species. Ensuring biodiversity.

4.   Non violence and inclusion of all people everywhere, including people with special needs and special abilities. Ensuring all nations have equal access to power and resources. Local people having control over their own destiny and resources. Increasing life expectancy, human welfare and per capita GDP in the least developed countries.

5.   Ensuring gender equity in all activities. Educating, respecting, empowering women and minorities.

6.   Ending current high mass consumption and overshoot of the planet's resources and returning to live within the comfortable bounds of nature in the climatic conditions under which humans built their civilisation. Choosing lifestyle changes over techno fixes and eco technology. Lowering our own carbon usage and living lightly on the earth. Changing how economics is done: from being an abstract mathematical exercise to embracing realism and the real world we all live in and share and in which we are all concerned stakeholders.

7. Valuing and respecting all people equally.

8.Poverty prevention. Climate change and instability prevention, adaptation, mitigation. Protecting the most vulnerable from risk. Ensuring the future of small island states.

9.Quickly reducing carbon per capita globally to 2 tonnes in the next 5 years and zero soon after. Limiting and reversing climate change. Moving to renewable energy sources.

10. Building a future-proofed economics to solve the current economic uncertainty and downturn which is suitable for the 21st century. Creating and nuturing an economy based on sharing, rather than greed and profit. Completely reshaping and reforming current economics.

1.5 What is Green Economics? The Green Economics Institute Team: Ideas for campaigning:

Ben Armstrong- Haworth, Dr Jeff Turk Phd Brussels and Slovenia, Paul Kennet South Africa, Volker Heinemann Germany and UK, Sophie Hengstridge, Miriam Kennet July 2008 Oxford.

Features of Green Economics for Campaigning:
Green Economics aims to work to create a fairer, more sustainable world by means of reforming economics practice, policy and theory. Green Economics has been acknowledged as becoming a school of economics and a new discipline in its own right. Green Economics is redefining what is termed " Economics" to make it more useful, more real and more sustainable.

- Green Economics is about provisioning for the basic needs, and the flourishing of all people everywhere, other species, the planet and its systems. Green Economics seeks to balance the impacts, effects and responsibilities of people, other species, and the planet and its systems. Green Economics is less concerned about distribution activities and rationale, than finding the means to ensure everyone has enough to meet their basic needs in a sustainable and equitable way.

- Green Economics is about the complex mesh of environmental and social justice together and at the same time.

- Poverty prevention and ending the current mass extinction of species and maintaining biodiversity are fundamental to Green Economics.

- Green Economics seeks to restore gender balance to provisioning, rights to assets and to power relations, economics activity and as a discipline. Green Economics uses means as well as ends. So it fundamentally requires for example equal numbers of men and women and minority groups and international working in the development of its economics policy, practise, implementation, and theory development. Green Economics involves access to economics for all and is about reclaiming economics for everyone rather than something which is done to us by remote or unaccountable bodies of elites, such bodies as the IMF.

- Green Economics takes a long term view reflecting earth

processes
Green Economics questions "civilisation" and seeks learning and
ideas from the whole of human history, pre- history and evolution,
and pre agricultural times and questions how to move forward
post agriculturally.

- Green Economics is part reflexive social science -economics of
provisioning and part natural science using pure science data
and models and narrative information, eg much as geography and
archaeology do. The Green Part – or environmental part is about
the management of our physical home and the social part is about
our human constructed home.

- Green Economics uses reality, and the real world as its data.
Models are only to inform us about reality.

- Green Economics aims to redefine economics, and make it more
successful than the current mainstream discipline. It does this by
providing more clarity into the use of specific terms by business,
academia, campaigners and policy makers and relating economics
definitions to the real world and to physical science and physical
aspects of reality and the real world rather than theoretical
models based on mathematical and other unworldy theories.

- It argues for democracy, and includes everyone in its calculations.
Indicators and counting will be informed by work of Waring- etc.
everyone counts equally. Reform of accounting and also
developing Green Accounting are important.

- Green Economics does not seek to impose one system globally
-and argues for diversity of systems, in which Green Economics
acts as a filter for checking systems are fairer and sustainable.

- Green Economics seeks to reform (main stream and other)
economics at the theory level by applying new filters of critique-
to existing theories on their own terms, but all grounded in the
real world. It seeks to improve global governance and a system of
global governance institutions which are democractically elected
and representative tasked with achieving sustainability and full
realisation of human rights and dignity.

- Green Economics questions all economics to check if its
requirements for social and environmental justice and real world
sustainability are met. Such questions might include:
Does a theory or practise contribute to climate change ?
Does the theory, practise or policy cause other global
environmental change?:
Does the theory or policy help with understanding reality?
How does the theory help or affect less able people?
How does the model impact minorities, etc ?

Does the theory create environmental refugees?

How does growth theory impact consumption patterns and resource depletion.?

How do theories impact resource depletion or biodiversity?

- Green Economics is international but works virtually and uses video and conference calling and the internet in order to keep its carbon footprint as low as possible as a matter of course in all its work.

- Green Economics questions " development concepts " and " under development" and the imposition of high mass consumption patterns on less developed countries in order to raise their GDP and linear development from " primitive " economies. It seeks to maintain diversity of systems and argues that each system has something to offer. Rather it seeks improvement in quality of life to meet basic needs for everyone on the planet as a rationale. It rejects Kuznet's which argues that a stage of hardship and poverty is necessary for development to follow.

- Green Economics is "Economics by Doing" in policy making, practise and theory and operates in 4 main fields: business, campaigning, academic and policy and will pursue these at the highest levels:eg in parliaments around the world Green Economics learns from and implements within all four -because these are the current power bases which need to change. Manifestations of current weaknesses include the complete lack of gender balance or high profile women in the academic disciplines of economics and geography which regulate and develop economics theory, policy and practice.

Homo oikonmicus must now start the process by sharing economics policy practise, theory development and implementation equally with Gyny oikonimika. This must be done in the practice and appointments to positions and in publications all becoming gender balanced and sustainable as fast as possible.

Green Economics seeks to " main stream" its ideas for economics replacing outdated mainstream economics with its more equitable, inclusive and accessible, and diverse discipline ideas.

Its ideas are now influencing mainstream terminology, practice, theory and policy and discipline contents.

1.6 Why it is important to change the current Economic System

Bente Teglgård Madeira

Introduction

This is a timely debate. Right now we have continuous problems with recognised climate change (floods, droughts, hurricanes etc.), oil shortages, water shortages, food security problems, pollution of air, sea and water.

Photo Miriam Kennet: At the St Pauls Cathedral protests.
"We apologize for inconvenience during essential global improvement works"

Also experienced is increased instability with the ' War on Terror', other wars for resources and the largest refugee movements ever - including internally displaced peoples.

Much of the analysis comes from the work & findings of Dr. Marilyn Waring, who has checked out all the volumes of rules, that governs the UNSNA. It also draws on the work and analyses by eco-feminists Dr. Maria Mies and Dr Vandana Shiva.
These truly remarkable women have shaped my thinking about the world irrevocably. They should be here with you. But with Maria

drastically reducing her talks (due to illness) and the distance Marilyn and Vandana would have to travel. I feel I need to try to further this work as best as I can.

Marilyn Waring came to RISC about 20 years ago and wrote to us in effect:
"I get the feeling that people want simple short answers to complex problems, but it cannot be done without hard work. This is not good for us and does not help the people, we seek to serve." Likewise, I recommend that you read the following books: Maria Mies's 'Patriarchy and Accumulation on a World Scale'. Vandana Shiva's 'Staying Alive' and their joint book 'Eco- feminism' published by Zed Books, Marilyn Waring's 'Counting for Nothing".

Most people assume that the economic measuring system is logical, even-handed, unbiased and that it measures a nation's well-being and success.
The aim of this talk is to explain the origins of the United Nations System of National Accounts (UNSNA) and some of the structures that underpin this system. It also illustrates how it considers the environment and unpaid work – mainly women's - as an unlimited free gift.

The only thing which counts in this system is money. An activity counts only if it goes through the marketplace. The system therefore excludes the environment and the unpaid work of women in particular, but also unpaid work of children and men.

Marilyn Waring shows how this links to the Global Economic System, which was created during the Second World War. John Maynard Keynes and Richard Stone co-wrote a paper entitled "The National Income and Expenditure of the United Kingdom, and how to pay for the war".
Keynes offered the general theory that the total amount of income in a country is heavily determined by a combination of the three factors: consumption, investment and government spending. Stone defined how each of the three elements could be measured and specified interactions between them.
The uniform accounting system was then developed to measure the national income of a country at war.

This system was designed for a western industrialised country, but is now forced on countries worldwide including countries, where the populations still live in a mainly subsistence economy, with disastrous consequences.

Richard Stone expanded on the above ideas, which were adopted in 1953 as the basis of the United Nations' System of National Accounts (UNSNA). All nations must conform to the rules of the UNSNA or they cannot belong to the United Nations, obtain loans from the International Monetary Fund, or be funded by the World Bank.

Milton Gilbert, chief of the National Income Division of the Department of Commerce in the U.S. government in 1941, presented a paper in December 1941 which is claimed to be the first, clear, published statement on Gross National Produce. Gilbert's paper did not insist that GNP was the one good & true concept. It states: " there is no one correct measure of income or output that can be used indiscriminately in every type of economic problem"
But Gilbert's purpose and economic problem was " how to pay for the war" He supported the use of GNP as a proper measure in analysing the economic relationship between defence expenditures and total output. The article was dealing with measurement rather than programming or feasibility. His conception of GNP was constructed for a specific political purposes: **How to pay for the war.**

The successes in the use of the national income and product statistics for war purposed made their use in post war planning apparently logical and inevitable. National income estimates everywhere continue, to this day, to be an assessment of *How best to pay for the war.*

Later in 1975 Sir Richard Stone drafted a system of Social and Demographic Statistics:
"Information about the environment is of obvious importance in connection with the subject matter of this report. Pollution of the air, sea and land and the disturbance of ecological balances are highly relevant to health, to feeding and otherwise providing for the worlds rapidly growing population, to the acceptability of unconstrained economic growth and to the choice of the techniques of production."

Despite this, the UNSNA still does not record the cost of poisoning the earth on which people and animals depend for survival.

Marilyn Waring writes:
"U.S. environmentalist and commentator Lewis Regenstein has written that the United States is being inundated with chemicals sprayed from the air, spewed from chimney stacks, applied to the crop land, showered over entire forests, buried beneath the earth and sea, and added to the food and drink. It may be too late, he writes, for most citizens to find antidotes to these persistent chemical poisons. It is projected that 56 million Americans will contract cancer annually, much of it as the result of the chemicals that surround them. Other

results of the poisons include vomiting, miscarriages, stillbirths, blindness, bleeding, insanity, and mercifully in some cases, death.

But with exception of those poisonings that are undeniable, such as the nuclear accident in Three Mile Island, these illnesses will not be visible to the UNSNA. They will be visible in the national accounts only as **consumption** of medical and other professional services and thus treated as **value-added** in national income accounting.

While it might seem logical that such costs should be subtracted from expenditures on Gross National Products, this is not the case. To get a net national product, all that is subtracted from GNP is the equivalent of the reinvestments necessary to maintain the Capital stock (such as stockpiles of Nuclear bombs) The goods and services involved in cleaning up an ecological disaster, just like cleaning up after a war, are said to be an expression of society's "preferences".

If our natural preferences are for clear air, fresh water, and standing forests, we cannot possibly express such desires, for they cannot be expressed in the market. No one and nothing records the permanent damage to water, air and the ecosystem as an income accounting cost.

National income provides for deficits in money but not deficits in natural resources. "

UPS AND DOWNS OF THE GNP/GDPPS AND DOWNS OF THE GNP/GDP
Gross National Product (GNP) & Gross Domestic Product (GDP) are derived from national accounts and can be estimated by using either the expenditure or income approach.

During the UN Development decade the GNP was quietly dropped from use by the UN statistics in favour of GDP. This is because they could not demonstrate growth in the 'developing' countries during the UN Development Decade in the poorest countries. In many cases especially in developing c ountries there is a big difference between GNP & GDP. The shift to GDP gives priority to economic growth and investment and obscures the needs of people. Political leaders agreed to this because they needed to demonstrate "growth" in order to attract more investment.

In other words if a country creates a positive climate with special tax exemptions to large foreign companies, it undermines a country's own development and smaller businesses and on top of this it takes the profit out of the country. It nevertheless increases a country's growth indicators and makes the country seem wealthier and therefore attractive to investors. This is particularly apparent in tourism. In Goa a fierce, local opposition has grown up to protect their beaches and the turtles that mate on them. They are reclaiming local people's access to the beaches and fishing in the sea.

The main difference between GNP and GDP is that the GDP measures production that generates income in a Nation's economy *whether the resources are owned by that country's residents or not.*

We have the bizarre situation where the 'GDP/GNP increases in the following situations:

• A growing forest becomes 'productive' only when cut and sold. It is not productive when it absorbs water, creates foods to a large variety of animals and people, provides firewood, reduces CO_2 emissions or creates life-giving rivers.

• When the giant tanker Exxon Valdes ran aground at Prince William Sound spilling 38,000 tons of crude oil, which covered 2,600square km it completed its most productive journey ever. The cost of cleanup operation, legal proceedings, publicity etc. increased the GNP. The company was fully insured and lost no money.

•Bottle feeding a baby is brilliant for the economy as it requires buying bottles, teats, milk powder, sterilising kit & fluids, bottle cleaner, heater etc. It is also good for companies such as Nestle, which continues to promote powder milk in countries, where people have no access to clean water. The deaths this causes of thousands of children is not measured anywhere.

The GNP/GDP decreases in the following situations:
•If a housekeeper marries her employer the GNP/GDP goes down as

she now does the same work for nothing. Yet this work is said to be difficult to give a monetary value.

• If people start to grow and consume their own food the GNP/GDP goes down.
The new interest in allotment and growing your own foods to gain the most optimum nutrition is not good. In other words the 'Dig for Victory' policy during the second World War was bad for the economy.

• Breast milk - the perfect food for a baby is not good for the 'growth indicators' despite the fact that it gives the child mothers' immunity during the first month of its life. It is always provided at perfect temperature and at right consistency – but it has no value. Any women who have tried bottle and breast feeding will know the difference.

The increase of the GNP & GDP bears no resemblance to a nations well-being, it does not measure the distribution of wealth or what national resources support the life of the poor. Yet it is continually used as a wealth indicator.

If you are not visible in the economy it is very difficult to make policy makers take account of your needs.
This economic system supported by the unjust rules of the International Monetary Fund, the World Bank and the World Trade Organisation will ensure that it will be impossible to meet United Nation's Millenium Development Goals by 2015.

In the words of Dr. Maria Mies

**" Life comes out of life – not money which is dead.
You can measure environmental destruction,
but no amount of money without life can repair it."**

We need to go back to basics: That is to say we need to devise a new economic system, which on the positive side includes:

•   Life sustaining,unpaid work such as care for children, the environment and household animals.
•   Growth of the natural (wild) environment such as forests, animals, clean water and fresh clean air. In other words the environment is not an unlimited free gift.
•   Reproduction   (life giving) both of animals, people and ecosystem
•   Unpaid activities that contribute to health of people and the planet

The negative side of the accounts should include:

- Destruction of the global commons e.g. pollution of air, water or land. This is often due to industrialisation, mal-development or unsustainable food production methods.
- Death, poverty, injury, destruction of infrastructure and starvation caused by war
- Any activity which causes ill health in people and animals.
- Any innovation that relies on unnecessary and unsustainable use of resources

This is not a complete list, but indicates in what direction we need to go. Many other types of indicators have been developed, but ultimately they are discarded, when there are other priorities unless they are intrinsic to the economic system. The system itself must therefore include the most important life-giving aspects.

Other ways of measuring quality of life indicators have been suggested such as the time it takes to do something. That would certainly improve women's status and may give a clearer more accurate picture of work.

Maybe now that there is increasing awareness of man-made climate change and over-exploitation of the Earth's natural resources it is the right time for people to sit up and take note.

I would certainly like to find an economic system which showed all the work of bringing up a child on the plus side of our National Accounts system (in other words as economically active) and a Soldier charged with the task of sitting in a bunker all day ready to press the Nuclear Button on the negative side of the National Accounts (as economically inactive)

I would welcome a serious debate on how we need to change the economic system so that we can ensure our children's and our children's children have a sane, clean and abundant world to live in.

References
Waring Marylin. (1989) Counting for Nothing, Speech at Reading.
Berkshire
Waring Marylin (1988) Counting for Nothing Allan & Unwin.
Reprinted 1990, 93,96 and 97 by Bridget Williams Books Limited.

P.O. Box 5482, Wellington, New Zealand
Stone, Sir Richard " Political Economy, Economics and Beyond" The
economic Journal (December 1980):
Keynes John. M. (1965) The General Theory of Employment Interest
and Money. London: Macmillan, New York: Harcourt Brace
Jovanovich.
Regenstein, Lewis (1983) America the Poisoned: how Deadly
Chemicals are Destroying Our Environment, Our Wildlife, and How
We can Survive! Acropolis
Mies M (2007) Patriarchy and Accumulation in International
Journal of Green Economics Vol 1 issue 3 / 4
Shiva V (1989) Staying Alive Zed Books

Photo: Professor Graciela Chichilnisky, one of the worlds top
economists and inventor of carbon trading speaking at Oxford
University at the Green Economics Institute's Conference on
economics methodology. 2011.

1.7 Rebalancing the world economy: Gender in green economics. Introduction to the era of women taking centre stage in economics

Miriam Kennet

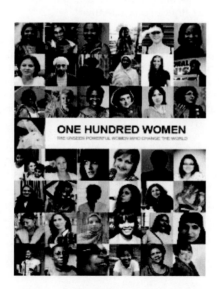

(Photos: belong to the One World Action campaign for 100 Global women who change the world)

Governing global money and gross indecency, sexual assault and attempted rape.
"The jolting of the worlds financial system and the course of French politics"
(Times May 16th 2011)

On the very same day as the protesters in the Occupy Wall Street received encouragement from the judiciary, as public opinion swung sharply in the protesters favour, I was struck by how the protesters nearly bit my hand off when I explained about green economics, an economics which is at core gender balanced and inclusive and a complete rework of economics. I was completely shocked – how having gone there an hour before -where bankers, clergy men and tourists from all over the world were taking part in Tent City University to try to make a completely new and different economics vernacular.
However not 10 minutes away- I then went to the "Green IT conference and was once again confronted with a panel of men -Not a single woman speaker at the entire conference and the men on the final panel congratulating themselves about how they were meeting new CSR Corporate Social Responsibility objectives, and how they were able to reduce some of their superfluous activities

and reduce their overall carbon footprint. The biggest problem ironically they mentioned was the population explosion and the fact that there are now 9 billion people on the planet! The fact that they hadnt even noticed the lack of women and that they still could talk about CSR -just served to highlight to me -that maybe we really do need a serious protest movement of world wide proportions to jog these people out of their comfort zone.

This idea that IT and population can be solved entirely by the worlds men with out reference to women would be a joke if it wasnt so serious and such a horror trip!

This article charts some of the changes behind the movements and what is really going on in the economy today.

In a year where the issue of women has risen to the very top of the tree in pretence of achieving a green economy is to be realised and what still needs to be done.

The very person charged with sorting out the Greek and Portuguese bailouts, was put in handcuffs and led away to prison for an attempted rape. This has actually thrown the entire IMF negotiations into turmoil —and in fact his position did enjoy full support from the global economics community so it may actually affect the outcome of the negotiations.

At first this seemed like a political stitch up by Sarkozy in the run up to important French elections. However, it turns out when we read deeper that Strauss-Kahn had a reputation as a complete womaniser who experts predicted would fall over a sex scandal. Indeed the allegation is that he assaulted a chamber maid in a hotel in the middle of the afternoon and dragged her down a corridor, raped her and hurt her so badly that she had to be treated in hospital! (Times May 16th 2011). Hardly a made up political tryst. No one was however surprised in the IMF and he was known for his sexual harassment of staff over many years. A French journalist Huguoette Nkoua said he had got her on the floor fighting and he was trying to undo her clothes and she was kicking him to get him off, hardly the stuff expected of the head of economics of the Western World (Sage and Pavia in the Times 2011). Surely we can do better than this. Surely such behaviour should not be tolerated in an important public figure and a person deciding the economic fate of millions of people globally.

What should concern us here, if he is the most powerful man in western economics, how is it possible that such a man was allowed to terrorise women over many years? How is it possible in public life that this is seen as compatible with mainstream economics? Surely, as economists deciding on the fate of nations and millions of people's well being, they should at least ensure they are dealing with consenting adults and the accepted use of force for sexual gratification by a "dominant ruling man" is positively medieval. So my question is: how did we ever get into such a situation and how do we avoid it happening again and again? The establishment condoned it or tolerated it at the very least. This is an opportunity for women to make a stand. If the mighty such as he can fall over such an event, then this may just give us the impetus to stop it happening in our own working lives.

The influential PWC who advise others how to do business—currently all its partners are male!

"PwC the biggest of the Big Four accountants is set to promote two women to its board, in a leadership reshuffle this summer. At present, all ten of the partners on its board are male." Gaenor Bagley, a tax specialist from London, and Stephanie Hyde, an audit partner based in Reading will both join the board as the first women! What is unbelievable is how long it has taken to get even one woman onto the board of this influential company. This is reported in the Times this week in the Business Dashboard (Spence 2011).

Male v female leadership styles

Similarly on a smaller scale in the UK, a major politician charged with our climate change defences has been accused of forcing his wife to take his own speeding tickets! His career is similarly damaged. But it points to systemic abuse of men in their dealings with women both at home and in the wider public sphere. It is time to stop this now. If we want economic power, we must take political power as well as power in the world's economics institutions, and if we want political power, we wont get it unless we get power in the world's economics institutions. There has never ever been a better time to put a woman in charge of the IMF and other world bodies.

One issue that is troubling: what happens if women don't want to have those roles? Are those roles only viable if people have these kinds of hierarchical in some cases abusive power relationships? Should we be looking for different forms of governance models which do not lead people to be abusive and charismatic and domineering leaders in the old fashioned way? What is a woman's way of doing this kind of role and can it be different? What makes a woman leader and what makes a woman economics leader? How many can we find and name, and how can we encourage more to come forward? How do we support them in that quest?

WE ARE THE 99%
WE WILL NOT BE IGNORED
WE STAND IN SOLIDARITY WITH
MADRID SAN FRANCISCO
MADISON LOS ANGELES
LONDON **TORONTO**
STUTTGART ATHENS SYDNEY
TOKYO **CHICAGO**
AMSTERDAM **PHOENIX**
ALGIERS TEL AVIV MONTREAL
MILAN **PORTLAND**
ATLANTA **CLEVELAND**
KANSAS CITY DALLAS ORLANDO **SEATTLE**
WE'RE STILL HERE. WE ARE GROWING.

OCCUPY TOGETHER
#OccupyWallSt #OccupyTogether occupytogether.org occupywallst.org

Or is something else at work: a casual glance at Oxford University's economics staff website reveals a shocking list of economists, which would be laughable if it wasn't so important or serious. They all have one startling feature in common! There is no gender balance—in fact only one gender is represented at all on the first few pages. There isn't much diversity either. If this represents the top governance of economics globally, no wonder women have started to take to the streets in some of the most powerful and unequal economies in the world. It is a further shocking fact that the Arab Spring was started by women and that it is really a movement: a backlash against this ridiculous imbalance.

With the IMF now headed by a woman, all this is about to change. The status quo of homo—and it really is deeply *"homo"* who are running the world economy—and new groups and forces are beginning to take it over. Hence our own, very global and very strong campaign, which we hope will be just as successful in putting women at the helm, or at least take their own rightful place at the top of economics, as it was in raising the Green Economics issue globally and getting governments everywhere to start to address it.

The shadow market: The powerhouse of the sovereign wealth funds and the new economic world order:
The world has changed considerably since our last conference on women 2 years ago. The drivers of the world economy are now partly from new sovereign wealth funds which in an unregulated market, are driving herds and hoards of the worlds wealth and cash instruments into dismembered investment with little or no conscience.

The most potent force in global commerce today is not the Federal Reserve, not the international banks, not the governments of the G7 countries, and certainly not the European Union. Rather, it is the multi-trillion-dollar network of super-rich, secretive, and largely unregulated investment vehicles—foreign sovereign wealth funds, government-run corporations, private equity funds, and hedge funds—that are quietly buying up the world, piece by valuable piece. According to Weiner (2010), the shadow market doesn't have a physical headquarters such as Wall Street. It doesn't have a formal leadership or an index to track or a single zone of exchange. Rather, it comprises an invisible and ever-shifting global nexus where money mixes with geopolitical power, often with great speed and secrecy (Bookstore website 2010—accessed 2011 May 15th 2011).

Led by cash-flush nations such as China, Kuwait, Abu Dhabi, Singapore, Saudi Arabia, and even Norway, the shadow market is hiring the brightest international financial talent money can buy, and is now assembling the gigantic investment portfolios that will form the power structure of tomorrow's economy.

Taking advantage of the Great Recession, or Great Contraction as its often called and subsequent liquidity problems in the United States and Europe, the major players of the shadow market are deploying staggering amounts of cash, controlling the capital markets, and securing not only major stakes in multinational companies but huge tracts of farmland and natural resources across the world. Yet that's not all; they're also pursuing political agendas made possible by their massive wealth and are becoming increasingly aggressive with the United States and other governments.

This wealth, with very little conscience, was based largely on oil money in the beginning in countries like Qatar. Such funds own 15% of Barclays Bank and also a large percentage of the London Stock Exchange. It is very difficult to unravel and to impose any governance. (Weiner 2010).

The symbol of this change played out at the Copenhagen COP15 where the world changed forever, since China started to act upon its new financial wealth and flex its new-found muscles. The USA has become powerless in the face of these massive wealth and power blocks and has lost its own muscle in a very public way. Power went to the new sovereign wealth funds. There is a huge increase of young wealthy consumers. The debate about globalisation has evolved into this debate.

Many governments in the West have borrowed substantial amounts of money. The European debt problems in 2010 and 2011 of Greece, Ireland and Portugal confirm that. China, UAE, Saudi Arabia and a number of other nations control vast amounts of capital. Some of the largest funds are from China, the Middle East and Norway. But many of the deals are very rational from the perspectives of the funds and countries themselves.

Many of the large purchases made are 'behind the scenes' and make few if any headlines. Many countries have purchased large pieces of farmland, to ensure that their faraway population can be fed in times of ever greater competition for food. Large mines, mineral deposits and other strategic raw materials guarantee that construction and manufacturing can continue into the future. Prime commercial and residential real estate in most of the major cities of the world are hollowing out much of the western economies, who will own very little of it and are increasingly loosing control and ownership of it it!

The character and size of the shadow market is truly astonishing. The main holder of foreign currency is now China, with £1.6 trillion of foreign exchange. Other major holders include Russia, now with a high global GDP growth of 3%, India, South Korea, and Brazil. China is the largest holder of American securities in the world. Since 2007 more than 605 of USA debt is owned by rich Asian nations, such as China, Japan and Singapore. China holds £600 billion of US debt as of April 2010 (Weiner 2011).

£2.3 billion of global capital is now run by sovereign wealth funds. The largest are Abu Dhabi, Saudi Arabia, China, Singapore, Kuwait, Russia, and Norway. The Abu Dhabi government in 2009 owned 15% of Barclays Bank, 9% of Daimler and 38% of Spain's oil company. Qatar owns 15% of the London Stock Exchange and more than half of London's Canary Wharf, and pumped in more than £2 billion to bail out Barclays Bank. This was the reason Al Magrahi was released. The G7 has now evolved to the G20 with China and India and Brazil as major players, but eventually this will give way to USA and China with Europe being largely excluded from decision making (Weiner 2011 page 219).

The needs and requirements of the American and European governments for liquidity are driving it, and sovereign wealth funds have lots of liquidity and many others are willing to sell prized assets to maintain it. This is driving such events as the imprisonment in China of western negotiators for Rio Tinto Zinc (itself no slouch in contravening human rights stakes), the use of funds for regimes such as Egypt's Mubarak and Libya's Gaddafi. It is also propelling the likes of the London School of Economics, Oxford from Rafsanjani in Iran (Turner 2011) and St Andrews University to accept unchecked (at the very least) and most probably knowingly the sons of some of the worlds worst despots and to provide them with academic and even economics doctoral validation in exchange for large amounts of money and getting caught doing it! How has it come to this that even a PhD from these learned institutions now has a price and a very unpleasant one, with no regard to human rights of any kind?

Child poverty has fallen and the UK government now requests information about women when considering its budgets. However the main consideration is the large and unstable and unsustainable budget deficits existing and issues such as women's well being are not being acted upon. Food investment by these wealthy funds include, surprisingly, grain baskets of the world. In the past five years Bahrain, China, India, Japan, Kuwait, Libya, Malaysia, Qatar, Saudi Arabia, South Korea and the UAE have spent billions of dollars buying up farmland from Brazil, Tanzania, Uganda etc. Saudi Arabia in particular has bought arable farmland in Ethiopia, Turkey and the Ukraine.

The downturn
The big issue is currently which countries will need bail out help from the IMF, and in the austerity packages women's issues are not generally considered and so get shunted out of the picture. Greece's GDP fell by 3%. The VAT rate went up to 23% and the retirement age was raised to 67 years. The exposure of Greece's economics position, having already received a massive bailout from Germany and the EU is now becoming clearer and is threatening to destabilise the entire Eurozone. It is very easy for the issue of women's equality to get lost in this new and challenging situation for the European Union, although the most powerful politician in the EU currently is Angela Merkel in German—a woman trusted as a leader around many nations.

Ireland was forced to cut teachers and police pay by 15% and welfare payments were slashed by 45%. The Prime Minister's salary was cut by 47,000 Euros. In Spain there was a pay cut for civil servants and no rise in pensions. VAT was put up to 18%, while in the UK VAT was raised to 20%. In Portugal there was a freeze on public salaries and income tax was raised by 1.5%. In Hungary the 13-month salary was abolished and there was new bank tax and cuts to railways and local government. In France there were riots when the retirement age was raised. The deficit in Ireland is 14% of GDP; in the UK the deficit reached 12.9%; in Germany it was 5%; in Hungary 4%; in Greece 12.2%; France 8.25%; Spain 10.1% and in Portugal 8% (The Independent 8/6/2010). Austerity Europe EU forecasts government borrowing and how nations plan to correct it (Lawson and Richards 2011).

The main areas of public spending are now social protection, health care, education, debt interest, defence, public order and safety, housing and environment and transport.

Estonia's GDP fell during the recession by 15%, while Ireland and Spain have experienced a large fall in the value of their wealth in real estate. Portugal has contracted by -.1.5%, Ireland's growth is now 0.5%, Spain's is 0.8%, Italy 1.1%, the Netherlands 1.5%, France 1.6%, Belgium 1.7% and Czech Republic 1.7% (Times May 13th 2011 Flemming and Hopkins). The largest economies are the USA and China, which overtook Japan recently in the no 2 slot. The fastest growing economies in Europe are worryingly Belarus at 6% and Russia at 4.8%, neither of which are known for the transparency or openness! Both are known for their issues with human rights. After them comes the Baltic nations—Poland on 3%, Sweden 3.8% as well as Latvia, Estonia, and Finland. Luxembourg has 3% growth and then comes Norway at 2.9%. The Mediterranean European countries are slightly contracting or with very low growth (Flemming and Hopkins 2011).

The Bank of England's Chief Melvyn King has this week revised its forecast downwards. Recovery from the recession is much slower than predicted and this will affect poverty. In fact many of the cuts have yet to be implemented in the sectors affecting women. The notices of redundancy in the private sector were sent out on the last day of the year 2010 and will be implemented in this current month, therefore will start to show more strongly in the forthcoming employment figures.

Photo Miriam Kennet at no 11 Downing Street advising the Chancellor about our campaign

However according to Carolina Lopez (2011) one prominent claim is that feminist economics argues that the Gross Domestic Product does not adequately measure unpaid labour predominantly performed by women such as housework, childcare and elder-care. Since a large part of women's work is rendered invisible, they argue that policies meant to boost GDP can in many circumstances actually worsen the impoverishment of women and even if the intention is to increase prosperity. For example opening up a state owned forest in India to commercial logging can increase India's GDP but women who collect fuel from the forest to cook may face substantially more hardships (Lopez 2011).

There will be many negative effects, including the effect of pensions changes in European countries, the effect on older women and also the difficulties of younger women when faced with being the target of many austerity packages focusing on areas heavily populated by women workers such as the public services, caring and education and healthcare, and being left out of the stimulus packages (Rugieri 2011).

We as the Green Economics Institute have taught on this this subject in the UK Treasury, lectured in the House of Commons and in the the United Nations and we are active in the economics at the COP Kyoto Climate Conferences and many governments and universities around the world. We specialise in spreading the word globally about how women's equal pay and opportunity are core to implementing a green economy and creating a wave of sustainable change today. There are also implications in the Middle East as many of the uprisings are actually beginning with women's dissatisfaction with their economics status, so this issue is beginning to drive world policies as well. There has never been a more topical time to address this issue—we do hope you will come and participate!

Activities of the Green Economics Institute in raising the issue in powerful forum around the world
The Green Economics Institute has been active in driving the debate for change and improvement in this area in the UK and in Europe and globally, using every opportunity to raise the issue, especially when economics policy is being created or designed. We have placed women's equality at the heart of our design of Green Economics.

Green Economics is Progressive Economics, reclaiming economics for all people everywhere, especially women, nature, other species, the planet and its systems. (Kennet and Heinemann 2006)

We raised the issue at the influential Fiscal Studies Institute national budget briefing for Ministers, financial journalists and economics commentators. We raised it with the UK Chancellor of the Exchequer and we raised it with top civil servants at the national government school. We also raised it in the formulation of the European Greens Economics policy debates for all the greens in government—now a considerable number around European economies and represent the women's group in the writing of economic policies adopted around Europe.

We also raised the issue in the UK Treasury with training officials there and in the UN in Geneva, when we launched the green economy there in December 2008. We raised it for the TEEB Report, the successor to the Stern Report, which this time covers the immense global economic cost of biodiversity loss and we requested that the issue of the cost to women is included in that budget assessment. We also challenged the Royal Economics Society to revamp its women's group and to include more women on its panels and committees. We raised it at the women's dinner "Women Changing Lives at Oxford University" November 2010. We took part training and running the high profile Women Leaders' Day for the very top of the UK civil service in March 2010 to investigate the issues and to ensure that the UK government officials really understood what the issues were and could implement effective change in their departments (National Government School 2010). We even found that the International Labour Organisation—the very EU and global organisation charged with ensuring women's access to jobs—has a very poor record of applying women's rights in the work place and the decent work programme itself is very light on the rights of women too. It has a low number of women's representations at all levels in the organisation, even though they were instrumental in setting it up in the first place!

Youth Unemployment
Recent graduates and many young people are one of the biggest casualties of the current downturn, with some countries reporting up to 50% youth unemployment. In the UK nearly 1 million of young people under 25 are unemployed, and thousands are underemployed or forced to take part-time work or a job that is not commensurate with their abilities. Long term unemployment is at an all time high. The Office for National Statistics showed youth unemployment at 941,000 for 16-24 year olds in 2010, and Spain even worse with nearly half of graduates believing that they wont get a job after graduating (Sarah Cassidy 2010).

Institute of Fiscal Studies
The Institute of Fiscal Studies is the leading commentator on the UK economy to which most economics journalist attend events and take a lead from. However, when I raised the issue and asked about compilation of women's statistics after the budget in March 2011, they said they had no statistics at all on the position of women and its effect on them! They do however research other kinds of inequality, but the situation of women is often not considered a necessity (IFS budget report event March 2011 Drill Hall London).

UK Child Poverty
Surprisingly, in the UK child poverty has fallen under the last Labour establishment, according to a report. Official poverty figures show that the number of children living in poverty fell by 200,000 to 20% of all

children in 2009–2010, down from 22% the year before. Poverty for pensioners has only fallen in 3 years within the last 50, and half of those pensioners are women. Research however shows that child poverty will increase once more between 2013 and 2014. But once again women's economics' wellbeing was treated as a subset of this other consideration, as if women only count in their role as mother. Women are often conceptualised as daughters, mothers and crones, instead of people in their own right with a whole life cycle (Times newspaper 2011 May 13th).

Citizens Income
One suggestion that is popular with some greens in the UK and Germany is the idea of a citizens' income which would provide a minimum but realistic wage for all citizens. So far, this has been tried in Alaska with the oil fund and was successful. Such a system would ensure that gender would not be a limiting factor in a person's economics life outcome.

However one of the big stories in 2010 and 2011 is the Green New Deal, a post-Keynsian stimulus package which has been adopted as an economics rationale by governments including Korea. This provides for new jobs in the expanding green sectors, and there will be a green investment bank set up in the UK, but there are no overt plans to include women's issues within it.

Women and citizenship and as global actors and as mothers; the identities of women
Interestingly as proposed by Natalie Bennet in our previous conference, women are not just mothers, but are people in their own right and so the description of "citizens" is empowering. Many of the current quests for revolution have women driving or participating for the first time in many societies. In the world of the internet, no one knows if the writer is a man or a women and it does really matter. This has perhaps enabled women to become more powerful actors (Bennet 2009: 20). She quotes Petra Kelly: *"women must lead the efforts in peace awareness, because only she I feel can go back to her womb her roots her natural rhythms her inner self for harmony and peace, while men, most of them anyway, are continually bound to their power struggle, the exploitation of nature and military ego trip."*

Photo – with the Treasury Minister inside no 11 Downing Street.
Supporting the women's budget group campaign

Pension changes

The EU has changed pension rules so that women who are often forced to retire early have to wait for their pension. Women, as we know, earn less over their working life and so the cohort of women now in their 50s are being told to wait for their planned pension for several more years. In a recession like this, however, many women are being laid off, as many are part time workers and in the target industries of public sector (health, education and care work). Therefore they are unable to earn more to compensate. Women's poverty was already a feature of old age and this has now got worse (Fawcet and women's budget group). So overall the position of women, for example in the UK, has got worse.

Academia

In academia there are still problems, especially in economics as a profession. The Royal Economics Society's conferences even have men presenting the gender sessions and in the gender working group. Very few sessions have women speakers at all and many of the panels are all male.

Photo Miriam Kennet: The Royal Economics Society, April 2010: a
nearly all male affair

Publishing
In addition there are rapid changes in technology and publishing,
which will make part-time non-tenured women even less likely to
publish than they are already. Several recent studies have noted that
women are not usually editors of academic journals and are not on
editorial boards, which seriously affects what gets accepted as truth as
academic journals are considered to be the arbiters of such truth.

Photo: Women in the Cameroun by Pauline Mouret

Photo: Inspecting a green energy plant in Estonia

Women in the media

There have always been issues about how women are represented in the media, but the issue of women owning and controlling the media affects how they are portrayed. One issue was Sarah Palin in the USA as a contender, whose media role was not presented in the same way. Although it is difficult to argue that her ideas are in any way progressive, but more alarming was the portrayal of Hilary Clinton as a presidential contender. More women-owned media might affect the outcome of gender parity.

Women in NGOs as leaders

Whilst many women work in the not for profit sector, many NGOs have very few women on the boards and many panels of speakers in all sectors are men-only. Women are discounted as "experts" in favour of men. In particular the climate change discourse and the technological green and other platforms are frequently men-only, including IPCC which has mainly men.

Speaker panels frequently men only

The visible face of expertise, both in public life and academia, form role models and emphasise the image of women as amateurs and non experts. The Nobel Prize for Economics finally went to a woman last year, Elinor Ostrom. However, the number of men-only panels is very high even in the green area: renewables, anything technical, companies and CEOs, and finance as well as green.

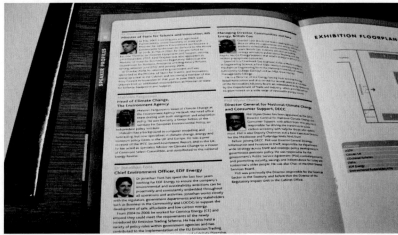

Legal status
There are two main issues which could alter this situation: firstly, the legal status and recourse to redress for infringement of equal rights. Our last conference established that the barriers and difficulties of complaining about unequal rights treatment were so high that no one really wanted to use the law to get redress. This means the law is used only in high profile more extreme cases and pay outs are so huge in those cases that it has the opposite result, meaning that businesses can be reluctant to recruit women so that ordinary every day discrimination cases go unpunished and unresolved. The barriers to speedy resolution via protection and access to law need to be removed.

Participation of women in Politics
Secondly, the participation of women into politics needs to be redressed. The UN is currently keeping figures of the percentage of women in each country active in politics, as this is one of the best indicators of progress in women's equal pay and opportunities as women can advocate politically to ensure women's interests are represented (Stevens 2009).

Participation of women in the Green New Deal Proposals
It was brought to our attention that even in the green new deal proposals, when they were presented in Estonia to green ministers and officials, the panel was all male. However in its wording it does mention the gender pay gap and that women earn less than men (an estimated 17.4% less and in some member states 33% less; the gap is

greater in the private sector than in the public sector). The employment rate of women falls when they have children by 12.4 points and rises by 7.4% when men have children, reflecting the unequal sharing of care responsibilities and lack of child facilities. Also increasing at the other end is the number of middle aged women caring for older relatives (European Commission Equality between men and women 2008, COM 2009.077. in The Green New Deal p.6; The employment dimension of the Green New Deal. 2011: European Greens). Women also are at a disadvantage collecting more employment points for pension and other social welfare benefits.

Poverty
Nearly 20% or 18 million children and young people under 18 are at risk of poverty. One out of six elderly people (a majority of them being women) live in poverty and the risk of poverty is highest among single-parent households (35% of EU average), 85% of which are headed up by women. Women over 65 are also at serious risk of poverty. Low-skilled workers are at high risk of being forced out before the retirement age. There is also a clear link between environmental damage and poverty, with the poor much more exposed to environmental damage and less able to protect themselves against it (GND employment Lamberts 8: 2010). In one of the Green New Deal Papers on employment and the Green New Deal, they aim for 60% female employment. They advocate minimum standards regarding working time, closing the gender pay gap and revising the EU Directive 75/117.EEC. They also advocate proper implementation of the directive 2002/7 with equal access to vocational training, employment, promotion and working conditions, and sanctions against those members states who do not implement these directives. They propose the Nordic Model but which includes some flexisecurity. They support flexible and reliable contract arrangements for workers which focus on employability, comprehensive life long learning, model social security systems and strong social dialogue. Similarly in an article in the Sunday Times (06.06.2010) on green engineering, all the pictures were of men and no women were mentioned at all as the assumption is that "green" engineering will help the men—with no consideration for women in engineering (Gareth Huw Davies 2010 Sunday Times).

Access to education
Additionally women's education is an important issue in this whole process too. Access to education is a prerequisite for participation in political and economic life and independence, and in far too many countries women are not included at all in political life. Women in some countries do not even have the right to vote yet. It was however the extreme discontent of women in these situations that began the

uprisings, i.e. the 'Arab Spring' which is still on going. Much of what happens in Afghanistan appears to be a war on women – where their rights are completely eroded by some parties in the conflict and the symbolism of women being excluded from education as a first act in this scenario of eroding women's rights. However it was in Afghanistan, Egypt, and Yemen and Iran that women became major players in the fight for democracy or participation. Women are becoming much more active in Lebanese politics in addition.

Iceland
In Iceland after the credit crunch and collapse of the banks, women actually took over the running of the country and the country's banks. This has allowed it to recover. Gender became an important and overt issue in its recovery.

Women into business
India has the lowest level of women in business and economics life, and one of the most challenging rates of women's maternal mortality—are these two linked? (The exact figure is 23%, followed by Japan, Turkey, and Austria at the bottom of the larger economies – source WEF 2010) and the most women in business is Norway 40%, and 52% USA (WEF 2011), Spain, Canada, Finland (WEF).The CEO picture was much worse: Finland 13%, Norway 12%, Turkey 12%, Italy 11%, Brazil 11% have the highest number of female CEOs. In the study by WEF there were no responding companies with female CEOs in the UK, Czech Republic, France, Greece, the Netherlands, India, Mexico, the Netherlands, Switzerland.

Women on the Boards – the law in Norway
Norway has a particular issue in the huge sovereign wealth funds and its very high welfare state provisions which are invested ethically. As a result, women's status and pay in Norway remains especially high in one of the wealthiest and most equal societies in the world. Very strong family policies protect women's opportunities. Additionally since our last conference a very important change happened: the makeup of company boards was changed by law to include 40% women, and this has perhaps helped Norway to ensure its place at the very top of the rankings. This has apparently allowed Norway to invite young women onto the boards of, for example, music recording companies. This has actually given the companies a further competitive advantage and helped make Norway one of the richest and most equal countries in the world. Overall, Nordic countries Iceland (1), Norway (2), Finland (3) and Sweden (4) continue to demonstrate the greatest equality between men and women according to the World Economic Forum's Global Gender Gap Report 2010 (WEF 2010).

The Global Gender Gap 2010 Rankings - Top 15				Change	
Country	2010	Score*	2009	Change	
Iceland	1	85.0%	1	0	→
Norway	2	84.0%	3	1	↑
Finland	3	82.6%	2	-1	↓
Sweden	4	80.2%	4	0	→
New Zealand	5	78.1%	5	0	→
Ireland	6	77.7%	8	2	↑
Denmark	7	77.2%	7	0	→
Lesotho	8	76.8%	10	2	↑
Philippines	9	76.5%	9	0	→
Switzerland	10	75.6%	13	3	↑
Spain	11	75.5%	17	6	↑
South Africa	12	75.3%	6	-6	↓
Germany	13	75.3%	12	-1	↓
Belgium	14	75.1%	33	19	↑
United Kingdom	15	74.6%	15	0	→

World Economic Forum Website (May 15th 2011)

According to the report's index, the level of gender equality in France (46) has sunk as the number of women in ministerial positions has fallen over the past 12 months. The United States (19) closed its gender gap, rising 12 places to enter the top 20 for the first time in the report's five-year history. The climb reflects the higher number of women in leading roles in the current administration and improvements in the wage gap (WEF 2011).

Photo : The importance of women's contribution to the economy and
high competitiveness

"Nordic countries continue to lead the way in eliminating gender inequality," said Klaus Schwab, Founder and Executive Chairman of the World Economic Forum. *"Low gender gaps are directly correlated with high economic competitiveness. Women and girls must be treated equally if a country is to grow and prosper. We still need a true gender equality revolution, not only to mobilize a major pool of talent both in terms of volume and quality, but also to create a more compassionate value system within all our institutions."* (WEF 2011). This finding is supported by the OECD in its report by Stevens in Kennet (2009).

GGR report criteria

The Global Gender Gap Report's index assesses 134 countries on how well they divide resources and opportunities amongst male and female populations, regardless of the overall levels of these resources. The report measures the size of the gender inequality gap in four areas:

1) Economic participation and opportunity – outcomes on salaries, participation levels and access to high-skilled employment
2) Educational attainment – outcomes on access to basic and higher level education
3) Health and survival – outcomes on life expectancy and sex ratio
4) Political empowerment – outcomes on representation in decision-making structures

Ireland (6), Switzerland (10), Spain (11), Germany (13) and the United Kingdom (15) are among the European countries dominating the top 20. Luxembourg (26) and Greece (58) made the biggest improvements in closing their gender gaps, climbing 37 and 27 spots respectively, owing to gains in political and economic participation (WEF 2011).

Corporate inequality globally

The Forum's Global Gender Gap Report has found that although more women are in employment than ever before, major corporations are still not capitalizing on their talents. Pay equality is not there either. So why are women still not equally represented in major multinational companies and, when they are, why aren't they being paid equally? (WEF 2011) The report shows that much progress is being made, but there is a lot of ground to catch up on. Its co-author Ricardo Hausmann, Director of the Centre for International Development at Harvard University, says countries have to adjust for the fact that marriage and motherhood are not at odds with women's advancement in the workplace (WEF 2011).

Education and Health
Hausmann said: *"We have found that gaps are closing between women and men's health and education – in fact, current data show that in the 134 countries covered, 96% of health gaps and 93% of education gaps have been closed. And, yet only 60% of economic participation gaps have been closed. Progress will be achieved when countries seek to reap returns on the investment in health and education of girls and women by finding ways to make marriage and motherhood compatible with the economic participation of women."* (WEF 2011) This is supported by the paper by Kennet (2011) on women's higher mortality rate in India, for example, where this is affected by women's lower economic outcomes. If women have a lower education and economics status, this directly affects life expectancy and health and infant mortality.

Gender pay gap and national growth and competitiveness
Fellow co-author Laura Tyson, S.K. and Angela Chan Professor of Global Management at the Hass School of Business, University of California at Berkeley, reflects: *"The Global Gender Gap Report demonstrates that closing the gender gap provides a basis for a prosperous and competitive society. Regardless of level of income, countries can choose to integrate gender equality and other social inclusion goals into their growth agenda – and have the potential to grow faster – or they can run the risk of undermining their competitive potential by not capitalizing fully on one-half of their human resources. The economic incentive for closing the gender gap in health, education, economic opportunity and political power is clear."* (WEF 2011)

Is my work valued the same?
European Commission campaign 2009 -2011

References
Bennet Rosemary (May 13th 2011) Child Poverty declined under Labour but income gap grew. (Times Newspaper)
Corporate Gender GAP (2010) Instead for WEF Accessed web May 15th 2011
Cassidy Sarah (2010) recent graduates employ new tactics to tackle the job market. Times
Huw Davies (2010) Plugged in motors, Sunday Times P;10
Huw Davies (2010) E car + smart grid = clean transport. Sunday Times
The Green Budget Report (2011) Institute of Fiscal Studies 2011
Dominic Lawson D and Richards. S (8.6.2010). The axe falls across

Europe: Austerity Europe EU forecasts for government borrowing and how nations plan to correct it. Independent Newspaper

Kennet M.,Eds. (2009) Proceedings of the Green Economics Conference Empowering women women's economics, women's poverty, and the impact of unequal pay and unequal opportunity – empowering women, solutions to the credit crunch workshops-cracking the concrete ceiling for women at work and at pay. Saturday 7th March 2009. Reading International Solidarity Centre. Editor Miriam Kennet.

Kennet M and Heinemann V.(2006) Green Economics Setting the Scene. International Journal of Green Economics Vol 1 issue 1/ 2 Inderscience Publishers

International Labour Organisation Decent work: various publication 2010 : ILO Turin

Lopez Carolina (2011) Post-feminism, motherhood and the welfare state

Reader Store -Sovereign wealth funds- Weiner -book review- (2011- web access May 15th 2011)

Pavia Will, (2011) IMF chief is charged over sex attack on hotel maid. French presidential hopeful held on eve of Euro crisis meeting. The Times. Front Page.

Sage Adam and Pavia Will, (2011) Everyone knows his weakness is seduction and women. It all a plot. P.6.

Spence Alex. (May 16 2011) Business big shot, Gaenor Bagley Age 46 position partner PwC in Business Dashboard. Page 32, The Times

Stevens C (2008) OECD Gender and sustainable development maximising the economic and social and environmental role of women. OECD 2008

Taylor M. (2010) India, in International Journal of Green Economics and also Taylor M(2009) India in Proceedings of womens conference Reading International Solidarity Centre. March 2009.

Editorial (2011) He Kahn't any more The arrest of Dominique Strauss Kahn is not just a scandal. The fall of the IMF boss will jolt the worlds financial system and the course of French Politics. Times Editorial May 16th 2011.

Turner C. (2011) Don swears oath that Rafsanjani hired help.in Cherwell May 13th 2011 volume 263 No 3,Weiner E.J. (2010) The Shadow Market: How a Group of Wealthy Nations and Powerful Investors Secretly Dominate the World WEF report (2011) accessed web May 15th 2011

Chapter 2 Finance

2.1 Green Investment Bank:Driving transition to a low-carbon economy

Winston Ka-Ming MAK

Supporting the UK Government's green policy objectives, the Green Investment Bank (GIB) is a new and enduring institution being established to finance environmental and clean energy projects for which the mainstream banks are currently reluctant to take the early risks. The United Kingdom will be the first country to create a bank dedicated to the low-carbon revolution. Ambitious to leverage billions of pounds of extra private sector capital, the bank will work to a 'double bottom line' of both achieving significant green impact and making financial returns. It will gain market credibility by operating at arm's length from Whitehall.

Financial market failure

In fact, many energy efficiency projects and ventures face a plethora of barriers to financing as they are too small and/or risky to attract the attention of large financial institutions. (World Bank, 2008) Today, not to mention various business projects of high profitability competing for capitals, the banking sector, in financing green energy projects, usually perceives the transaction costs and risks around new technologies, creditworthiness and revenue security, etc. to be unbearable. A number of scholars and energy professionals agree that these market failures necessitates a government-backed bank acting in the public interest, if the UK is to go ahead with the scale of the low-carbon infrastructure required to meet the national carbon reduction targets. Thus in 2009-10, the UK Government accepted a proposal by the Sustainable Development Commission for a green investment bank that will unlock private finance to accelerate a wide range of green infrastructure projects.

The Green Investment Bank Commission estimates that £550 billion could be required for investment in supply chains and infrastructure in order to meet the national climate change and renewable energy target between now and 2020. (GIB Commission, 2010) Meanwhile, evidence given to the Environmental Audit Committee suggests that the UK will need to raise £200 billion and £1 trillion over the next two decades, but traditional sources of private fundraising are likely to deliver between £50 and £80 billion only. (BBC News, 2011)

The 'commercial' bank for green economy

The GIB is now being capitalised with £3 billion taxpayers' money, of which £2 billion will be injected on top of the initial £1 billion capital according to the Budget 2011. The bank is expected to have catalysed an additional £15 billion into the green economy within four years, making money for clean energy projects more cheaply. According to the Deputy Prime Minister, Nick Clegg, some of the bank's priorities will be offshore wind, non-domestic energy efficiency and waste. (Kinver, 2011) Work is being done to explore other sectors that would be eligible for intervention. A further boost to green campaigners is the possibility that GIB helps finance the green deal scheme, where householders will have access to loans for energy efficiency refurbishment to be repaid in instalments through their energy bills.

The GIB Commission has proposed that the primary focus of the bank should be on lowering risk for investors, rather than simply providing capital. It could help catalyse low-carbon investment by:

(a)Unlocking project finance through equity co-investment, first loss debt and insurance products;

(b) Creating green bonds to access to very large pools of capital held by such institutional investors as pension funds and life insurance companies and which would provide the scale of capital needed; and

(c) Selling green ISAs that enable retail investors to contribute to the funding of green infrastructure. (GIB Commission, 2010)

An independent institution

To ensure the green bank is an enduring and independent institution, it will be free from governmental and political interference as well as able to reinvest the proceeds from its investments. The GIB will be set up as a Companies Act company and follow best practice corporate governance. Its public roles, interim governance structure and independence will be enshrined in legislation as soon as the state aid approval is achieved. (BIS, 2011) Actually, the independence of the bank from ministers has been a major concern for investors, who are worried about the Treasury's plan to avoid legislation and retain control over the bank would result in years of damaging political interference. The Deputy Prime Minister has reassured the public that it will be part of the institutional architecture of the country and translated from an idea to a flow of investment to Britain's clean energy industries in under two years. The GIB will have powers to borrow from the private money markets from April 2015.

Downing Street's decision to delay the bank's power to borrow from the capital market until the public sector net debt has fallen as a targeted percentage of GDP attracted criticisms. Some urged the Government to needs to say legislation will happen next year at the latest, and make clear the bank can borrow from the capital markets from the outset. (Kinver, 2011) Earlier, the heads of 15 green campaign groups have written to the Prime Minister and pointed to delays in giving borrowing powers to the new green investment bank. (BBC News, 2011) "Setting up a Green Investment Bank without the power to borrow would be a bit like trying to buy a house without first getting a mortgage offer. George Osborne has got the deposit, but if he doesn't allow the bank to raise extra capital, the sums are going to fall far short of what is needed," said Joan Walley, chair of the Environmental Audit Committee. (BBC News, 2011) Many believe the most effective form to stimulate and promote green growth is to let the bank raise money in a similar fashion to regular banks that can leverage huge funding from the private sector.

Timing

The Green Investment Bank will begin operating in April 2012, according to the latest statement of the Government in the House of Commons in May 2011. The legislation for the bank may take longer than a year, but funds would be released within 11 months so that companies can start planning their applications for funding for green projects, including offshore wind farms, waste and industrial energy efficiency. Now, Edinburgh and Bristol are bidding to be the home of the bank's headquarter and a decision will be made later this year.

The way forward

Vital to driving a transition to a truly low-carbon economy is the development of well-designed, long-term and stable policies that provide incentives for businesses to invest in new, green infrastructure. The Green Investment Bank will unlock the major new streams of investment and give greater certainty of meeting the climate change targets. It will work over the long term in the national interest with its focus on innovative risk aversion, sending a strong signal to investors that the UK is serious about its low-carbon transformation. This is a tremendous opportunity to realise sustainable growth by rapidly scaling up the green investment, creating green jobs and industries of our future. If the green bank model is a success, this will be another great contribution from Britain to the world's economy.

Bibliography

BBC News. (2011, May 14). Coalition 'losing way' on green policies - campaigners. *BBC News* .

BBC News. (2011, March 11). Green Investment Bank must not be compromised, say MPs. *BBC News* .

BIS. (2011). *Update on the design of the Green Investment Bank*. London: Department for Business Innovations & Skills.

GIB Commission. (2010). *Unlocking investment to deliver Britain's low-carbon future*. London: Green Investment Bank Commission.

Kinver, M. (2011, May 23). Clegg: UK green bank 'to begin investing in April 2012'. *BBC News* .

World Bank. (2008). *Financing Energy Efficiency: Lessons from Brazil, China, India and Beyond*. Washington DC: World Bank.

2.2 Finance and instability: re-focusing the economic policy agenda

Maria Alejandra Caporale Madi

Introduction

In the last few decades there has been broad recognition that the current operation of the financial markets has not generated sustainable economic and social development. Otherwise, it has promoted financial vulnerability (Akyüz, 1993). According to Minsky (1986:5) "the economic instability since the late 1960s is the result of the fragile financial system that emerged from the cumulative changes in financial relations and institutions over the following World War II".

This long-run process of financial expansion turned out to be characterized as the "financialisation" of the capitalist economy where monopoly-finance capital became increasingly dependent on credit and financial bubbles (Foster, 2009). As a matter of fact, the international economy suffered 244 financial crises between 1975 and 1998: 158 currency, 54 banking and 32 twin (currency and banking) crises happened (Kaul et al., 2003). These crises were more frequent in emerging countries that faced 116 currency, 54 banking crises and 32 twin crises. After 1998, Brazil, Turkey, United States and many European countries, among others, also presented financial instability. Output and employment losses partially illustrate the economic and social costs.

In the context of unrestricted market flexibilisation, good governance practices refer especially to sound policies (fiscal and monetary) besides prudential financial regulation that could favour macroeconomic stability (Madi, 2004). In this setup, the concept of credibility is decisive to understand the potential of success of this economic agenda. In other words, governments should adopt not only the right macroeconomic policies but also implement prudential financial measures and efficient supervision practices in order to be supported by the global "investors" (Grabel, 2000).

The recent global crisis has shown sources of financial fragility: the financial innovations regarding asset, liability and capital management in the banking sector, the movement toward securitized finance, the growing importance of institutional investors in the management of "financial savings" within the shadow banking system, besides the random investors´ behaviour in a context of capital account openness (The Economist, 2011). As a matter of fact, economic systemic contradictions and tensions in the political and social spheres have been created by financial globalization (Guttmann, 1998) .

Green economics looks beyond the dynamics of the financial markets in order to take into account a "long-term, earth-wide and holistic context" where equity and inclusiveness could be understood within a multidisciplinary range of knowledge (Kennet and Heinemann, 2006). Considering this background our main concern is to reflect on the interactions between finance and instability in contemporary capitalist and enhance further understanding of financial policy issues. Section 1 considers the relationship between finance and instability. Section 2 presents the main features of the policy debate on financial regulation. Finally, we underline the importance of Green Economics in facing the effects of financial globalization on livelihood conditions and suggest the need of a reassessment of the economic policy agenda.

Finance and instability

In the last decades, the free-market pressures turned out to deepen the instability of the domestic financial systems. If we look at the current global economic downturn in terms of the lessons from Minsky, we can observe that outstanding features of this crisis should be focused within the financial sector. The recent American financial crisis is an example of how the financial industry encouraged speculation dependent on future housing prices, the future price of securitized assets and the renewal of lending operations. This conduct was supported by the banking system in a context where lending requirements were liberalized and banks managed the capital requirements adjusted to risk by means of enhancing further securitized operations. The banks were interested in selling credit so as to enhance credit and liquidity risk management within a new profit pattern where they stopped requiring income, assets or even job verification. The banking system was encouraging speculative and Ponzi operations that depend on the future prices of houses, future prices of the securitized assets and the renewals of the lending operations.

Under the perspective of Minsky, it is especially important to understand the current challenges to the financial markets as he emphasized that the financial institutions play a crucial role in determining investment through the business cycle. The process of financial deregulation has been overwhelmed by transformations in the investment pattern since corporate decisions have been increasingly subordinated to speculative financial commitments (Minsky, 1975). The financial conception of investment has increased in the context where financial innovations aimed to achieve fast growth with lower capital requirements could be used by managers to favour short-term financial performance (Fligstein, 2001).

Financial instability is viewed as a result of speculation and uncertainty. Growing investment puts pressure on the demand for funding – a function of bankers' expectation of future incomes. Increased investment leads to higher profit rates and present value of capital assets. The credit boom intensifies while liquidity preference declines and the resulting portfolios are extremely vulnerable to changes in interest rates and asset prices. When profits decline, as they inevitably do, credit and external funding becomes restricted.

From the Keynesian tradition, Hyman Minsky considered the role of finance in the business cycle and developed the financial instability hypothesis which states that financial crises are inherent to the capitalist economy after financial deregulation in the 1970s. In his own words: "..it is finance that acts as the sometimes dampening, sometimes amplifying governor of investment. As a result finance sets the pace of investment" (Minsky 1975:130). In the capitalist economy, there is a set of interrelated balance sheets and cash flows between the income-producing system (hedge, speculative and Ponzi firms) and the financial structure that affect the valuation of the stock of capital assets, the evolution of credit and the pace of investment. The pace of investment, in turn, determines income and employment (Madi, 1993).

While considering the factors that determine investment, the autonomous component of aggregate demand, Minsky stated how credit markets affect investment transactions which are financed initially through debt and ultimately through profits resulting from the previous levels of investment and asset prices. His approach relies on the endogenous nature of financial instability and criticized the competitive market paradigm of neo-classical economics. Under Minsky's perspective, the investment dynamics is based on the existence of a monetary economy where credit relations, speculation and uncertainty are decisive to affect the investment path, leading to endogenous credit crunches. When profits and the asset prices begin to decline, the credit crunch also restricts external financing for those transactions. In this scenario, the liquidity crunch might be dampened by the Central Bank interventions as a lender of last resort while the Big Government supports private profits in order to enhance the recovery of aggregate demand (Madi and Gonçalves, 2008).

What Brunhoff, Chesnais and Flassbeck add to our understanding is that another consequence of liberalized system is that financial crises have shown the fragility of exchange rate regimes and balance of payments vulnerability in the context of current international financial architecture where the determination of exchange rates depends on the hierarchy among monetary policies and the arbitrage/speculation made by financial markets. Brunhoff (1998) points out that financial instability means price instability in financial asset markets. The instability of exchange rates is a co-related question since domestic currencies assume the role of financial assets. Chesnais (1998) also emphasized the interactions between monetary and exchange rate markets while explaining that: "A pattern of high financial return was universally imposed by financial markets, with local variations, depending on the influence of financial arbitrages on domestic monetary policies. The evaluation of domestic currencies in exchange markets was submitted to this new financial regime, as well as the practices of Central Banks" (Chesnais, 1998:51). In this set up, the level of domestic interest rates is subordinated to the main features of the new international financial pattern - high returns and low inflation.

This idea is also discussed by Flassbeck (2002) who analyzes the viability of unilateral options of exchange rate regimes in a multilateral world where the advance of market globalization continues despite the lack of global institutions or yet the absence of a global approach to economic policy. Under his perspective, the canonic discussion between fixed or flexible exchange rate regimes sets aside the essence of the current financial global problem, that is, the destabilizing effects of the increasing capital mobility and the loss of autonomy of economic policy.

As a matter of fact, in the current international financial architecture, exchange rate crises may also happen as result of abrupt reversal of capital flows. This is explained in a context of uncertainty where portfolio decisions are not submitted to stochastic behaviour, that is to say, they are not predictable: the process of decision making, in truth, is based on conventions. Considering this background, the vulnerability of domestic currencies, as a result of changes in market opinions, is not independent of the global financial cycle that threatens the sustainability of the exchange rate regimes.

Debating financial regulation

As Keynes pointed out in the 1930s the organization of capital markets increases the risk of predominance of speculation and instability since these markets are mostly based upon conventions whose precariousness affects the rhythm of investment and increases pressures on the political sphere (Belluzzo and Almeida, 2002). Keynes (1936) suggested a reconsideration of the understanding of the relations among individuals, society and state within the market where institutions and conventions could shape rationality. Expressing concerns about the 1930 Great Depression fragile institutional set up and its effects on income and employment, his proposals aimed to promote economic and social transformations. Aware of the need to overcome the economic vision centred on the caricature known as the rational Homo economicus, his contribution enhances a more extended vision on individuals´ behaviours and a more fruitful analysis on the real-world financial complexities that prevent full employment.

These questions have long been ignored in the competitive market paradigm of neo-classic economics. Mainstream economists assume that financial markets efficaciously transfer funds; and furthermore that financial deregulation was necessary to increase efficiency and the supply of loanable funds. Financial crisis are a monetary phenomena: expansionary monetary policies do not favour domestic and external equilibrium. The ex-ante saving-investment disequilibrium is stimulated by the money supply and credit expansion and causes financial imbalances. In other words, the roots of the crisis are related to the attempt to keep the domestic income level too high vis à vis its non-inflationary level (Madi, 1993). Under this approach, the monetary policy, aimed to stabilize prices, subordinates the evolution of fiscal policy: the financing of the public sector, trough monetary expansion or public debt, must be compatible with the inflationary targets. Besides, the autonomy of the monetary policy requires flexible exchange rates in the frame of capital account openness.

From the mainstream perspective, the financial crises would be the result of wrong economic policy options. This approach foundations rely on the exogenous nature of money supply and the duality "real versus monetary" when analyzing the dynamics of the capitalist economy. As a result, it does not consider the active role of money and financial institutions and their speculative and destabilizing behaviours. Under this view, financial market imperfections might be avoided and, eventually, corrected, since adequate monetary and financial policies would be implemented.

This approach has supported the frame of the current financial regulation. Among the financial policies, the Basle Agreements have shaped an institutional set up in order to improve the efficiency of financial markets in the allocation of resources by means of the commitment to better risk and capital management practices in the domestic banking sectors (BCBS, 2001). The Basle "codes and patterns"- based on the conception of capital adjustment to risk in the banking sector – focused the reduction of asymmetric information in credit and capital markets, maximize investors´ returns and dampen the arising agency problem. As a matter of fact, the Basle Agreements have been voluntary adopted to spread out mechanisms of protection to avoid the financial systemic risk and favour informational transparency (disclosure). Thus, the prudential measures might be supported by the dissemination of information, transparency, contingent strategies and better supervision practices. These practices, aimed to overcome the "asymmetric information" that overwhelms the contracts within the financial markets, would enhance more efficient financial leverage systems and greater transparency to financial regulators and investors (Fligstein, 2001).

However, these financial international agreements have supported the "status quo", that is to say, the expansion of universal banks, private money and liquid capital markets under the World Trade Organization´s defence of financial services liberalization (Guttmann, 1998). As a matter of fact, the efficient financial liberalized model presents limits and failures in face of the empirical reality. In addition, the idea of autonomous monetary management has collapsed under the 2008 global financial crisis. Domestic monetary systems, in a context of financial liberalization and inconvertible currencies, do not face financial disturbances easily. The financial crises and the erratic movements of key-currencies have shown that the Central Banks do not have control on the complexity of global, innovative and speculative markets. Otherwise, the Central Banks´ actions are not independent from private and public pressures.

The financial crises observed in the last decades gave strong reasons to think about systemic problems. From a Keynesian perspective, the understanding on financial crises and regulation highlights that the scope of domestic policies to prevent and manage crisis is limited. The global financial integration has augmented the exposure of countries to global macroeconomic and financial vulnerabilities. In this set up, domestic prudential financial regulation presents challenges to success. First, the banking assets and liabilities are vulnerable to changes in global macroeconomic conditions. Second, the universal scope of banks ´ operations reveals the conflicts behind the segmentation of domestic supervision. Third, there is a delay between new regulation patterns and banking practices. At last, the consolidation of larger financial institutions, stimulated by capital adequacy requirements, information technology, the elimination of geographic restrictions and changes in the composition of financial savings have favoured the action of the Central Bank as an agency that arbitrates the competitive settlement (Campilongo et al., 2000). As a result, domestic financial regulation can induce to better practices but cannot eliminate the possibility of crisis. It is also necessary a global action with coordination and coherence among the objectives and practices of multilateral institutions.

Taking into account this background, it is decisive to underline the importance of supervision of global financial risk. The recent American crisis exposed the inner economic, social and political tensions that overwhelm the outcomes of the reality of the self-regulated markets. Nevertheless, one of the main challenges to restructure the international financial architecture and promote sustainable growth is the absence of a common project with the compliance of all countries so as to achieve the adequate provision of liquidity, the recognition of the need of stable financial flows and new forms of debt negotiation (Griffith-Jones, 2002). The Great 2007-2009 crisis has restated the menace of deep depressions among the current challenges (Foster, 2009) while livelihood conditions turned out to be subordinated to the bailout of the domestic financial systems.

Mainly concerned about the challenges to prevent deep depressions, Minsky (1986) urgently emphasized the need of shaping a thorough agenda of institutional reform so as to control the working of a capitalist economy. In his opinion "finance cannot be left to the free markets". As the organization of economic and social institutions helps to define policy goals and outcomes, his proposals stimulates a reflection on how to promote: a financial reform aimed to favour hedge financing; an industrial policy; an employment strategy based on the creation of an infinitely elastic demand for labour by the government that that could act as employer of last resort; a taxation policy that could have allocational, distributional and macroeconomic outcomes toward inclusive growth (Madi, 2004).

Under this perspective, the role of monetary policy could be highlighted through the participation of Central Bank in redirecting flows of credit. It is necessary to influence the flows of credit and articulate them within the framework of the industrial policy that would search for alternatives to the market power of giant corporations (Minsky, 1986). A new relationship between the financial and industrial spheres is required to promote growth and income distribution. In this attempt, the economic agenda involves aggregate demand (fiscal and monetary) and income policies besides the articulation of financial flows in both credit and capital markets.It is also time to think about capital controls that might reduce the effects of sharp reversal short-term capital flows. Globalization has not been a miracle way to achieve growth. We need to look forward new perspectives to search for more coherence in the relationship among finance and sustainable development.

Final considerations

Green economics could favour a reflection on the changing nature and rhythm of the transformations of society, knowledge and values (Kennet, 2007). The speed of these changes enhances the search for new connections to offer new alternatives within a more satisfactory understanding of the reality. Time and space are not neglected as they shape the possibilities of observation, analysis and intervention to configure the society where the individuals live.

Thus, Green economists could support proactive interventions based on a theoretical framework that can explain the current financial instability as an outcome of the private accumulation process. In this attempt, the Green Economics´ principles highlight the pillars of a holistic framework where the social, ecological and environmental challenges could be thought as the result of the interactions among institutions, state and society in the context of contemporary Sand concepts. Therefore, the participation of the Green Economists is required to build alternatives for a new regulation should express a holistic approach to finance.

Taking into account the current social and economic challenges, it is necessary to re-focus the economic policy agenda. Investment, employment and finance cannot be left to the free markets. In his attempt to re-shape the world order in the 1940s, Keynes pointed out the need of an international currency system that might only work by means of a "wide measure of agreement", that is to say, by means of the creation of a new international convention. In Keynes´ time, this convention would rely on multiple needs: an international currency, a stable exchange rate system, redistribution of international reserves, stabilizing mechanisms, sources of liquidity, besides a central institution to aid and support other international institutions related to the planning and regulation of the world economic life.

As uncertainty is inherent in all economic decisions, Keynes relied on the concepts of credibility and degree of confidence on a conventional judgment that is historical and socially built in the markets. In his own words: "More generally, we need a means of reassurance to a troubled world, by which any country whose own affairs are conducted with due prudence is relieved of anxiety, for causes which are not of its own making, concerning its ability to meet its international liabilities; and which will, therefore, make unnecessary those methods of restriction and discrimination which countries have adopted hitherto, not on their merits, but as measures of self-protection from disruptive outside forces" (Keynes, 1987).

Thus, the solution to enhance financial stability has to be holistic and based on a historic understanding of the international inequalities. In our times, new convention-conducing institutions could foster financial re-regulation and re-shape domestic policies to enhance sustainable inclusive growth. The Central Banks´ actions should be subordinated to this must.

2.3 New trends in energy finance in Brazil: challenges to sustainable investment

Maria Alejandra Caporale Madi

1. Introduction

Latin American market deregulation has opened up new investment opportunities in sectors where private enterprises and foreign companies were formerly subject to restrictions such as mining, energy and telecommunications. New energy finance has increased in a context where private equity funds have assumed active role in the selection of investments of high profit potential and in the process of fundraising (Gonçalves and Madi, 2011).

In the current global crisis, Brazil continued to attract investors and private equity funds that are looking to emerging markets for opportunities of returns. The fundraising by private equity reached U.S. $ 6.1 billion in 2009, 6.4% over the amount fundraised in 2008. As a matter of fact, Brazil has presented an important development in fundraising among emerging markets: in 2005 the share was 6.9% and peaked in 2007 with 15.9% (ABDI, 2011).[1]

Considering this background our main concern is to highlight the financialisation of the private equity funds´ management practices that aim short-term profits (ITUC, 2007 and IUF, 2007).[2] As a result, financial restructuring, cost adjustments to achieve economic efficiency and owners changes could threaten the long-run sustainability of energy investments in Brazil.

An overview of the private equity fundraising and investments and the recent trends in energy private equity in Brazil are presented in Section 1. Section 2 questions private equity funds´ management practices. Finally we underline the challenges to sustainable energy investment in the long-run and suggest the need of a reassessment of the economic policy agenda.

1. **Private equity funds and energy finance in Brazil: recent trends**

The private equity funds in Brazil have been gaining more relevance in the country's economy (GVcepe 2008). In 2009, the committed capital corresponded to 2.33% of GDP, against 1.8% of GDP in 2008 and 1% in 2004. The capital committed is concentrated in closely held companies where investments in expansion stage companies are more common than early stage financing. However, private investments in public equity and leveraged buyout are turning out to become more common.[3] Currently, there is a trend towards diversification of the types of investors, such as government-controlled companies, insurance companies, other investment funds, banks and family offices. However, pension funds remain the most active type of investor, representing 22 per cent of the total committed capital existing in Brazil (Pinho et al., 2011).[4]

In 2010 fundraising for Brazil reached US$4.5 billion, surpassing the 2008 peak of US$3.6 billion. This amount shows a 400 per cent increase over 2009. Emerging markets seem to return to pre-crisis fundraising levels: 119 funds raised US$23.5 billion in all of 2010. Asia (led by China) continues to dominate the private equity fundraising capturing US$23.7 billion (EMPEA, 2011).

The private equity industry in Brazil operates in a broad range of economic sectors (GVcepe, 2008). Nevertheless, IT and electronics are historically the leading sectors. When analyzing the distribution of new private equity investments in 2009, the largest distinction between the periods (assuming 2005-2008 as reference to comparison) is in the amount of investment in energy and oil, which represented 5 per cent of the value of new investments made by private managers and represented 54 per cent of new businesses in 2009 (ABDI, 2011).[5]

The energy industry has been particularly attractive to private equity investors, especially renewable fuels projects such as wind power, small hydro-electric plants and "co-generation" by sugar and alcohol mills burning the remains of sugar cane stalks to generate electricity (Wheatley, 2010). In 2010 some examples of these investments include:

1. Qatar Holding, the emirate's sovereign wealth fund, signed memorandums of understanding with Vale (the world's biggest iron ore miner), Previ (the pension fund for government-controlled Banco do Brasil), and the BNDES (the national development bank) in order to invest in energy, agribusiness and real estate;

2. First Reserve, a US private equity group with US $19 billion under management, committed US $500million to an oil and gas start-up - Barra Energia Petróleo e Gas;

3. The Brazilian firm Omega Energia entered into an investment agreement with Warburg Pincus, a leading global private equity firm, and Tarpon Investimentos, in order to fund the transform Omega into one of the leading renewable energy platforms (LAVCA, 2010).

At the end of 2010, private equity investments in Brazil were distributed as shown in Table 1. Energy and oil private equity investments corresponded to 9.7 per cent of the total. As matter of fact energy and oil are the second most relevant sectors regarding private equity finance.

In 2011, US $1.9 billion was fundraised by the Brazilian asset manager Gavea Investimentos in order to expand investments of its fourth private equity fund. Almost one-third of that amount of capital has already been committed in buying stakes in four companies: car rental agency Unidas, oil and gas operator Odebrecht Oleo e Gas, food company Camil Alimentos and men's clothing company Camisaria Colombo (LAVCA, 2011). Besides, Banco Votorantim SA (the financial services unit of Votorantim Group[6]) plans to fundraise US $768 million for three private equity funds that will invest in renewable energy projects.[7]
The funds will invest in small hydroelectric projects, biomass plants and wind farms.
The fund is considering other technologies like photovoltaic solar energy projects and biogas plants.[8]

In the period between 2005 and 2008 were reported 181 disinvestments. Only in 2009, 40 disinvestments were reported by 22 fund managers (ABDI, 2011). The largest number of disinvestments was recorded in the computers and electronics Sector, representing 29% of the total. The sector includes software, hardware, internet and other technology-based micro-sectors. Secondly, the sector of diverse industries accounted the 34 disinvestments. This sector represents industries such as steel ,automotive, chemical, textile etc. The communications industry was the third most significant sector in the number of disinvestments. It is observed that, in the period between 2005 and 2009, private equity exit strategies included: buyback, followed by public secondary sale, trade-sale (strategic buyers) and IPO (public offering). These evidences also reflect the period of financial crisis, in which the exit through IPO would not be profitable (Pinho et al, 2011).

2. Management practices and challenges to Sustainable Development

It is worth noting the substantial increase in activities of international fund managers in Brazil. Fund managers' services include fund raising, financial statement analysis, company selection, restructuring implementation and ongoing monitoring of investments. Fund managers centralize endowments from investors, such as financial institutions, institutional investors - also pension funds - and high net worth individuals, among others, in order to assume key roles in acquisitions of high profit potential (Gonçalves and Madi, 2011). According to Pinho et al. (2011), the private equity fund manager could charge a management fee on a yearly basis (which varies from 1 to 3 per cent of the committed capital) or of the equity held by the fund (fixed fee). Besides, there is a performance fee (success fee).[9] No limitation for the establishment of the management and performance fees usually charged by the fund managers is imposed by regulation. [10]

Private equity firms are considered a financial phenomenon (Cullen and James, 2007). The process of financial deregulation has been overwhelmed by transformations in the investment pattern since corporate decisions have been increasingly subordinated to speculative financial commitments (Minsky, 1975). In a private equity firms´ portfolio structure, a company acquisition is equivalent to an addition to a stock of financial assets. This investment is generated by expectations about short-run cash flows, mainly anticipated dividends and non–equity based fees. Thus, the selection of the portfolio companies has been influenced by potential market growth and profits, besides legal and incentive structures, among other factors. Exit conditions become crucial in the investment decision making process because capital mobility shortens the maturation of energy investments.

The Brazilian evidences emphasize the relevance to highlight the business model of private equity funds, as energy private equity has been growing in importance in the country, despite the global crisis. As private equity interest in energy investments involve predictable returns, financial restructuring and cost adjustments could be part of the set of the fund managers´ practices. Private equity fund managers are spreading, in truth, a business model in energy projects where the target is to trade the companies up to bigger investors years later (Wheatley, 2010). As an increasing part of the energy investment flows in Brazil turns out to be subordinated to the evolution of expected financial returns and exit conditions of private equity firms, it seems likely that private equity investors will not take a role in building the large-scale energy projects that Brazil needs to ensure sustainable economic growth and inclusiveness.

As a matter of fact, the management practices of private equity funds enhances the expansion of monopoly- capital in the context of financialization. In this setting, great concerns arise since the fund managers´ practices could pass down social and environmental safeguards. Decisions taken by private equity fund managers - strongly influenced by short- term returns– could turn out to challenge sustainable energy investment in the long-run.

4. Final comments

Green economics looks beyond the dynamics of finance in order to take into account a "long-term, earth-wide and holistic context" where growth and inclusiveness could be understood within a multidisciplinary range of knowledge (Kennet and Heinemann, 2006). Taking into account the current global scenario, it is still difficult to assess the full impact of the crisis but investors seem to continue looking to emerging markets for opportunities of attractive returns such as Brazil. The future scenario for the Brazilian economy (which includes major sporting events and the Pre-salt oil fields) is creating expectations of a huge expansion in investments on energy, oil and gas, transportation and logistics services and infrastructure, among others industries (ABID, 2011).

The entrance of private equity firms into the energy industry highlights the tensions between the fund managers´ commitment to short-term returns and the long-run nature of energy investments. In this setting, it is important to reassess the importance of public policies regarding further regulation in private equity energy disinvestments. The sustainability challenges suggest a possible research agenda for expanding energy private equity fund performance assessment to include green developmental as well as financial metrics.

References

Agência Brasileira de Desenvolvimento Industrial, ABDI, (2011) A Indústria de Private Equity e Venture Capital, [The Private Equity and Venture Capital Industry] 2º Brazilian Census (Brasília).

Cullen, A. and James, S. 2007. Private equity and Business Information. Part 3: Business Information Services and Private equity: North American Involvement. *Business Information Alert;* Nov/Dec, vol. 19, issue 10, p.1-4.

Emerging Markets Private Equity Association (EMPEA). 2011. *EMPEA Q3 2011 PE Industry Statistics.* http://www.empea.net/

Foster, John Bellamy. 2009. "Monopoly-Finance Capital." *Monthly Review* 58 (December) : 1-14.

GVcepe. 2008. *Panorama da indústria Brasileira de private equity and venture capital*, research report [Overview of the Brazilian industry of private equity and venture capital], (São Paulo, Fundação Getúlio Vargas).

Gonçalves, J. R. B.; Madi, M. A. C. Private equity investment and labor: faceless capital and the challenges to trade unions in Brazil. In: Serrano, M. et al. (ed.) *Trade unions and the global crisis: Labour´s visions, strategies and responses.* Geneve, Intenational Labour Office, 2011

International Trade Union Confederation (ITUC). 2007. *Where the house always wins: Private equity, hedge funds and the new casino capitalism* (Brussels).

International Union of Food, Agricultural, Hotel, Restaurant, Catering, Tobacco and Allied Workers' Association (IUF). 2007. *A workers´ guide to private equity buyouts* (Geneva).

Kennet, M. and Heinemann, V. Green Economics: setting the scene. 2006. Aims, context, and philosophical underpinning of the distinctive new solutions offered by Green Economics *Int. J. of Green Economics,* Vol. 1, No.1/2 pp. 68 – 102.

LAVCA. 2010. *Investments in renewable energy. Warbug Pincus funds Brazilian Energy firm.*

http://lavca.org/2010/09/22/warburg-pincus-funds-brazilian-energy-firm/ .

LAVCA. 2011. *Brazil's Gavea Raises $1.9 Bln for Private Equity Fund.* http://lavca.org/2011/11/18/brazils-gavea-raises-1-9-bln-for-private-equity-fund/

Pinho, L. F. et al. 2011. Brazil. http://www.latinlawyer.com/reference/topics/50/jurisdictions/6/brazil/

Wheatley, J. 2010. *Capital markets: Private equity funds explore the market.* Published: May 6 2010. http://www.ft.com/cms/s/0/cbfe7ce6-571c-11df-aaff-0144feab49a.html#axzz1ezwgqbFE

[1] In Brazil, the private equity industry include a) private equity funds that acquire companies in the phases of restructuring, consolidation and/or expansion and b) venture capital funds for start-ups and other types of seed capital. Private equity funds have been more relevant in terms of fundraising and number of deals (Gonçalves and Madi, 2011).

[2] The long-run process of financial expansion turned out to be characterized as the "financialization" of the capitalist economy where monopoly-finance capital increasingly affect social and economic reproduction (Foster, 2009).

[3] Taking into account the legal structures in Brazil, there is predominance Fund for Investment in Equity Participation (FIP) and Fund for Investment in Emerging Companies (FMIEE). The taxes levied on gains, regulated by CVM, are usually less burdensome in theses vehicles. Nevertheless, private equity canbe conducted through other structures, such as holdings companies, direct investment and corporate venture (Pinho et al.,2011).

[4] Pension funds can apply the maximum of 20 per cent of their

capital in private equity structured funds.

[5] Almost 46 per cent of Brazil's energy comes from renewable sources, and 85 percent of its power generation capacity due to its great hydropower resources and long-established bioethanol industry.

[6] Votorantim Group is one of the largest conglomerates in Latin America, operating, among others, in sectors like finance, energy, sideurgy, steel, pulp and paper.

[7] In spite of the global crisis, investment in clean energy during 2008 surpassed 2007's record investments by 5 percent. In large part this performance is the result of China, Brazil and other emerging economies´ energy investments. See http://www.livescience.com/5497-investment-green-energy-quadruples-4-years.html.

[8] See http://www.stockmarketdigital.com/financial_services/banco-votorantim-to-raise-768-mln-for-brazilian-pvt-equity-funds

[9] This fees variable and is calculated on a pre-established percentage (normally 20 per cent) over the obtained earnings basis.

[10] According to ICVMs n° 391 and n° 209, the responsibilities for the fund managers mainly derived from the fault or negligence in managing the fund. Divergences between the shareholders and the company, or between the controlling shareholders and the minority shareholders are resolved by means of arbitration (Pinho et al, 2011).

Chapter 3 Development of Green Economics

3.1 Greening the Academy – Economics: The Latest Developments and Issues in Environmental and Green Economics

Miriam Kennet and Michele Gale D'Oliveira

1. Introduction to the concepts and competing frameworks in green economics
"We are living in an age of transformation, an age of Green Economics" Ban Ki Moon, UN General Secretary in Newsweek November 2008.

"If the bee disappears off the surface of the globe, then man would only have four years of life left," attributed popularly *to* Albert Einstein:*(Lean and Shawcross 2007).Colony Collapse Disorder is leading to bee losses at 30%. One third of the world's agricultural production relies on the European Honey Bee Apis mellifera. Climate change has forced the once common great yellow bumblebee (bombus distinguendus) to now cling only to the north of Scotland."* (Savage:2009: 15)

"Anyone who believes exponential growth can go on forever in a finite world is either a madman or an economist." – Kenneth E. Boulding.

97

This year, the City of London and many other cities, saw mass demonstrations against the role of casino banking and the damage caused by capitalist economics speculators to the rest of society. St Paul's Cathedral was closed for the first time since the second World War as it was surrounded by protesters. Nowhere has this frustration been more evident than in Egypt with the significance of the Arab Spring movement which was actually focused on (and largely unknown outside Egypt) the hideous corrupt back handers, President Mubarack extracted from every single economics transaction made in the country.

"Meanwhile, Egyptian courts have charged former President Hosni Mubarak with corruption and sentenced in absentia his former finance minister, Youssef Boutros-Ghali, to 30 years in prison on charges of corruption and embezzlement of public money. Frustration with cronyism and corruption is a key grievance of those protesting in the streets in Libya, Syria, and Yemen as well." (Levey BBC 2011).

The protests, this year, have had far reaching effects, from the "Indignants" in Spain , to the *Occupy Wall Street* movement in the financial district of New York, USA.

2. What is wrong with main stream economics and how we are changing it together Occupy Wall Street, which began in September 2011, is a large scale and significant protest and movement at the heart of the financial sector in many cities in the USA and is supported by over 50% of Americans. Its slogan is "we are the 99%" which is the described as the difference in wealth between the very richest who are regarded as causing and benefiting from the boom which led to the current "great economic contraction and downturn." The ordinary people are being forced around the developed world, to pay for it with austerity measures, possibly the last denouement of a failing capitalist system, which is turning on finances of *"the people"* to bail them out. The focus of the protest is against the power and influence of corporations, corporate greed and the banks as international corporations and the revolving door between them, the financial sector. Governments which are powerless in the face of enormous funds these banks and corporations wield, mainly composed of the misappropriation of ordinary people's money in the name of shareholding and trickle down wealth theory. The Green Economics Institute also point out the revolving door between the large energy companies, media corporations and governments. Add to this mix, which is predicated on inequalities, the complete and disastrous corruption of representative democracy and its impotence in the face of a hollowed out western economy outsourced to countries with low human rights standards and slave labour conditions in a race to the bottom. The Green Economics Institute argues for a reinstatement of local or regional production, investment and reduction in the volumes of trade and volumes of speculative investment, and an increase in its quality and standards and a reversal of this "Global shift" in world trade and financial flows.

In 2012, the Earth Summit RIO + 20 will focus on the *Green economy and Rethinking growth*. This chapter will explore how the above mentioned problems and characteristics of the current global economics system are all related. It will investigate how a Green Economy is one of the only solutions for creating a global economy providing social and environmental justice and which can help us to avoid a dangerous swing towards protectionism and "me first" solutions to a challenging era for human kind. Although complex and new, it is one of the solutions which has managed to really gain ground with governments around the world. It is also remarkable as this is a very radical solution which has arisen almost entirely from activist and campaigners, almost entirely green activists! Its stance is creating nothing less than a new world order! It no longer accepts that men own 99% of the worlds assets or control the corridors of power and money. Its contribution amongst other things has been to create a climate in which it is now considered time to put a woman at the head of the IMF and world global financial institutions and to create an economy where the resources of the world, the global commons are truly shared and where nature and other species are given legal standing and the care and understanding to play their role on the earth.

Our system of capitalism and neo liberal economics has for the past 60 years encouraged and measured itself according to the paradigm of ever increasing economic growth fuelled by speculation and consumption, (and overconsumption) as well as capital betting on ever increasing GDP in developed countries. With the repeal (1999) of the Glass -Steagal Act the final regulatory firewall to prevent the speculation with the ordinary public's money was allowed to become the stock for this huge betting ring. This capitalist investment was based on an ideology of an ever increasing growth, consumption and as well as consumer and governments vociferous demand so much so that it used up much of the worlds resources and natural capital and started to eat up most of the worlds economic capital.

Ever more inventive and complex instruments were created to bolster up ever more needy GDP growth. Many of these instruments were not even understood by the traders themselves.Unnoticed this casino capitalism started to extrude far beyond the real economy of the mature economies and of more developed countries, who began outsource their entire sections of their economies,especially production activities and such repetitive jobs as call centres and with them any social and environmental standards. This led to ever cheaper labour costs, a race to the bottom, and the only means to continue to satisfy this hungry machine was for it to use a form of slave labour from countries with very low standards of ethics or CSR or social provision. This became the cheapest form of labour on the planet and we now have more slaves on the planet than at any time in history. Far from abolition, the capitalist casino economy has been driven by commodities such as sex, war, guns, and car industries. These all make huge amounts of money and feed the capitalist machine.

However this very unpleasant machine itself is starting to implode with Austerity measures being imposed on such ancient economies as Greece and such developed economies as Ireland, and formerly rich countries such as Iceland. The resultant unrest has been experienced from outside the European Commission's Charlemagne Building at the heart of Europe, into the streets of Greece and young people are protesting all over Europe from Spain to Italy about the drastic fall in jobs and living standards.

This machine, this capitalist system had at the head of its main institution, the IMF, a man, well known for taking sexual advantage of women, with a string of affairs and coercion behind him. It seemed that this main stream global economics machine was comfortable with a testosterone driven image and a driven and selfish raison d'etre. Nothing else mattered except neo liberal GPD growth and ever increasing expansion.. The annual bounty of the entire planet, (some even say 2 planets worth of bounty) was eaten up and destroyed in the Lust for Greed and Greed for Lust and testosterone driven, (and lots of it,), economic gain. The saying went around that " If Lehman Brothers had been Lehman sisters, the banking crisis would not have happened." The Deputy Prime Minister in the UK raised the issue of gender inbalance and unequal pay and influence in the financial sector, in Parliament as being a factor in the cause of the current economics crisis.

All that has changed- the machine was exposed for the unpleasant entity it was and now there is a woman in the role, and the IMF- the former imposer of austerity measures on others has reached the limit of its own excesses and can't raise enough bail out funds to stop the rot.

Whilst this denouement – of capitalism has been going on- there have been stirrings of what is really driving the world economy.

2.The environmental economics umbrella: The Green Economy begins to stir

As with the dinosaurs before them, a small tiny and seemingly insignificant movement began to stir about 16 years ago. This is slowly and quietly now threatening the very survival dominance and very logic and future of the capitalist machine. Green is the new black and its the green dialogues which. are being regarded as the way forward-the design of the economies of the twenty first century

The green economy is a fascinating place at present with several competing dialogues currently going on. Pro growth, anti growth, limits to growth, green growth, austerity, life style changes, techno-fixes and many more. Some of these prevailing ideas will be introduced and discussed here. Even the credit rating agencies may be including environmental risk in a countries credit rating. As with many human activities these ideas and competing dialogues are fiercely debated.

2 a) The Green Growth School: The wolf in sheeps clothing

Masquerading as green economics -(which is actually based on social and environmental justice and a concern to benefit all people everywhere, other species, nature, the planet and its systems) -is the idea of Green Growth - which is the business and main stream backlash and the skewing of the concept to mean the opposite to what is intended. It follows from green consumerism- the idea you can have your cake and eat it at the same time. The Green Growth School advocates a bit of greening and environmental greenwash around the edges and maintaining control and doing Business as Usual. Here we find the fascinating - (but alarming alliance) of the Price Waterhouse Coopers heading up WWFs initiative on green economy and entire alliance of companies and some larger corporate NGOs allowing the agenda to be set to " green the economy" with business - (and they mean business, corporate or capital – or capitalism – depending on your own point of view) but in any case, in an alliance which is similar in structure to that of the World Council of Business and Sustainable Development. We found such an alliance at the Copenhagen COP 15 conference where every single NGO registered in the USA had come via the (WCBSD) The World Council of Business and Sustainable Development , which if you investigate is an alliance of all the worlds largest businesses and the voice of its capital (and it is designed to keep it that way) -whilst tweaking some environmental greenwashing. There is no room for dissenting voices, as all the little NGO signed up without checking.

Green growth theory is powered through the London School of Economics, the OECD, the Korean Government and United Nations Environment Programme, and its theory is that green is good for growth, and growth is good for green.Stern delivered a speech in October 2009 arguing that the world will see the fastest growth it has ever seen in the next 50 years and that this will fund the environmental clean up.

In fact it is probable that green companies are the main companies that will probably last but that is not the rationale of green economics and it misses its most important parts. This view, which I documented in my paper in (Kennet 1997)- I called the *wolf in sheeps clothing*- (Kennet 182: 1997) it makes all the right noises but misses the guts of the changes. This view differs little from the Friedmanite theory of the firm, as the most important entity and at all costs its survival must be assured. However measuring "social and environmental bads"- is introduced by environmental economics into this view and although it is in effect a red herring, actually delaying underlying structural change, its is probably better than doing nothing at all.

2b) Green New Deal and Keynsian stimulus

b)The most popular alternative at the moment in Europe and with the European greens (Green European Foundation) is the Keynesian green stimulus Green New Deal which largely wants to switch consumption from market laissez faire capitalism to a more managed green public project based approach for public works and infrastructure. This is called the Green Deal in the USA and in Korea and Europe, the Green New Deal. However its meaning can vary, for example the UN include for example the manufacture of more cars -albeit ones using eco technology or what purists might call a techno fix. This is in part the impetus for carbon storage and sequestration and for carbon scrubbers and green tech and those products that use rare earth metals mainly sourced from China. This view argues that a programme of cuts and austerity won't work and that a technological evolution in the economy has always worked well before and so advocates that a stimulus of spending and green quantitative easing are the answer, without the need for lifestyle. changes.

Green New Deal Proposed (Elliot et al. 2009) *A sample of £10 billion in green* quantitative easing invested in the energy efficiency sector could:

- Create 60,000 jobs (or 300,000 person-years of employment) while also reducing emissions by a further 3.96Mt-CO_2e each year;

- This could also create public savings of £4.5 billion over five years in reduced benefits and increased tax intake alone;

A sample of £10 billion in 'green quantitative easing' invested in onshore wind could:

10. Increase wind's contribution to the UK's total electricity supply from its current 1.9 per cent to 10 per cent Create over 36,000 jobs in installation and direct and indirect manufacturing This is a total of 180,000 job-years of employment -. Create a further 4,800 jobs in the operations and maintenance of the installed capacity and other related employment over the entire 20 year lifetime of the installation (equivalent to 96,000 job-years)
11. And, if this directly replaced energy from conventional sources, it could decarbonise the UK economy by 2.4 per cent – reducing emissions from the power sector by up to 16 Mt-CO_2e each year **This corresponds to a £19 billion reduction in environmental damage**

Or, a sample investment of £10 billion could:

- re-skill 1.5 million people for the low-carbon skills of the future, bringing 120,000 people back into the workforce, and increasing the earnings of those with a low income by a total of £15.4 billion.

- *A £50 billion programme in 'green quantitative easing' in the short term to rebuild the economy. Next, planning must begin for all of the new forms of bond finance detailed in the Group's report to ensure the long-term stable funding needed for the long-term transformation*

Measures on tax that are explicitly designed to re-gear the UK economy and transform energy infrastructure:

- **Tax incentives on green savings and investment**, *so that future ISA tax relief – costing more than £2 billion a year – is only available for funds invested in green savings*
- **A general tax-avoidance provision** *to end the abuse of tax allowances* **A Financial Transaction Tax, comm**only *known as a "Tobin Tax". Such a* **tax, applied internationall**y *at a rate of about 0.05 per cent has the potential to raise more than £400 billion a year..*

New savings mechanisms that support the greening of the economy now, create thousands of new jobs and guarantee stable returns into the future:

- **Green bonds**
- **Local authority bonds, Carbon linked bonds, to align in-**vestment *returns with carbon* **A new publicly owned 'Green New Deal Investment Bank' to allocate the capital provided by green quantitative easing, and new bank lending to government:**

- **Green New Deal Investment Bank, a publicly owned bank to hol**d *and disburse capital provided by 'green quantitative easing'. It will be used exclusively to fund companies and projects designed to accelerate the transition towards a low carbon economy.*
- **Treasury Deposit Receipts**, *like those issued during the Second World War, a mechanism whereby banks were forced to use their ability to create credit to lend to government.*

2c) The green economy school

This year 2012 the UN RIO + 20 global conference is entitled Green Economy rethinking growth. The world is taking up this challenge. Their definition of the green economy is according to the United Nations General Secretary (2012) for the first Preparatory Meeting of the UNCSD identifies four strands:

United Nations Definition of a Green Economy

> a) end market failure and the internalization of externalities.

> b) systemic view of the economic structure and its impact on relevant aspects of sustainable development.

 c) social goals (jobs, for example) and examines ancillary policies needed to reconcile social goals with the other objectives of economic policy.

> d) the macroeconomic framework and development strategy with the goal of identifying dynamic pathways towards sustainable development" 2012 Earth Summit 2012 (2011

United Nations Policy Options Proposals for Rio + 20

(a)Getting prices right, including removing subsidies, valuing natural resources and imposing taxes on things that harm the environment (environmental "bads") in order to internalize externalities, support sustainable consumption and incentivize business choices

 (b) Public procurement policies to promote greening of business and markets;

(c) Ecological tax reforms based mainly on the experience of European countries. The basic idea is that shifting the tax base away from "good" factors of production such as labour to "bad" factors such as pollution will allow for a double dividend: correcting environmental externalities while boosting employment

(d) Public investment in sustainable infrastructure (including public transport, renewable energy and retrofitting of existing infrastructure and buildings for improved energy efficiency) and natural capital, to restore, maintain and, where possible, enhance the *stock of natural capital. This has particular salience within the current recessionary context, given the need for public expenditure on stimulus packages;*

(e) Targeted public support for research and development on environmentally sound technologies, partly in order to compensate for private underinvestment in pre-commercial research and development, and partly to stimulate investments in critical areas (such as renewable energy) with potentially high dynamic scale economies, and partly to offset the bias of current research and development towards dirty and hazardous technologies;

(f) Strategic investment through public sector development outlays, incentive programmes and partnerships, in order to lay the foundation of a self-sustaining process of socially and environmentally sustainable economic growth;

(g) Social policies to reconcile social goals with existing or proposed economic policies. (2011 UNEP)

2d)The lower growth school

The foundations of this approach can be found in Malthus (1817) and issues raised by Hardin (1968) in *The Tragedy of the Commons*. The debate also questions the root of technological fixes to ecological problems and, one might argue, Environmental Economics and Corporate Social Responsibility.

In *The Limits to Growth* (1972),Meadows argues that rapidly diminishing resources force a slowdown in industrial growth due to a rise in the death rate and a decrease in food supply and medical services. Despite greater material output, the world's people will be poorer than they were. This collapse occurs because of non-renewable resource depletion. Growth would be stopped well before 2100, caused by overloading of the natural absorptive capacity of the environment. These models were influential, and Meadows suggested the use of technology to circumvent problems.

Rachel Carson's book *Silent Spring* (1962) shows the devastating effects of chemicals on the natural world. She highlights the effects on bird's eggs which led to a silent spring. Carson writes that the obligation to endure gives us the right to know and to stop using such chemicals. This genre is also featured in such books as *Chemical Children* by Mansfield and Munro (1987) and Paul Ehrlich's article on the dangers of an increasing population, *The Population Bomb* (1969).

UK Government departments have started exploring staff's capacity to deal with today's crises, plunging into changed economic and ecological problems. Surprisingly, this has opened radically new ground, focusing on economic management through The Green Economics Institute. Radical approaches such lower-growth economics, degrowth economics and Redefining Prosperity are being taught and discussed in government departments as they gain in popularity as an approach. Important work under the banner of Redefining Prosperity has been done by Kennet and Heinemann (2008), Victor (2008), and Anderson (2008), with Jackson leading the Sustainable Development Commission in this area Serge Latouche, whose focus is not dissimilar to the work of Green Economics is the leading thinker in this movement.

2e) Green economics and reality – unravelling the sovereign wealth funds and debt in a post oil phase

Sovereign wealth funds started slopping capital wizzing around the world and with national banks becoming exposed to debt, in an unregulated way, and property hopelessly overvalued in many countries, then the die was cast for a global economics catastrophe perhaps on a scale never seen before and almost impossible to unravel.

The new problem today is that capital has morphed into this new form due to the herd spending and several countries investment, stubborn arch dependence on fossil fuel economies. Much of the worlds capital has already taken flight into a few major economies creating a small number of ultra powerful sovereign wealth funds, a kind of power oligopoly and unfortunately most of them(with the sole exception of Norway) have horrific human rights standards. Failure to understand this important structural change in capital and capitalism means the inability to either reverse this situation or to change or improve it.

2e) Green economics and lifestyle changes

On the other hand a " green economics agenda " argues for a life style change which provides less consumption, less resource use and alternatives to the consumption patterns and high mass consumption of Rostow and the Kennedy administration – the main economics policy paradigm of the last 60 years.(Jorion2011) It argues for lower growth – in developed countries- contraction and convergence for everyone. This view allows for degrowth shifts to be included as it reduces overall economic activity and lowers GDP and typically the GINI coefficient and other measures of well being go up in advanced economies, above a certain level of satisfaction of the basic physical requirements of living. The emphasis on growth as an end itself disappears. The alleviation of poverty, education of everyone especially girls, the participation in democracy, the halting of climate change and sea level rise and the halting of biodiversity loss are all important aims of such an economy. The equality within and between countries and between generations becomes much more interesting in such an economy.
This method allocates more to less developed countries and less to more developed countries.

Green Economics intrinsically is supportive of the *Contraction and Convergence*, based on the principle proposed by Aubrey Meyer of the Global Commons Institute initially for reducing global carbon emissions by a consensus of contracting larger emitters and expanding emitters who are not using enough. This elegant solution is based on social and environmental justice and so is attractive to green economists. It has been adopted as a principle for carbon by the UNFCC. As economists green economists also regard it as a key idea to implement a green economy. In practise less developed countries can still grow to meet in the middle range of basic living standards but those over consuming countries need to contract to meet in the middle to ensure that there is enough to go round.

The role of the commons, ownership of air, water and soil is important as well as resources which we all need to live. The substituting of carbon increasing private goods such as cars for public goods with the replacement by the commons such a publicly owned and lower carbon train transport is important **Slow travel**. as a change in lifestyle and of as ways of reconstituting economics life and using bicycles and walking more within the community are also a feature with prominent green economists taking the *No Flight Pledge*. In particular green economics changes the emphasis away from capital intensive gadget driven short life produced goods for consumption and capital accumulation economics, with demand artificially stimulated by advertising and marketing, towards more labour intensive longer term durable and sustainable goods. The taxation system would disencentivise short term, social and environmental " bads" and encourage with incentives " goods" and the protection and creation of the global commons. It argues for home production for local and smaller scale needs where necessary and remaining within the limits to growth and the limits of the planets resources and an awareness of and visibility of the total supply chain and the manner and place of production as well as how what we consume is produced. Green Economics deals with social and environmental justice and the provisioning for the needs of all people everywhere, nature, other species, the planet and its systems.(Kennet and Heinemann 2006). It integrates the physical environment and its data into a real economy perspective together, with social science, to create an economics discipline fit for purpose for the 21st century. More recently it is clear it is intensely practical having first expanded in the governments of many countries and the attempt to implement it around the world.

It has thus been called the economics of doing, the economics of caring and the economics of sharing- sharing with each other, sharing with other species and sharing the planet and its resources. (Kennet 2010). The other strands of policies which do form an integral tool kit for a green economy- include regulation, techno fixes, incentives, and taxation. Even in some cases rationing of use where it benefits the community. Green Economics is about doing more with less and in some cases avoidance and finding an alternative.

Reuse, reduce, recycle, repair are also useful aspects of policies. Green Economics is an inclusive discipline, for all people everywhere, especially women, minorities, pelple with special needs, and those hitherto without a voice, nature, other species, the planet and its systems as beneficiaries rather than throw away imputs to the economics sausage machine. It is NOT about the greatest happiness of the greatest number. It seeks to value everyone and everything on the planet. It seeks to enhance and allow to flourish rather than to destroy as main stream economics sometimes does as is claimed a predestined " inevitability in economics mainstream logic."

In particular two umbrella terms are relevant here, firstly the Heterodox schools of economics containing elements from the Neo keynsians, the Austrian , and Marxist schools but also increasingly a home for the Green Economics school and to an extent the ecological economics schools.

Additionally, although confusingly, the umbrella term of Environmental Economics does contains the ecological economics school and the green economics schools, the specific term environmental economics when used to describe a school itself (as opposed to the terms use as an umbrella term), has been criticised for being too close to the mainstream, neo liberal and business as usual methodology and in that sense lacking ambition for radical change.

In 1989, after the fall of the Berlin Wall, capitalism seemed to be unrivalled in its ascendency and to have won the political and moral battle for the future of economics. Governments and banks allowed themselves to believe that the era of cycles of boom and bust was actually well and truly behind them and that we had moved into a period of continued economic growth and ever expanding GDP which could last forever. They believed that a deregulated international, free trade, consumption driven, capitalist economy would always continue to deliver ever expanding growth led by Anglo -Saxon stock markets .

We were personally worried about this, as we clearly saw

behind this facade certain facts and truths and problems which were not being addressed at all. Firstly all the economics models were very one dimensional and ignored reality in favour of a certain mathematical and statistical, purism and elitism. The main problems seemed to us to be:

a) One fifth of humanity was still starving in life threatening poverty (Sachs 2005) even through this period of unparalleled plenty- and this seemed to question the distributive theory of economics

b) Climate change was ratcheting up and sea level was rising and the evidence from the latest IPCC scientific consensus appeared to suggest this was largely anthropocentric and we thought the increase in carbon was caused by a consumerist, fossil fuel, car driven economy which needed amending.

c) This capitalist economy was very uneven and unequal and consisted largely of intrafirm trade, behind closed doors which even then, had a turnover larger than many countries and it also seemed to be driven by unelected invisible power elites and to be leading to catastrophic decline of the worlds natural capital. In fact this process has now resulted in an oligopoly of world capital power resting in a tiny number of sovereign states' wealth funds able to mobilise and dominate the entire globe's resources at will. They include such entities as the oil states in the middle east- (This latest trend began in Kuwait) and in Singapore, Norway and above all in China, with the

BRICS coming up the rear -Brazil, India and Russia, all accelerating fast in terms of their trade and a group of CIVETS also doing well – Cambodia, Indonesia, Vietnam, Egypt and Turkey and South Africa. Whilst on the other side, the PIGGS and - the Euro zone, are struggling as they have bought products and moved production to these newer countries, to such an extent as to hollow out their economy and are unable to refinance their enormous debts. The world's largest economy the USA has even fallen into this trap and now is unable to call the tune when trading for example with the owner of much of its debt China. As a result, downgrades of many of the more developed economies have occurred recently in the credit ratings agencies such as Standard and Poor. This is a warning that dumping our social, environmental and production standards comes back to haunt us. What goes around, really does come around!

       d) We never believed that the boom could continue in a world of finite resources

       e) Miriam Kennet had watched the developments in China from the start when she was involved in putting in the telecoms infrastructure in the early 1990s and saw the few were benefiting at the expense of the many and it was becoming more unequal.

       f) She noticed the global shift (Dicken 2009) and the rapid changes in the balances of trade and huge outsourcing as the west grew more lazy and arrogant (like the fall of the Roman Empire identified by Gibbon in the 20th century.). She was alarmed by the developed economy as it outsourced its core activities and practised social and environmental dumping, just at the very time that explicit standards were rising legally, (with lots of talk about environmental and social improvement). The reality was rather different -and happening a long way away. For example the contents of mobile phones contain a mineral that is largely mined by children in the DRC Congo and is the cause of wars and serious genocide in DR Congo and Rwanda which would horrify many of the mobile phone users if they stopped to think about it. It is solving such dynamics and making the public aware of their own responsibility and actions,as well as and changing and shifting such trade flows that is the stuff of green economics. This double speak- standards, normative books and speeches were happening but on the quiet the energy was being put into hiding all the dirty linen in poorer and less developed countries. We now know this included borrowing from them to the extent that the USA is largely in debt to such countries completely. The hollowing out of western economies and companies seemed to me an unsustainable economics system and one doomed to failure. On the other hand the human rights were being eroded in the production of unnecessary luxury goods to an alarming rate.

References

Anderson V., (2008)Victor Anderson's opinion piece on the

economic growth and the economic crisis. Prosperity without growth at http://www.sd-commission.org.uk/publications.php?id=832 accessed August 10th 2009 Sustainable Development Commission UK Government Independent Watchdog Paper 10 11 208

Andrioff J and Waddock S (2002) Unfolding stakeholder engagement in Andrioff J and Wardock S Husted B and Sutherland Rahman S Unfolding stakeholder thinking Theory responsibility and Engagement Greenleaf Publishing Ltd Sheffield

Ban Ki Moon (3rd December 2007)Time for a New green economics A test for the world in Bali and Beyond Washington Post http://www.washingtonpost.com/wp-dyn/content/article/2007/12/02/AR2007120201635.html acessed August 10th 2009

Barry J., (1999a) The environment and social theory London Routledge

BBC Occupy London in Protest October 16th 2011 http://www.bbc.co.uk/news/uk-15322134

http://www.bbc.co.uk/news/world-asia-pacific-15319924 October 16th 2011 Rome protest against cuts descends into violence

Boulding K (1966) The economics of the coming of spaceship earth. In H.E Daly Towards a steady state economy, San Francisco W H Freeman and Company 1973.

Brundtland G. H. (1987) Our common future.World

Commission on Environment and Development OUP 1-11.

Carson R (1962) Silent Spring. Houghton Mifflin

Carroll A (1993) Business and Society : Ethics and Stakeholder Management OH South Western Cincinatti

Carroll, A.B. (1979.) A three-dimensional conceptual model of corporate social
   performance; Academy of Management Review 4.

Commoner B.(1971) The closing circle Nature Man and Technology Kopf NY (267-276)

Daly H., (1974) The economics of the steady state in American Economic Review (Papers and Proceedings) May vol 64 no 2 (15-21)

Dobson A (2000) Green Political Thought London Routledge

Ehrlich P (1969) The Population Bomb Ballantine

Feiner S. (2003) Reading Neo classical economics towards an erotic economy of sharing in D. Barker and E Kuiper (Eds) Towards a feminist philosophy of economics. Routledge.

Freeman, E. R., 1984, Strategic management: A stakeholder approach, Pitman, Boston. Stakeholder Theory

Goldsmith E (2005) Rewriting economics www.greeneconmics.org.uk accessed 17th january 2006.

Gramsci A(2006) Some theoretical and practical aspects of economism at www.marxists.org accesses 17th January 2006.

Elliott E, et al,. (2009) Green New Deal Group demands http://www.greennewdealgroup.org Accessed 23rd October 2011

Hardin G (1968) The Tragedy of the commons Science vol 162 (1243-1248)

Henderson H (2006) in International Journal of Green Economics Growing the green economy – globally in International Journal of Green Economics- Vol 1 issue 3 4 (2007: 276) Inderscience

Hussen A. (2000) Principles of environmental economics. London Routledge

Paul Jorion, (2011)"Le capitalisme a l'agonie (2011)"

Kaul N., (2003) The anxious identities we inhabit positivisms and economics understandings in Kuiper and Barker (Eds) Towards a feminist philosophy of economics Routedge London ..

Kennet M (1997) Green Backlash strategies. In Green Economics Beyond Supply and Demand to meeting peoples needs. Green Audit

Kennet M., (2007) Editorial Progress in Green Economics: ontology concepts and philosophy. Civilisation the lost factor of reality in social and environmental justice. International Journal of Green Economics. Vol 1 issue 3 4 (225: 2007).

Kennet M., and Heinemann V., (2006) Green Economics Setting the Scene. International Journal of Green Economics Vol 1 issue 1 /2 p 68- 102 Inderscience Geneva .

Kennet M., and Heinemann V., (2008) The second opinion piece for the Redefining Prosperity, third seminar "Confronting Structure - achieving economic sustainability" Prosperity without growth at http://www.sd-commission.org.uk/publications.php? id=772 accessed August 10th 2009 Sustainable Development Commission UK Government Independent Watchdog Paper 10 11 208

Kennet M., (2008) The Economics of Doing No 13 e :   51 Green Economics for European Green Activists Berlin December 2007 Green European Foundation : The Green Economics Institute European Commission

Kennet M., (2009) Green Economics and Pedagogy, Developing Teaching Green Economics. In Proceedings of the 4th Annual Green Economics Conference, Oxford University Part 1 (2009: 118). The Green Economics Institute

Kennet M., (2010) A Green Economics Reader The Green Economics Institute

Kennet M. Black K., Gale M., Bouquet, and A., Pipinyte I (2011) A Handbook of Green Economics: A Practitioners Guide

Lean G., and Shawcross, H., (15 .4. 2007) Are mobile phones wiping out our bees?

Scientists claim radiation from handsets are to blame for mysterious 'colony collapse' of bees

Meyer A.(1995) Contraction and Convergence.The Global Commons Institute

Leopold A(1997) A sand county almanac Oxford University Press

Levey S (2011) Fighting Corruption After the Arab Spring: Harnessing Countries' Desire to Improve their Reputations for Integrity (2011) .http://www.foreignaffairs.com/articles/67895/stuart-levey/fighting-corruption-after-the-arab-spring accessed 16th October 2011 http://www.foreignaffairs.com/articles/67895/stuart-levey/fighting-corruption-after-the-arab-spring

Meadows D., (1972) The Limits to Growth: A report for the Club of Rome's Project on the Predicament of Mankind 2nd Ed New York Universe Books

Mies M (1998) Patriarchy and Accumulation in Scot Cato and Kennet Green Economics.Green Audit

Mies M., (2007) Patriarchy and accumulation on a world scale revisited International Journal of Green Economics -Vol 1 issue ¾ (2007:268) Inderscience

Mill J.S.(1848) Principles of Political Economy

Mansfield P and Munro J (1987) Chemical Children London Century

Naess A. (1995)Deep ecology for the 21st century Shamballa

Nelson J., (2009) Teaching Economics as if Time Mattered

in The Handbook of Pluralist Economics Education Edited by Reardon J., Routledge

Savage P.(2009) A bee in our bonnet. You bet: The plight of the bumble bee, in Roundabout RG8 R and A. August 2009:(13-15.)

Salleh A Ed (2009)Eco sufficiency and global justice. Pluto

Sachs G(2005) The end of poverty How we can make it happen in our lifetime London Penguin

Sessions G. (1995) Deep ecology for the 21st century Shambala Publications.

Singer P. (1994) \\defence of animals in Singer Ethical Studies Practical ethics in Bowie Business Ethics. Nelson Thornes 1994

Sukhdev P (2008) TEEB Interim Report UNEP. Geneva

Springett D.(2006)Managing the narrative of Sustainable Development "discipline" of an inefficient concept : Vol 1 issue 1 /2 (2006: 50) International Journal of Green Economics.Inderscience

Stern N. (2007) Stern Review. The economics of climate change. HM Treasury

Turk J.(2010) Green Economics Methodology in A green economics reader Green Economics Institute 2010.

United Nations Earth summit (2011) http://www.earthsummit2012.org/workshops-meetings-and-events acessed October 16th 20111.

Victor P. (2008) Managing without Growth Slower by Design

Edward Elgar

Ward, Barbara and Rene Dubos, Only one earth: the care and maintenance of a small planet, 1st Ed., New York, Norton: 1972

Waring M., in Salleh A. (2009) Policy and the measurement of women in Eco sufficiency and global justice.Pluto

Welford R. (2007) Examining discussing and suggesting the possible contribution and role of Bhuddist economics for corporate social responsibility in International Journal of Green Economics Inderscience vol 1 issue 3 4 .(2007: 341)

Chapter 4.
Methodology

4.1 What is Green Economics? A new discipline

Volker Heinemann

Green Economics is a new academic discipline that is based on the innovations in the society that started to emerge in the 1960ies and attempted to replace the consensus based on traditional values and aims for society that existed at that time. The 'Green' agenda developed into a new set of thinking similarly to the conservative, liberal and social democratic/socialist traditions already existing.

A common misunderstanding is still that 'Green' is primarily focused on the environment, which is not the case. The ecological issues raised are part of a wider set of concerns that have at its core a rejection of conventional values and aims for society, the environmental issues follow from this core request for change in attitude similarly to the emergence of other movements like peace, feminism, social justice and human rights economic development. All those new and already existing subjects were combined to a new holistic strategy based on the unifying concern for a new consensus for society beyond conservatism.

Over the past 30 years this new set of thinking has matured and comprises a wide variety of issues and disciplines. Green Economics is a newly founded discipline within academic economics that is systematically assessing problems and questions in that original spirit. These new ideas have a defined set of basic principles that are particularly important as far as economics as a key social science is concerned. Green Economics is influenced by its historic roots concerned with the problem that existing structures are defined or seen as value free and objective whereas they are in fact a particular value or ideology based concept that just happened to be the starting point for the development of the society.

A strong belief in the benefits of evolution of society renders this new discipline truly innovative and it works to replace the existing ideologies and conventions with a wider set of options. It does so by accepting that ultimately a value free social science is not possible but in accepting this fact the discipline is therefore less normatively biased than conventional economic thinking which bases its claim to be value free because it is predicated on maintenance of the status quo and reflects majority thinking. Furthermore, all innovations in society were once in a minority position.

The outcome of such conservative thinking is a strong normative bias in economics towards explanations and concepts that have no longer any future.

As a consequence of this awareness of normative influences Green Economics is set up in the most holistic way possible. Discoveries from other sciences are actively incorporated into the own work to really make sense of the complex phenomenon called society. This stands in sharp contrast to the reductionist and overly quantitative mathematics and assumptions on which conventional mainstream research is based. Conventional economics creates an artificial world of how things could optimally be, based on the values it inherently includes. Green Economics tries as an alternative to incorporate a wider set of potential behaviour and allows for systems and institutions to be designed so that this degree of freedom is maintained and rather than a particular set of rules accepted as unavoidable. Along this way the language, methodology and terms used are reassessed. Freedom, optimal, growth and justice are all terms that have a surprisingly intentional use in conventional economics. Terms like competition, are used as if competition itself is freedom, something that is desirable, where in fact competition only occurs when people cannot achieve all their goal simultaneously. Green Economics gives people back the sovereignty over their decisions and life rather than pushing the language used, not to mention the methodology, into areas where an objective assessment of the matter considered is no longer possible.

Green Economics is practically focused and deals with all economically relevant phenomena of the modern society. Significant findings from other areas of science like for example the awareness of absolute limits to resource use are comprehensively incorporated in the approach taken, rather than a continuous attempt to rescue as much from conventional methodology and definitions as possible.

There are some similarities of Green Economics with Ecological Economics. But Ecological Economics remains focused on the environment and Green Economics does not. This is the basis for calling Green Economics a new and independent discipline from all other existing economic disciplines so far.

As it appears to be the case that the original spirit of the new value set, that gave rise to the wider green movement and finally to Green Economics, is as relevant as ever considering current issues that require addressing, it is of prime importance that this new discipline is developed further in the near future to balance the views and opinions publicised that are based on conventional thinking. It is of particular concern, as conventional economic thinking is always surrounded by scarcity up to the point that scarcity is actively promoted. This is in order to maintain a reality that can be explained within the existing framework and concepts. People are advised how to behave accordingly, so that with such outdated methods the current economic challenges will not be met. It should be emphasised that Green Economics is as a consequence not only developing an alternative view to economic issues that might or might not be normatively desired depending on the viewpoint. The research develops the tools and methods that are required to master today's economic problems in society. This is because conventional economics evolved in the nineteenth century in a different set of circumstances and was designed and is still designed to meet those previous needs and is unable to solve the problems of today. Green Economics is truly the future of economics not just a niche addition to the discourse.

4.2 Methodology Tools and Instruments:Green Economics: Research and disciplinary developments. Background, instruments and tools

Miriam Kennet, Volker Heinemann and Michelle S. Gale de Oliveira

Green Economics has become the focus of much interest over the past year. It is increasingly clear that the standard neo-liberal model of economics is in urgent need of not only a major overhaul but a replacement with more sophisticated concepts.

These new concepts, that still need to be developed fully, are however beginning to emerge in more detail and a significant increase in alternative, pluralistic contributions is emerging against the persistent strong hostility from mainstream economics. One particular area has been the pioneering field in economics where changes to traditional concepts have been demanded and were developed already some time ago. It is the area where ecological principles were introduced into the economic discourse, where much ground has been covered in identifying the deficiencies and limitations in scope, methodology and contents of conventional economics. This area of economics is transforming itself at the same time and more recently a newly emerging concept of 'Green' or 'Progressive' economics is widening the scope of the search for an alternative economic framework even further, extending the scope and methodology of environmental and ecological economics. In doing so it is trying to reform mainstream economics, rather than adding a discipline too mainstream economics regardless of how critical this discipline might be of the existing conventional thinking. Green Economics is not niche economics, and is likely to be a major contribution to the development of a more sophisticated understanding of economics as a social science and our current economic situation and prospects for the future. There will be some examples of how economic concepts can already now influence the economic debate and transform existing policies and decision-making and will explain some of the new approaches and methodologies that have developed in this field.

Evolution towards 'Green Economics'

For quite a number of decades, environmental concerns have had a significant influence on public debate, including economics, which have recently, with the recognition of climate change as a global and highly significant environmental problems, enhanced their importance. The significance of such environmental problems for economics is in fact very simple. It introduces absolute limits into a science that has traditionally been based on the concept that more is better than less and which was considered as a permanent given and undisputed as the basis of all economic thinking. People have now realized that the world has an end and this existence of an absolute limit introduces the concept of evolution of society into economics. The world cannot continue forever on the basis of unchanged principles or paradigms, linear thinking has to come to an end and new concepts are required. As a consequence environmental issues are still one of the most profound areas of criticism of mainstream economics as in the standard discourse, typically referred to as 'environmental economics' the tendency persists that ecological questions are seamlessly incorporated into existing economic thinking with the aim to preserve as much as possible from the standards concepts. Conventional economics attempts to explain all ecology related decision-making based on standard economic assumptions about human behaviour assumed without looking at the impact of the newly recognized absolute boundaries that might well require people to change their behaviour, rather than just aggregating the observable human activity and presume optimal solutions from it.

Such deficiencies in the conventional 'environmental economics' approach where the environment is costed and introduced with that price into the unadjusted decision-making procedures was quickly criticized as it is in many areas missing the point that made the whole subject relevant in the first place, namely that ecological limits require a reassessment of how economic decisions can be derived based on an objective assessment of what is required rather than taking unadjusted opinions for granted. This environmental economics approach was soon criticized and led to the development of ecological economics, which aims to address the above mentioned deficiencies and to a certain extent widens the scope of its analysis by including similar issues like social justice into its discourse.

A great number of important insights can be derived that consider the natural environment and other related spheres in the discourse of Ecological Economics. There is however growing awareness that even this wider scope is still not sufficient, and that there are other issues, unrelated to ecology, that are of equal importance to make their impact in economics. There are issues of strategy, of how to implement change in mainstream economics given the fact that ecological economics concerns are experiencing a backlash or widely ignored. Most importantly that ecological economics cannot fully explain the reason why such resistance persists and the necessary reform of mainstream economics has still not taken place, despite clear deficiencies that become right now in the current economic crisis caused in part by deregulation and is very apparent.

What is required is a more comprehensive understanding of current mainstream economic thinking and of how only one specific discourse, the neo-liberal agenda, could become so dominant despite an apparent lack of sophistication in many areas. The answers to this are very complicated and require a detailed historical assessment as to how the economic discourse is formed and how it is influenced.

Green Economics is the term given to this progressive approach that is developing an alternative to conventional, conservative economics based on a more fundamentally holistic approach that identifies economics as a social science, as well as a natural science. It shows that economics as a whole cannot be explained by simplistic, typically linear, mathematics and fixed preferences of individuals.

Green Economics searches far beyond ecological economics and in fact ecological issues to wider considerations of ideology, history of thought, evolution of society, the level of objectivity and the time specificity of solutions in a social science environment to be taken into account that provide a much stronger basis to criticize current mainstream economics and eventually lead to a replacement of this doctrine. Green Economics is, with this approach, not only a very recent and advanced form of criticism of conventional 19th century economics, in addition, it has the potential to enact a comprehensive reform of this science which could and is starting to equip political decision-makers with a much more sophisticated and ideologically unbiased set of tools and insights to manage the economy more successfully. It has the capacity to widen the scope to include all relevant stakeholders rather than continuing the narrow focused reductionist economics of the past. Green or Progressive Economics results from the acceptance of society as an evolutionary process an inherently innovative and undogmatic exercise. It will help to develop true economic freedom for a much wider range of individuals including non human species concerns and those of the natural environment, nature and the planet as well as its systems. . As such it is an innovative approach to economic theory and an extremely timely and relevant contribution to the development of economics as a social science which incorporates natural and biological science data. This is in sharp contrast to the extremely un-innovative and repetitive contributions from mainstream economics. It is becoming a most significant contribution to a reform of economics, most importantly, because it does not try to reform economics by introducing ecological concepts into economics but by reforming economics in a much wider sense so that this science can correctly assess economic realities, and is as a consequence embracing a wider set of values including ecological values. -The conflict is not between economics and ecology but between the conservative conventions that have shaped a specific economic discipline that is narrow minded and those wider ecological and social and physical science concerns that are by definition not part of the conventional science of economics.

Scope, methodology and contents

Ecological and green, progressive economics are contributing to changes in economics as far as scope, methodology and contents is concerned. The contents side is of the highest relevance from a practical point of view and here we focus on some of the issues and changes in practical economic policy making. We summarise a selection of such methods that are currently shaping the discourse and already contributing to a gradual shift away from neo-liberal objectives.

We can summarize the main criticisms, concerns and areas that require change to give an overview of how the practical examples fit into this progressive framework and why the changes are necessary. In respect of the scope of economics, the major issue is methodology and the contents of economics itself, and a sample of reforms will be discussed for each category.

Scope

Economics can no longer only deal with goods and services in a narrow sense, it has to embrace a wider set of values. Ecological, cultural and social values have to form an integral part of the science.A less anthropocentric view is required to incorporate the concerns of non-human species as ultimately humans rely on the wider web of life.

Economics needs to be aware of the historic dimension. Economic models may work at a certain time but as society moves on, such concerns and concepts become irrelevant and others take their place. Non appreciation of this evolution makes models dogmatic or even worse, reality is changed or restricted -unbelievably simply to fit with the models. Efforts are made to make people behave in a certain way so that the conventional wisdom remains correct! It is this process which causes some of the disasters from economics. Reality is messy, fuzzy and complex. Economics as a discipline has attempted to be tidy, limited and linear. The two are currently mis -matched.

Economics is a social science, as well as a natural science but not a formal science like mathematics. This gives rise to a very complicated issue of what is fact and what is normative and how the normative views that influence human behaviour change over time. Economics cannot be blind to such considerations in its reasoning.

Methodology

Many economic phenomena are qualitative in nature rather than quantitative. This needs to be reflected properly and limits the usefulness of especially simple mathematics. Considerations on the quality of data are neglected. In physics it is of prime importance to get proper unbiased data. In economics very vague datasets are used as the foundation of highly formalized models without concern on how sensitive the findings are in respect of the assumptions.

Empirical data in a social science is not the same as measurements in physics. What is measured is the current activity and behaviour of human beings. This can however change and the empirical data now is not indicative on how the future of society might be, nor whether the activities of human beings based on their opinion are in any way objectively right. Empiricism has a tendency to be conservative, explaining that the world has to be as it is because this is how it currently is.

Related to this, economics requires a higher level of objectivity rather than just using current observations. Such demoscopic economics is able to identify how people behave now or what people think, but opinion is not equal to facts. Precisely an objective science has for example to be able to identify necessary changes to human behaviour to, for example balance an ecological deficit, regardless whether the public opinion accepts such a problem.

Contents

Most of the above deficiencies result in a very simplistic picture of society and very crude suggestions of how people behave and why. As a tendency a wider set of values is off the radar. The price (not the value) is the prime variable, or it is assumed that the price is always a correct approximation for value. This however ignores any intrinsic values of incorrect reflection of the full scope that should determine decision-making. The theory of external effects can obviously rectify this partly but precisely such findings are pushed to the side as soon as important proposals are made. The main criticism by Green Economics is the ideological bias of mainstream economics with the aim of using it to derive a conservative society which ignores current important trends as far as ecological, cultural and social limits or considerations are concerned. Mainstream economics is not pluralistic and it is the aim of Green Economics to add to the pluralistic and progressive spectrum by focusing on and incorporating facts derived from other sciences to overcome this bias.

In relation to this concern, current economic discourses are still highly influenced by battles between political concepts from the past. The axis of the battle with socialism is still contributing to retention of to a tendency that markets need to be deregulated ever further. This is contrary to the evidence available and can be regarded as political propaganda rather than objective science about the differentiated advantages and disadvantages of particular methods that contribute to the advancement of society.

Modern, highly sophisticated developed societies require a high level of investments that appear to be mainly 'public' in nature or are for various reasons provided publicly. Under those circumstances it appears questionable to continuously argue for the trend of reducing the public involvement and suggest that tax reductions will always contribute to economic development. Such arguments are designed to avoid all shaping of society, which is done by economic policies, and they suggest that a simplistic competitive market outcome is all that is needed. This is an attempt to prevent a simplistic materialistic economy from developing into any culturally or socially higher state, and it thus most importantly excludes any and all options which would be able to initiate any responsible lifestyle changes to balance ecological or social imbalances.

Photo Miriam Kennet- the economics of doing, the economics of sharing, the economics of supporting each other! 2010

129

Chapter 5 Climate change

5.1 Green Economics: 10 Key Points for avoiding further catastrophic runaway Climate Change
Miriam Kennet

1 Participation is vital in the COP Kyoto Climate Conferences and agreement processes and IPCC.
The Green Economics Institute has a delegation that it sends to every United Nations Kyoto Climate Change Convention COP (UNFCCC) meeting. In December 2010, three of our representatives (Prof Graciela Chichilnisky, the inventor of the carbon market, Michelle S. Gale de Oliveira and Katie Black) attended the COP16 conference in Cancun as delegates, where progress was made towards a global climate change agreement. Durban COP 17 is a vital step to renewing Kyoto too. Partner with other organisations to achieve our goals more easily.

2 The markets which have driven the global economy, have failed in 2 respects, they have failed to prevent dangerous runaway climate change which now threatens the future for our children and for coastal peoples, and they have failed to prevent the 6th ever mass extinction of species which will probably have even worse consequences for humans. Therefore the reliance on the markets alone must end. The Kyoto Protocol should continue but the abuses and inequalities within it must end and new fairer and more efficient instruments within it must be developed. The global commons must be valued and the abuse of them as externalities must be concluded. We need to instigate a global culture of sharing and doing and of supporting each other and not rely on markets which tend to always favour those in possession of assets at the outset. Therefore regulation and rationing are considered to be more effective tools in situations which really matter. No reward should be made in global agreements for those already in possession of or which high previous use of carbon credits. Everyone should begin at one level and no trading should take place whereby large companies can buy up smaller companies or individuals allowances. There should be no dumping of carbon or green house gas activity in poorer countries. They are NOT carbon sinks and they are not carbon dumps

and they are not to be used as an excuse for more developed countries to carry on business as usual. All large energy provider groups should immediately be disbanded. It should become an offence for heads of large energy companies to run entire governments- or to finance members of parliament as has been the case in many countries from Russia, to Venuzuela to Kuwait to Nigeria to the USA etc. This must be regarded globally as a crime against humanity and there must be a global court to police it. All energy companies large and small must have boards which are gender and representative diversity and inclusion based in correct percentages with young people from the next generations on them at a high level. Tools must now include taxes and caps and limits on carbon usage and this should include the fast growing use of IT and aviation and alternatives found.

We regard further climate change as a massive and show stopping cost for our global economy and therefore to be prevented at all costs. For example one of the governments of a small island state ran its government cabinet meeting under water to highlight what the future holds for them if it continues to cause sea level rise. Future proofing of a companies impacts, rights and responsibilities must now be included in every company report. All households should report their total energy usage right down the supply chain. All companies must do likewise and no outsourcing of energy usage will be permitted.

3 The only real solution is to change our life styles so we consume less in the more developed economies and don't over consume more than our fair share. For less developed countries they might need to consume enough or more -within the 2 tonnes of carbon to survive better which may constitute an increase. This policy is known as contraction and convergence both within nations where huge inequalities exist and between nations. No nation and no business and no person should have incomes from the top to the bottom more than 7 times the smallest to the largest.

4 Poverty and refugees and displaced peoples, people lossing their home and means of agriculture are vulnerable and this is made worse by elite and business decisions on projects of deforestation or removing protective mangrove swamps or other natural barriers. More and more people are becoming displaced due to climate change or live stock dying of drought or people dying of more frequent famine is to be prevented. Often this is more as a result of war and disputes over territory ultimately over wealth power and money an resources and the grab between powers to take over resources and are fights between elites with the victims local people who do not receive the benefit. Green Economics does not think this is a good use of economics. The costs of climate change such as droughts and harvest failures should now be kept as a global register and figures issued monthly so that

everyone on the planet can see the impact of their activities aggregated and how it impacts the local global micro and and regional climate status.

5 Lifestsyle changes are the best policy choice against risk from climate change- to do more with less, and less emboddied carbon and less energy. Reuse, recycle, reduce, avoid all unnecessary usage. Avoid using carbon intensive activities, for example choosing the train or bus would make quite a difference as would turning off computers and lap tops when not in use and weaning ourselves off reliance on computers and mobile phones and their rapidly accelerating non essential recreational use. Sort out the global train ticketing once and for all and provide bicycles and safe point to point and walking routes with special needs and women and vulnerable people and children in mind. Include these people in all planning and infrastructure provision and design. Stop building out of town shopping malls.

6 Reduce our carbon usage for each of us to 2 tonnes of carbon each with 2 years and to zero carbon within 3 years and to remove it or drive it to negative within 5 years. We should take care not to use an another unsafe technology in our haste to wean ourselves off our carbon.

7 We should switch all our households and businesses and work to green energy, local generation and neighbours generation schemes and feed in tarrifs using renewables where-ever possible and avoiding altogether where it is possible. Everyone should have an energy audit every year and everyone should be reducing their energy use and green house gas use by 5% per month every month. Energy and travel should be rationed.

8 Smart grid – is to be supported and investments should be encouraged in true renewables solar, wind biomass and they should be promoted. Nuclear is NOT a renewable. Carbon storage is Not a renewable and is not a long term solution. China and all other nations should be weaned off using oil and gas and any fossil fuel and massive investment globally should go into developing viable renewables especially local generation. New technologies such as carbon scrubbers to be immediately employed to start to remove carbon but these must be placed in more developed countries. Not dumped in poorer ones. No new developments should be made without checking the climate impact. Green Building and planning must now be a compulsory part of development and all homes to be switched to green energy and green materials in a massive global switch which every country begins at once as a global human project. There should be an immediate cessation of mining exploitation of less developed countries and minerals and other

132

resources should become the property of the people in those countries. NO elite in any country and NO foreign power can ever again claim them or to keep the profits for themselves using violent regimes. This should become a crime against humanity. There should be an immediate cessation of all investment in nuclear except for decommissioning and an immediate cessation of all deep sea oil exploration and production. The profits from any such exploration should be given out as a citizens income and converted to a sovereign wealth fund shared by the whole country and whose use should be voted on but used to fund conversion to greener technologies infrastructure and lifestyles and to fund the removal of anyone in the country from poverty.

9 We should use all tools at our disposal- so regulation, markets, lifestyle changes and business mechanisms to try to preserve a more hospitable climate for all people everywhere, nature, other species, the planet and its systems !Most importantly, women in all countries should be educated which reduces the birth rate as the more educated a woman is the fewer children she generally has. Women should be given equal economics opportunity as this will also reduce the overall global birth rate.

10 We should share all technologies and smaller countries should get help and technology transfer to achieve a change. Projects that remove carbon from one place or activity and dump it in another in order to claim a reduction or money are to be stopped. We should reduce, reuse, recycle repair and more importantly avoid the use of anything that contributes to increased greenhouse gas use. Anyone cutting down rainforest should pay into a global fine fund commensurate with their ability to pay and constituting 99% of any profit made on the removal of the forest or trees. There should be immediate investment globally for non aviation and car based travel. If such infrastructure were put in place fast enough it would stimulate world trade.

A plan for the planet should be drawn up with key tipping points for the climate and action should be planned on a global scale. For example if small island states go under water or become uninhabitable new rationing should come into place. If the climate changes by more than x % or reaches x amount of warming above 1990 levels then rationing or caps should be triggered globally until the earth's systems revert.(which could be several 100 years). Everyone should join in the effort with global elites leading the way- no longer should the rich and famous be encouraged and rewarded for using gaz guzzling limousines as a symbol of power- on the contrary global elites should now lead the way with low carbon usage of transport and huge palaces and buildings. If they fail to show such leadership they should be removed and sanctioned.

A Green Economy should be adopted everywhere, to enable to above to work and to fit with other suitable democracy and economies so there is a local flavour with a green economy as a quality and standards filter for everyone. So it can work with indigenous economies, advanced economies and subsistence economies- the idea is to maintain diversity and local and peoples power and sharing but have universal ways of sharing and doing and supporting each other, other species, nature and the planet and its systems!

Symbols of earthly power should be the lack of use of displays of conspicuous consumption and overt flaunting of power-using frugality and constraint as beacons for our age of green economics as with Ghandi and Nelson Mandela. As a species we can wean ourselves off material displays of power and into a period of sharing and another way of displaying wealth and power. We need to do different things, by different people inclusion and diversity and gender balance- nurturing sharing and supporting each other an and create a true age of green economics -an age of doing, (our own energy- not the earths or someone else's- we need to end the sedentary age we have created) an age of sharing- an age of supporting each other as we go into one of the most exciting and challenging for at least 10 000 years!

5.2 Tackling Poverty and Climate Change: an opportunity for China

Sandra Ries and Lu Wei

The two defining challenges of our century are tackling poverty, and climate change. Tackling global poverty and extreme inequality have, in a serious sense, been on the agenda of most governments and development agencies for the last 70 years. What is striking about the development trajectory now is that from a sustainable point of view, the goals for development should in many ways be significantly different to the earlier development models that aimed for industrialization, and economic growth. The western way of living has come to be seen as the epitome of development, and currently we still see countries imitating this image of development. It is now, however, important that action is taken to combat the effects of climate change. This is why green development is so necessary. This chapter outlines the role of China, and its position and possible developing role in tackling poverty and climate change.

Issues of contemporary poverty reduction strategies

Eliminating poverty is an imperative goal that world leaders have committed to tackle. The Millennium Development Goals (MDGs), adopted by world leaders at the UN Millennium Summit, September 2000, reveal the widespread view that deep poverty is immoral, can be prevented, and needs action. The MDGs set out time bound targets with the deadline of 2015, and the goals range from reducing extreme poverty, hunger, disease, promoting gender equality, education and environmental sustainability. In many ways the MDG"s reflect international and national development policy. They emphasize the idea, and acknowledgement, that people over the world are seen as living in a single social space, and in this space, their well being is compared. The MDGs have furthermore provided a basis for a new development consensus during the last decade. In themselves, the MDGs do not constitute a development policy paradigm, but are nevertheless seen as the foundation of a particular approach to development and poverty in the last decade. They are not only the foundation for an international development cooperation approach, but also applied within an analytical and policy description, about how development and poverty reduction should be achieved. The message of this strategy is to advocate the best national strategy for achieving poverty reduction, which is largely achieved by promoting close integration with the global economy, through deep liberalization, and through the harmonization of global standards (Gore, 2008; Bendana, 2004). This contradicts sustainable development. Climate change is already a serious problem in many countries, and predicted by scientists to become ever more threatening if we do not change consumption styles soon. Poverty and climate change are intrinsically linked and part of policy making should recognize that unmanaged climate change would in fact harm the advances in development over the next few decades. In the example of China, we see how damaging economic growth has been for the environment, and the opportunities will be discussed.

China's Performance: MDG 1 (Reducing poverty) & MDG 7 (Environmental Sustainability)

China has been measured as quite a successful country on the United Nations Development Programme (UNDP) MDG assessments, with a high likelihood of MDG 1 being achieved by 2015. According to the UNDP, China has reduced the number of people living in extreme poverty from 85 million in 1990 to 26.1 million by the end of 2004 (UNDP). Due to the different methods of calculation and different standards of estimating the poverty line, there are huge deviations in the number of people who are actual living in extreme poverty. In 2008, Chinese Government readjusted the poverty line again. The new poverty line increased to 1196-yuan-a-year, about $180(Tang, Min 2009 ADB). Based on the new threshold, the number of Chinese living in poverty would be much bigger; about 43 million people were living below the poverty line in the country's rural area in 2007. The number in urban area was more than 22 million. However, the success of reducing poverty has come at the expense of the environment. At the moment, China is the world"s biggest emitter. Between 1994 and 2004 the annual average increment of greenhouse gas emissions was about 4%, whereas the share of CO_2 in total emissions increased from 76% to 83%. At the current rate of emissions, Chinas output is expected to double each decade. If this unit of output is to remain constant, China"s emissions will be around 30-35 billion tonnes in 2030, which is also the worlds global budget for 2030 (UNDP; Stern, 2010).

In the last 30 years China's economic development has been extraordinary. In just 3 decades, growth has averaged more than 9% a year. Despite its enormous growth, China is categorized as a developing country, and is still dealing with problems such as a weak social safety net, corruption, sustaining adequate job growth for its 1.3 billion citizens, and an ever-widening inequality gap, and of course environmental deterioration (OECD: Environmental Performance

Review: China). China has experienced a very fast industrialization, and focus on rapid economic growth has resulted in people moving to the urban centres for work. The increase in the urban share of the population in China has led to extremely high levels of pollution. The urban share of the population has recently risen from 17.9% to 44.9%. Industrialization and urbanization have led to an increased quest for natural resources which put pressure on land use, forest management and environment protection. The air pollution created by industrialization has caused many premature deaths per year, and the water pollution is a source of many health problems. Due to climate change and degradation of the eco system, the agriculture, water resources and bio diversity of china are facing severe pressure, which also leads to future risks of food shortages (OECD: Environmental Performance Review China).

China's goal is to build a moderately prosperous society, but the inequality gap is widening, and this is also a problem. The difference in per capita income ratio between urban and rural residents is about 3.3:1, which ranks china as second highest in Asia. According to a survey released by the Chinese Academy of social sciences, China"s richest 10% of the population own 40% of all private assets, while only 2% of total wealth goes to the bottom 10% (Sicular, Ximing, Gustafsson & Shi, 2007). Traditionally, China has had a very eco-friendly philosophy. According to the ancient Taoist philosophical-religious tradition, human beings are an integral and inseparable part of the natural realm. In this holistic view, development of any kind, could only occur in accordance with nature"s boundaries, and protection. This traditional perception of the environment was however heavily disrupted since China began its industrialization, especially since the reform that took place in 1978.

It is true that China is now the largest greenhouse gas emission country, but the rich or industrial countries had been for a long time by far the largest missioners, and because of the hysteresis in the climate change response, these countries are largely responsible for the majority of the stock of anthropogenic greenhouse gases in the atmosphere. Facing the truth and facts, we are not here to try to come to a verdict about whom should be more culpable, but rather to find the best ways for China to deal with the two issues that for the moment, at least technically, contradict each other: climate change and poverty the same time. As people in developed countries are trying to find ways to solve the economic problem of the Age of Austerity, people in developing countries like China, will have to choose the harder and less cost effective way, the environmentally friendly way, to get out poverty without causing pollution. It is therefore again at least technically, it will take a much longer time for China as well as other developing countries to eliminate poverty, and they will be less likely to achieve the MDG 1 by 2015. The poor who have done least to create the problem, now will w be forced to take the same responsibility.

In the 1970s, China experienced a radical transition from a self contained, centrally planned economy, to a more open and market friendly one. The leading motto „Development First – Environment Later", became very characteristic for this period. Several areas and cities situated mostly on the eastern part of the country expanded tremendously since the launch of the so called open door policy originally initiated by Deng Xiaopeng in 1978 (Han, 2006).

So what now?

The Chinese government is focusing on economic growth, featuring less input, less consumption, fewer emissions while maintaining high levels of efficiency. China is still set on economic growth, but is also increasingly becoming aware of the necessity for sustainable action and is working on decarbonisation. China has much of the world's viable resources of rare earth metals needed for green technology. The Copenhagen Summit December 2009 was the dramatic scene both of China's entry onto the world stage as keeper of the raw materials for powering the " green " technology revolution and also realising its own profound and critical powers to intervene. At Cancun COP 16, Kyoto climate conference, December 2010, China emerged from this intermediate, perhaps shocking phase both to itself and to the outside world and is now considering starting to take a mature position, possibly a lead and to participate fully. It is showing more understanding of and acknowledging its own pivotal role in this climax of human civilisation. China holds many of the key cards and is slowly starting to mature into the role. China is investing heavily in economic resources, research and development as a strategy which relies on technological advancement and innovation as a basis for tackling climate change. In 2008 China set aside 4 trillion Yuan (almost £380 billion) for a stimulus package for climate change mitigation projects. China has also made some progression in the area of renewable energies. China is currently one of the world's main producers of photovoltaic generators, solar water heating technology, and wind power plants (China's Government White Papers: III Strategies and Objectives for Addressing Climate Change; Xing, 2010). China has also begun to take the lead in investment in educational achievement and the knowledge economy which are characteristics of a mature green economy and she has made a very significant start in this respect. However there is still a long way to go, from political promises to real sustainable development. Green is also foundationally characterised by social and environmental justice and equity. There are still development issues concerning the approaches to

138

development, but there may be cause for optimism, as China evolves very rapidly. China could, if it desired, take the lead in green, sustainable development. Low carbon growth opportunities are vast, and China is in a position to compete, and to lead in this sector if it moves fast, considering its natural resources. The challenge is how to organize this transition in accordance with green principles in the round. Stern (2010) has suggested that public policies and public investment are key factors to creating a positive environment for innovation and change. This, for example, could be a policy on coal taxation, which would provide incentives for investment in alternative technologies. If China saw this moment as an opportunity- as investing in green technologies, as promoting their competitiveness in a time of serious environmental change, it would provide incentives for other countries to do the same, and fast.

This chapter started by introducing two defining challenges of our century, overcoming poverty and managing climate change. The MDGs are addressing important factors, but there are problems surrounding the approach taken to tackle the problems. A global development consensus needs to be agreed upon, on the notion of global sustainable development, bringing poverty reduction and climate change together, based on mutual interest, and economic development for the poorest. Where we would see 'global development means used to achieve global development goals', instead of the current national development means used to achieve global development goals" (Gore, 2008; Richards, 2003). If it were the case that global development means were used to achieve global development goals and also fulfil the guiding concepts of green economics, for simultaneous social and environmental development goals, then China, indeed would be in an impressive situation to take a leading role in combating climate change.

This chapter is based on a paper by Sandra Ries (Denmark)and kindly amended by Professor Wei Lu (China)and a previous version was originally published in the Autumn 2010 edition of the Green Economist. Published by The Green Economics Institute.

5.3 The economics of the anthropocene

Sir Crispin Tickell

What is the Anthropocene? It was well explained in a recent article in *The Economist*. Briefly it is the idea that humans have so transformed the land surface, seas and atmosphere of the Earth since the beginning of the industrial revolution some 250 years ago that we need a new geological epoch to describe it. Our not so little animal species has changed the character of soils, the chemistry of the oceans and atmosphere, the selective breeding of species of all kinds and their movement round the Earth to produce a world substantially different from what preceded it. Hence the Anthropocene.

It falls to this generation to try and measure the impact on society, and work out what might be done to mitigate or adapt to change in the general human interest. Little is more difficult than learning to think differently. Yet it is hard even to define the principal problems without upsetting longstanding traditions, beliefs, attitudes and the often unspoken assumptions on which we build our lives. It took a long time for previous generations to accept the antiquity of the Earth, the mechanisms of evolution, the movement of tectonic plates, the shared genetic inheritance of all living organisms, and the symbiotic and to some extent self-regulating relationship between the physical, chemical, biological and human components of the Earth system. Some still reject the whole idea.

The impacts which together constitute the Anthropocene can be defined in many ways. In broad terms we are exploiting and in some respects running down the Earth's natural capital, including the biosphere, and damaging the ecosystem services on which we depend. This is hard to reconcile with our experience of the bonanza of inventiveness, exploitation and consumption since the industrial revolution. All successful species, whether bivalves, beetles or humans, multiply until they come up against the environmental stops, reach some accommodation with the rest of the environment, and willy-nilly restore some balance. Are we near to those stops?

In September 2009 the magazine Nature published an article by Johan Rockstrom and others identifying nine scientific stops or boundaries which humans would cross at their peril. Three had already been crossed: climate change; loss of biodiversity; and interference with nitrogen and phosphorus levels. The other six were stratospheric ozone depletion; ocean acidification; use of fresh water; changes in land use; chemical pollution; and atmospheric aerosol loading.

But these stops, however important, are only half the story. There are six more general ones where the societal responses are critical. First we need to confront the effects of our own proliferation in all its aspects; next to work out new ways of generating energy; to manage and adapt to what is in effect climate destabilization; to give higher priority to conservation of the natural world; to create the necessary institutional means of coping with global problems; and not least to look at economics in the broadest sense and the way in which we measure things. As has been well said by Lord Rees former President of the Royal Society: in the future global village we cannot afford to have too many village idiots.

There is a lot to be said about all these issues, but today I want to focus on economics and what has been labelled socio-ecology. Much current economics is built on the assumptions of more than a hundred years ago. Resources then seemed limitless; shortages were more of labour and skills than of goods; technology could solve almost any problem: wastes could always be disposed of; the other organisms on which we depended could adapt to the demands we made on them; the good functioning of society was a product of what was called 'growth' (hence the increasing use of Gross National Product and Gross Domestic Product as measuring devices); and a kind of belief (I can think of no better word) in market forces as the main if not the only drivers of health, wealth and prosperity. With this comes the belief that economics are governed by reason (often mathematically expressed) rather than by animal - herd - instincts which otherwise rule.

It may be painful but indeed we have to think again. Our society, even our animal species, is in a unique situation: as the title of a recent book put it: we have *Something New Under the Sun*. Here are some broad propositions:

We should recognise that there is no such thing as a free market, and there never has been. All markets operate within rules, whether explicit or implicit. Together they constitute a framework which if it is any good should be in the public interest and to the public good.

The question, answered differently, in different societies is to determine the character of regulation, the nature of incentives and disincentives, how best to profit from enterprise, the avoidance of market failure, and in the long as well as the short term the stability and general health of society.

Somehow we have to bring in externalities (or true costs in social as well as economic terms). Indeed externalities could be more important than internalities. Markets are marvellous at fixing prices but incapable of recognising costs.

We should be ready to admit that human population increase is a major global problem, even if it is levelling off in some areas. Associated with it is increasing unemployment as technology enables us to produce more goods and services with fewer people.

We should challenge the current models of 'development' which underline the artificiality of the distinction between developed, developing, under-developed and even over-developed countries. The true distinction is between those who have set industrialization as an ideal within and between their countries, and those who look more widely and see the future in term of their people's resources and welfare. We have majority and minority worlds across the world as a whole.

In measuring health, wealth and happiness, we have to take into account the things we most value: safety, security, food, water, cleanliness and energy. Here we must recognise that despite continuing population increase we are producing more and more goods and services with fewer and fewer people. The social costs of unemployment are enormous, and we have to reckon properly with them.

Concepts of value are controversial. For example how do we value uncut rainforest, and reward those who do not cut it? Who should take the responsibility for human-driven climate change, and pay those who suffer most for it ?

None of these points is new. Change is already under way, even if sometimes obscured by the current economic crisis. In particular efforts have been made to establish new systems of measurement: for example through the Human Development Index, the Stern Review, and the recent report of the Stiglitz Commission. There is even a effort to measure GDH, or Gross Domestic Happiness, I suppose as part of the Big Society. But we are still far from the changes of attitude that are required.

Supposing, as I hope, that the message does eventually become more widely received and understood, what would be the implications ? Frankly they go so wide that I hesitate to be very specific. Individuals, local authorities, corporations, government at all levels would need to set very different priorities and human behaviour generally would change as a result.

A pivotal factor would be our use of energy. The flow of energy affects economics, indeed life itself, every minute. It was the uses to which we put the stored energy or sunlight known as coal, oil and gas, which directly caused the industrial revolution and the consequent transformation we now label the Anthropocene. I take energy as an example of how we need to think differently.

First we must recognize that supplies of energy from fossil fuels are limited. Estimates vary all the time as technologies develop, but deposits of oil, gas and coal are by their nature finite, and the environmental penalties paid in their exploitation will become higher than society can expect. There is also a changing balance of consumption between them. For example in the European Union, electricity supplies from gas have risen to 25% and from coal have fallen to 20%. There is increasing fear of dependence on certain suppliers, whether they be in the Middle East or Russia. Energy security is now high politics. In the meantime demand continues to increase worldwide. In China energy use doubled between 1990 and 2006, and is likely to double again by 2025.
The second new factor is better understanding of the cumulative effects of fossil fuel use and combustion on the chemistry of the atmosphere and the environment generally. The general relationship between greenhouse gases and the surface temperature of the Earth is well established, and although strenuous debate continues on the degree of public responsibility for the current increase in carbon dioxide in the atmosphere, many think that the consequences of our continuing dependence on fossil fuels are more serious than the prospect of their depletion.

Hence the new interest in making more effective use of what fossil fuels remain, and such measures as sequestration of carbon or global auctions of permits to emit greenhouse gases. But the main interest has been in developing alternative sources of energy. They include nuclear power, whether fission or fusion; solar energy on the ground or through geo-engineering; power from biofuels; tidal and ocean power; a return to wind and hydro power; geothermal power using the heat beneath our feet; and a range of new electrification technologies.

Of course there are many uncertainties and complexities. We can rarely identify tipping points until we have passed them. So far the societal responses have been mixed and uncertain with wide variations between countries.

The economics of the Anthropocene demand not just a new approach but a whole new methodology. Out of date economics should be recognised as a dangerous mental condition which is driving the world in an alarmingly wrong direction. In natural terms we are tiny parts of a gigantic system of life to which we are doing increasing injury. The human superorganism has to learn its place among other superorganisms. So far it has failed to do so. The impact of our species has been so great that the term Anthropocene is more than justified. Let economists reckon with it.

5.4 Understanding Environmental Degradation as a Cause of Conflict: patterns of Conflict and Cooperation

Max Marioni

All the numerous manifestations of environmental degradation deriving from mankind's tampering with the Earth's environment do not end with the damage meted out to the planet itself. Rather, the effects of human economic activity, from pollution contributing to global warming, from the excesses of the logging industry resulting in mass deforestation and soil degradation, or from overfishing and overgrazing resulting in the loss of biodiversity in the seas and on land interact in complex chains of causation which have as end-product severe repercussions on humans themselves and on the way we live our lives. The rationale behind this paper and the whole body of research into environmentally-induced conflict lies in the investigation of the effects which environmental degradation has on how humans pursue their social relations and how the latter change as a direct or indirect consequence of the former. It is clear that phenomena once attributed solely to the spatial environment have consequences on the social environment as well, and in the past few decades a new body of academic research in the social sciences has sprung up to accommodate this need for scientific inquiry into the social dimensions of environmental change.

Environmental change has consequences on the social interactions between different groups both at the national and supranational level; its transnational nature poses a challenge to the way we think about international relations and security in terms of state-centric approaches. These are global issues which require collective solutions, and no one state can tackle these issues successfully on its own. The negative consequences environmental degradation had on economic and social development as well as on human life have been recognised by policy-makers at least since the publication of the Brundtland report in 1987. The end of the Cold War and relaxation of traditional security concerns which characterised the bipolar era of superpower relations enabled a rethinking in academic and policy circles about the meaning of security, the nature of threats to human well-being and the relevance of environmental issues to security as well as for social and political stability in areas vulnerable to the effects of environmental degradation.

Early scholars of this emerging field of social inquiry developed a theoretical perspective which borrowed from the ideas of British economist Thomas Malthus, who famously predicted that rising populations would entail the reduction of the pool of natural resources available and an increase in competition among social groups and individuals over the exploitation of said natural resources. The contemporary combination of environmental degradation, with climate change, water degradation, deforestation and soil degradation, loss of biodiversity in the seas and on land all conspiring towards the depletion of a number of resources crucial to human survival and social cohesion, together with the demographic increases which the developing world has been experiencing in the last decade ensues in a situation of resource scarcity reminiscent of Malthus' vision. Resting on the Neo-Malthusian premises that Earth's resources are finite and their increasing scarcity will have detrimental effects on mankind, the main proponent is Thomas Homer-Dixon, who led successive projects on environmental scarcity and conflict. Environmental scarcity, driven by climate-induced renewable resource distribution, demographic pressure and uneven resource distribution, drives individuals and groups into competing for an ever scarcer pool of available resources, causing violent conflict in several regions of the world among developing countries, where environmental degradation already is severe and hits people at its hardest (Homer-Dixon 1991; 1994). Later research projects on the environment, population and security confirmed that "Environmental scarcity causes violent conflict" which "tends to be persistent, diffuse, and subnational" (1994:3) and a parallel project undertaken by the Environmental Conflicts Project (ENCOP) of the Swiss Federal Institute for Technology reached the same conclusion (Spillman and Bächler, 1995; Bächler, 1998). Neo-Malthusian theories have been used to explain numerous armed conflicts such as civil wars in Rwanda and the Philippines, Indian and Pakistani confrontations over Kashmir and tensions over the use of water in the Jordan valley between Israel and its neighbouring states (Homer-Dixon and Blitt, 1998; Kahl, 2006).There is ample archaeological evidence that the demise of the Easter island civilisation, as well as the Norse settlements in Greenland, were caused by a chain of events very similar to the Neo-Malthusian narrative (Matthew and Gaulin, 2001; Mazo, 2010).

This paradigm, however, has been cast into doubt by a separate strand of studies which have found no significant statistical correlation between environmental degradation and conflict (Binningsbø, De Soysa and Gleditsch, 2007; Esty et al, 1999; Gleditsch, 1998; Nordås and Gleditsch, 2007; Raleigh and Urdal, 2007; Thiesen, 2008). However, the existence of a link between environmental change and conflict, however indirect, is widely suspected, and has come to the attention of NATO, the EU and the US department of Defence. A report commissioned by the US Department of Defence revealed the cataclysmic consequences of a worst case scenario of abrupt intensification of global warming (Schwartz and Randall, 2003). Another report, signed by a military advisory committee of no less than 11 retired US Army, US Marine Corps, USAF Generals and US Navy Admirals highlighted the national security implications of Climate Change for the US and established the notion of climate change acting as a "threat multiplier", exacerbating pre-existing tensions in the social fabric of unstable regions (CNA, 2007), which has become influential and accepted in later interpretations of the subject (Kerry, 2008; Mazo, 2010). The German Advisory Council on Global Change also published an influential report on security threats caused by climate change, which concluded that, while "Climate-induced interstate wars are unlikely to occur, [...] climate change could well trigger national and international distributional conflicts and intensify problems already hard to manage such as state failure, the erosion of social order, and rising violence" (WBGU, 2007:1).

While the security concerns attached to environmental degradation are real and urgent, the above seems to suggest that rarely environmental issues alone are sufficient to trigger conflict. Other observers have pointed out to humankind's capability of adaptation to severe environmental conditions and to find peaceful solutions to situations of environmental scarcity. Richard Matthew and Ted Gaulin (2001) undertook an assessment of the social effects of environmental degradation on the populations of small islands. His findings show that, while the first case (Easter Island) followed closely the Neo-Malthusian model of anthropogenic environmental change leading to resource scarcity and in turn leading to societal breakdown and civil strife, the other two cases he considered, Nauru and the Solomon Islands, differ markedly from the assumed behaviour suggested by the theory. The authors found that the degree of social , political and economic openness, i.e. levels of trade, of democracy and participation in regional agreements and organisations have a large impact on the island's stability and prosperity, reducing its vulnerability to environmental degradation and making the possibility of experiencing conflict more remote.

Matthew's fresh approach (further elaborated in Matthew, Gaulin and MacDonald, 2003) focuses on the factors moderating the likelihood of environmentally induced conflict, factors which show the adaptation capability humans have when confronted by the necessity of cohabitation in areas prone to environmental scarcity, to avoid the societal breakdown and violence which can be traced back to environmental scarcity. The scope of research hence should be shifted towards issues of governance and resource management: in fact, the academic literature has moved more into the direction of investigating how cooperation can be achieved and which cooperative adaptation strategies can be used to put up with conditions of severe environmental damage and environmental scarcity. This debate harks back to one of the fundamental debates of international relations theory, between realists on one side, who maintain that the world is in essence a zero-sum game system dominated by balance-of-power mentalities, where actors (states) are self-centred units after their own relative gains at the expense of others, and liberals on the other, who believe that cooperation can be beneficial to all actors and absolute gains can be attained in a global system regulated by peaceful exchange and interdependence.

The central question is whether scarce resources can be successfully managed in areas susceptible to armed conflict, where the authority of the state is weak, inter-ethnic rivalries are already strong and the fabric of society already under stress. In addition, environmental degradation has all a series of destabilising consequences which go beyond state borders: one need go no further but think of the plight of environmental refugees escaping from situations of famine and drought. If the state, or other competent local authority, is unable to manage its critical renewable resources, collective action is required. Can transnational and regional cooperation succeed in managing renewable resources effectively, solving the issue of scarcity and removing the danger of civil and interstate conflict? There are a series of transnational and regional agreements which point to positive experiences in this direction. The Horn of Africa is an area particularly vulnerable to environmental degradation, above all suffering from the consequences of climate change and land degradation. The countries in this region are characterised by arid and semi-arid landscapes and have experienced an increasing rate of desertification, with reportedly 25% of Sudan's arable land at risk of further desertification (UNEP:2007), while witnessing large increases in their population. The majority of the local population are dependent on and involved in agriculture and pastoralism, which have been hit very hard by climate change-induced land degradation. This has left more people competing over decreasing quantities of food and good, arable land; the consequent phenomena of overgrazing and over-exploitation of land have made matters worse, exacerbating tensions between neighbouring groups and between pastoralist and agricultural communities, tensions which have often given rise to forms of organised violence. The civil war in Darfur, for example, has been defined by UN Secretary-General Ban Ki-Moon as the "first Climate Change conflict" (2007) and the UNEP Sudan post-conflict environmental assessment report concluded that "there is a very strong link between land degradation, desertification and conflict in Darfur" (UNEP, 2007:8). Kenya has witnessed bouts of violence between tribes in nomadic areas in the 1990s and 2008, Ethiopia and Eritrea have been at war with each other between 1998 and 2000, and Somalia has been locked in a state of semi-continous civil war since 1992 and is the clearest example of failed state in Africa. Disputes over land use and water management have played a significant role in fomenting each one of these conflicts. Environmental conflicts have been particularly harsh towards women, children, the elderly and the disadvantaged, as these are the groups that tend to be most vulnerabie to resource and food scarcity, and tend to be left behind in the battle over good land and water (Perry, Potgieter and Bob, 2010).

The state and national governments are often powerless in the face of these adversities as they lack the infrastructure, the resources and know-how, and the popular legitimacy in the eyes of the people to tackle these issues effectively. Various regional schemes have come into existence , also thanks to AU and UN assistance, to provide collective, regional solutions. One of the most active organisations in this sense has been the Inter-Governmental Authority on Development (IGAD), founded in 1986 to provide an organised intergovernmental response to the hardship and social unrest provoked by droughts and other forms of environmental degradation in the Horn of Africa. It has created a Conflict Early Warning and Response Mechanism (CEWARN) which focuses on establishing peaceful solutions for cross-border conflicts related to land use and encouraging more sustainable methods in agriculture and soil use. CEWARN has been successful in cases in Ethiopia and Kenya.

Tensions have been high over water rights over the Nile River, especially between the down-river states of Egypt and Sudan, who are the main beneficiaries of old settlements signed in colonial times, and the up-river states of Ethiopia and Kenya, who have limited access to the river and its tributaries notwithstanding the presence of the Nile sources on their territory and the Horn of Africa's dire need of water both for irrigation and personal consumption. The Nile Basin Initiative has been successful in preventing water-related conflicts in North-Eastern Africa and achieving sustainable socio-economic development through the equitable utilisation of the Nile Basin water resources. Similar regional agreements and organisations have risen about the equitable management of water resources around lake Chad, in the region of the Great Lakes in sub-Saharan Africa, as well as outside Africa, in the Middle East, East Asia and South America.

Environmentally-induced conflict, hence, can be stopped, and the ecological and socio-economic issues which cause this kind of conflict can be tackled through cooperation and the activity of regional organisations such as the Nile Basin Initiative, IGAD's CEWARN, and so on. A shift of emphasis by policy-makers and policy analysts from more traditional foreign and security policy would also be welcome, because the tragic social consequences of drought, desertification, famine and displacement are urgent and need attending to as much as, if not more than, other security priorities. As Lester Brown indicated in the lead article of Foreign Policy magazine some months ago in a special issue devoted to food security, "Civilisation can survive the loss of its oil reserves, but it cannot survive the loss of its soil reserves." (Brown, 2011)

References

Bächler, Günther, "Why Environmental Transformation Causes Violence: A Synthesis", *Environmental Change and Security Report*, Issue 4 (Spring 1998), pp.24-44
Ban Ki-Moon, "A Climate Culprit in Darfur", *The Washington Post*, June 16, 2007, http://www.washingtonpost.com/wp-dyn/content/article/2007/06/15/AR2007061501857.html_,_accessed April 25, 2011
Binningsbø , Helga M., De Soysa, Indra and Gleditsch, Nils P., "Green Giant or Straw Man? Environmental Pressure and Civil Conflict, 1961-99", *Population and Enviironment*, Vol. 28 No. 6 (2007), pp. 337-353
Brown, Lester R., "The New Geopolitics of Food", *Foreign Policy*, May/June 2011, http://www.foreignpolicy.com/articles/2011/04/25/the_new_geopolitics_of_food?page=full_, accessed 25 April 2011
Brundtland, Gro Harlem et al., (1987) *Our Common Future. World Commission Report on Environment and Development* Oxford: Oxford University Press
CNA (2007), *National Security and the Threat of Climate Change*, Washington, DC: Center of Naval Analysis, http://www.SecurityAndClimate.cna.org/
Esty, Daniel C., Goldstone, Jack A., Gurr, Ted A., Harff, Barbara, Levy, Marc, Dabelko, Geoffrey D., Surko, Pamela T. and Alan N. Unger, State Failure Task Force Report: Phase II Findings, Environmental Change and Security Report, Issue 5 (Summer 1999), pp. 49-72
German Advisory Council on Global Change (WBGU), "Welt im Wandel: Sicherheitsrisiko Klimawandel" – "World in Transition: Climate Change as a Security Risk", Springer Verlag: Berlin, (2007; transl. 2008)
Gleditsch, Nils P, "Armed Conflict and the Environment: a Critique of the Literature", *Journal of Peace Research*, Vol. 35 No. 3 (May, 1998)

Special Issue on Environmental Conflict, pp. 381-400

Homer-Dixon, Thomas F, "On the Threshold: Environmental Changes as Causes of Acute Conflict", *International Security*, Vol. 16, No. 2 (Autumn, 1991), pp. 76-116

Homer-Dixon, Thomas F, "Environmental Scarcities and Violent Conflict: Evidence from the Cases", *International Security*, Vol.19 No. 1 (Summer, 1994), pp. 5-40

Homer-Dixon, Thomas F, and Blitt, Jessica (1998), *Ecoviolence: Links among Environment, Population, and Security*, Lanham, MA: Rowman and Littlefield Publishers

Kahl, Colin (2006), *States, Scarcity and Civil Strife in the Developing World*, Princeton, NJ: Princeton University Press

Kerry, John, 'Climate Change and American Foreign Policy: Security Challenged, Diplomatic Opportunities', Conference, Council for Foreign Relations, New York, 15th June 2009, http://www.cfr.org/climate-change/climate-change-american-foreign-policy-security-challenges-diplomatic-opportunities/p19639, accessed on 25 April 2011

Matthew, Richard A. and Gaulin, Ted, "Conflict or Cooperation? the Social and Political Impacts of Resource Scarcity on Small Island States", *Global Environmental Politics*, Vol. 1 No. 2 (May, 2001), pp. 48-70

Matthew, Richard A., Gaulin, Ted, and McDonald, Bryan, "The Elusive Quest: Linking Environmental Change and Conflict", *Canadian Journal of Political Science*, Vol. 36 No. 4 (September, 2003), pp. 857-878

Mazo, Jeffrey (2010), *Climate Conflict: How Global Warming Threatens Security and What to do About it*, London: International Institute for Strategic Studies

Nordås, Ragnhild and Gleditsch, Nils P., "Climate Change and Conflict", *Political Geography*, Vol. 26 No. 6 (August 2007), Special Issue on Climate Change and Conflict, pp. 627-736

Perry, Edwin C., Potgieter, Cheryl and Bob, Urmilla, "Environmental Conflicts and Women's Vulnerability in Africa", *African Journal of Conflict Resolution*, Vol. 10 No. 2 (2010), pp. 121-136

Raleigh, Clionadh and Urdal, Henrik, "Climate Change, Environmental Degradation and Armed Conflict", *Political Geography*, Vol. 26 No. 6 (August 2007), Special Issue on Climate Change and Conflict, pp. 674-694

Schwartz, P., & Randall, D. (2003). *An abrupt climate change scenario and its implications for United States National Security*. Washington, DC: Environmental Media Services, Department of Defence

Spillmann, Kurt R. and Bächler, "Günther, Environmental Crisis: Regional Conflicts and Ways of Cooperation", Report of the International Conference at Monte Verità, Ascona, Switzerland, *Environment and Conflicts Project (ENCOP)*: Occasional Paper No. 14,

September, 1995
Thiesen, Ole M., "Blood and Soil? Resource Scarcity and Internal Armed Conflict Revisited", *Journal of Peace Research,* Vol. 45 No. 6 (November, 2008), pp. 801-818
UNEP (2007), *Sudan: Post-Conflict Environmental Assessment,* Nairobi: United Nations Environmental Program

Chapter 5. 5 Responses to climate change and their implications for green jobs: Techno fixes or lifestyle changes?
Katie Black

Working from the premise that anthropogenically-induced climate change is real and occurring, the ensuing major challenge facing us, the human race, is the formulation of an appropriate response. This article seeks to explore and summarise the available options to deal with the issue and to examine some of the implications that pursuing different options may have upon the creation (or retention) of "green jobs".

With June 2010 recently confirmed as the warmest June on record and the 304th consecutive month where average global land and surface temperature were above the average for the 20th century (NOAA, 2010), the trend towards a warmer world is indisputable. This is not something that can be ignored – if left unchecked, climate change is predicted have dire consequences for most occupants of the earth (OECD, 2008).

Human-induced climate change is caused by the emission of greenhouse gases into the atmosphere. These gases are by-products of processes used in agriculture, energy production and as a result of deforestation (Stern, 2006). Responding to the impacts of climate change is a controversial topic which has been much discussed, although there still remains a lack of consensus on the best way to tackle the problem at every level, from world leaders to the general public. Do we grapple with the roots of the problem and attempt to make wide-ranging lifestyle changes in order to reduce our carbon

153

emissions? Do we place our faith in greater efficiency in the way that we use energy to change the relationship between carbon output and economic activity? Or do we grin, bear it and try to actively adapt as best we can? Many rightly point out that none of these strategies will work in isolation, it is too late.

"Adaptation and mitigation are not alternatives, we must pursue both" (Stern, 2006) .

Although adaptation and mitigation are the most commonly identified methods for combating climate change, according to some there is a third, more contentious, component which has also become necessary to complete the overall approach, namely geo engineering. There is no universally accepted definition of the term "geo engineering", although the National Academy of Sciences has described it as "options that would involve large-scale engineering of our environment in order to combat or counteract the effects of changes in atmospheric chemistry" (COSEPUP, 1992).

Some geo engineering techniques such as Carbon Capture and Storage, which does actually seek to reduce the amount of CO_2 in the atmosphere, may be classed under the heading of mitigation. Other proposals seek only to combat certain effects of global warming, such as Solar Radiation Management (SRM) projects, which aim to reflect some of the sunlight hitting the earth and therefore prevent it from heating (whilst not actually reducing the atmospheric concentrations of greenhouse gases, therefore doing little to assuage the other effects such as ocean acidification) (Royal Society, 2009). In 2009, a review published by the Royal Society (2009) emphasised that lower risk carbon dioxide removal techniques should be regarded as preferable to SRM techniques and called for a 10 year geoengineering research program to be funded. The current problem with geoengineering stems from the fact that no large-scale projects have been carried out, and hence their effectiveness and/or downsides remain unproven.

Research is undoubtedly needed to ensure that in solving one aspect of the problem we are not creating another.

There are devotees of all of the above approaches, from those who seek to minimise their own carbon footprint in choosing to adopt low-carbon impact lifestyles to others who advocate large-scale geo engineering as a potentially effective way to deal with the consequences of climate change. The Institution of Mechanical Engineers is one organisation promoting geo engineering as an essential component of the move towards a de-carbonised economy. They highlight three options in particular as promising: artificial trees, which remove CO_2 directly from the air to be sequestered, algae-coated buildings, which will naturally absorb CO_2 and reflective buildings, which could serve to provide a cooling effect in urban heat islands (IMechE, 2009).

Equally, there are fierce opponents to most strategies, who range from complete climate change deniers who refute the need to do anything, to those point out the downside of particular techniques, to those who appear fundamentally opposed to certain means of fighting climate change. For example, the Swedish Society for Nature Conservation has branded geoengineering "an act of geopiracy" (Lamb, 2010).

Danger also lies in allowing companies to push their own agenda. We must ensure that companies seeking to make a profit out of (as yet) unproven geoengineering technologies are properly regulated. Concerns of this nature were raised in an open letter signed by many civil society groups expressing unease at a conference held by the Climate Response Fund in April 2010, which focussed on "the development of risk reduction guidelines for climate intervention experiments" (CRF, 2010). They argue that allowing companies to set their own rules concerning controversial approaches to climate change is worrying.

"This public debate must, at the very least, include the peoples and countries that are most vulnerable and likely to be affected by geoengineering, not only those who stand to gain. ... Determining guidelines for geoengineering research and testing in the absence of that debate is premature and irresponsible." (ETC 2010)

It is also worth recognising that climate change brings potential opportunities as well as threats, not least in the domain of green employment opportunities. UNEP, the United Nations Environment Program, has defined a "green job" as:

"work in agricultural, manufacturing, research and development (R&D), administrative, and service activities that contribute substantially to preserving or restoring environmental quality. Specifically, but not exclusively, this includes jobs that help to protect ecosystems and biodiversity; reduce energy, materials, and water consumption through high efficiency strategies; de-carbonize the economy; and minimize or altogether avoid generation of all forms of waste and pollution." (2008)

Green jobs, "the key to a sustainable economy" (Chaal, 2010), are often touted as one of the welcome consequences of taking action to counteract climate change and have rapidly become part of environmental discourse. UNEP also states that:

"(the) green job has become something of an emblem for both a new and sustainable economy and a more just society" (2008).

It is political choices which will, in part, be responsible for removing some of the barriers to a "Just Transition" (UNEP 2008) towards a low carbon economy and drive the creation of these "green" opportunities. Different climate change strategies will have different effects on economic growth and job opportunities in particular sectors. Whilst the creation of new (or retention of existing) jobs in more sustainable industries is undoubtedly a positive and necessary thing, policy-makers must be careful about using the creation of green jobs to add weight to arguments in favour or against particular climate change options. We must be careful to ensure that a job labelled as green is actually working towards the benefit of the environment and develop real ways to measure this (Walsh, 2010).

Just as there is dispute surrounding the controversial approaches towards combating climate change, there must also be a fresh debate on how we define and measure "green jobs", and how we can ensure that stakeholders do not use the creation of such jobs as a bargaining tool for helping to promote their own interests.

References
Chaal, N., *Green jobs the key to a sustainable economy* [Online]. European Parliament. 2010. [Accessed 19 July 2010]. Available from: http://www.europarl.europa.eu/news/expert/infopress_page/048-78672-193-07-29-908-20100712IPR78671-12-07-2010-2010-false/default_es.htm
Climate Response Fund (CRF). *Asilomar International Conference on Climate Intervention Technologies* [Online]. Climate Response Fund. 2010. [Accessed 19 July 2010]. Available from: http://climateresponsefund.org/images/stories/announcement.pdf

Committee on Science, Engineering, and Public Policy (COSEPUP). 1992. Geoengineering. *In:* Committee on Science, Engineering, and Public Policy. *Policy Implications of Greenhouse Warming: Mitigation, Adaptation, and the Science Base.* Washington D.C.: National Academy Press, 433-464.
ETC Group. *SIGN ON! Open Letter Opposing Asilomar Geoengineering Conference* [Online]. 2010. [Accessed 19 July 2010]. Available from: http://www.etcgroup.org/en/node/5080
Institution of Mechanical Engineers (IMechE). *Geo-engineering: giving us the time to act?* [Online] Institution of Mechanical Engineers. 2009. [Accessed 19 July 2010]. Available from: http://www.imeche.org/NR/rdonlyres/448C8083-F00D-426B-B086-

565AA17CB703/0/IMechEGeoengineeringReport.pdf
Lamb, G. M., *Should geoengineering be used to address global warming?* [Online]. The Christian Science Monitor. 2010. [Accessed 19 July 2010]. Available from: http://www.csmonitor.com/Environment/2010/0503/Should-geoengineering-be-used-to-address-global-warming
National Oceanic and Atmospheric Administration (NOAA). *June, April to June, and Year-to-Date Global Temperatures are Warmest on Record* [Online]. National Oceanic and Atmospheric Administration. 2010. [Accessed 19 July 2010]. Available from: http://www.noaanews.noaa.gov/stories2010/20100715_globalstats.html
Organisation for Economic Co-operation and Development (OECD). *Climate Change Mitigation: what do we do?* [Online]. Organisation for Economic Co-operation and Development. 2008. [Accessed 19 July 2010]. Available from: http://www.oecd.org/dataoecd/30/41/41753450.pdf
Stern, N., What is the economics of climate change? *World Economics*, 2006, 7, 1-10.
The Royal Society. *Geoengineering the climate: science, governance and uncertainty* [Online]. The Royal Society. 2009. [Accessed 19 July 2010]. Available from: http://royalsociety.org/Geoengineering-the-climate/
United Nations Environment Program (UNEP). *Green jobs: towards decent work in a sustainable, low-carbon world* [Online]. 2008. [Accessed 19 July 2010]. Available from: http://www.unep.org/PDF/UNEPGreenjobs_report08.pdf
Walsh, B., *What is a green-collar job exactly?* [Online] Time. 2010. [Accessed 19 July 2010]. Available from: http://www.time.com/time/health/article/0,8599,1809506,00.html

5.6 European SuperSmart Grid: Great opportunities for renewable energy sources

Winston Ka-Ming Mak

In December 2010, the European Commission formally presented the proposal for a Super Smart Grid (SSG), which joins up the electricity networks of the European Union's member states and North Africa by 2050 as part of its energy infrastructure priorities for the next two decades. Super smart grids are a type of infrastructure perceived by the European Parliament as indispensable to improve the efficiency of using renewable energy sources. SSG will decarbonise the Pan-European electricity industry and economy and hence combat climate change; enhance security of energy supply; realise a single energy market; and in particular, increase the scale of renewables portfolio. (Prodi, 2011) A low-carbon Europe is in the making.

Smart grid

Run parallel with the EU, the UK Government are committed to reforming British electricity networks and developing a smart grid by 2050. Different from conventional grid systems, 'smart grids' will revolutionise the way our power is generated by allowing electrical devices to communicate accurately with utility firms on energy use and, thus, reducing carbon emission by at least 211 million tonnes. The basic idea is to connect different parts of the electrical grid – from a single home to the largest of power stations – with a customised network based on internet protocol (IP). Smart grid will be able to handle the bi-directional flow of data and electricity, facilitating renewables micro-generation capacities around the world. (BBC News, 2009) The core elements of Europe's Supergrid investment through 2020 include: transmission system upgrades, smart meters, distribution automation and substation automation, as well as electric vehicle management system (in later years).

Policy drivers

The world today is facing increasing energy prices, diminishing fossil energy resources and rapidly growing energy demand. Now, the price of oil has hit the record high of US$130 per barrel. Production has already peaked in over 60 oil-producing countries. It is expected that the exploitation of world oil reserves continues to outpace the discovery of new resources and the world energy demand will increase by further 50% by 2030. To reduce GHG emissions by 20-30% by 2020 and 80% by 2050, the EU has decided to increase the use of renewable energies to 20% of total energy consumption by 2020, 33% by 2030 and 50% by 2050. Therefore, stronger regulations and limitations on greenhouse gas emissions are expected, the possibilities to use even the remaining, expensive fossil energy resources will be severely limited.

Promoting the extensive use of renewable energy sources is the way out. Potential is spread across Europe with wind in the North and sun in the South, biomass and geothermy in Central and Eastern Europe, as well as ocean energy around. According to the European Wind Energy Association, over €57 billion of cumulative investments in wind energy is expected by 2020 for 40GW of generating capacity. (Reuters, 2010) Given the international consensus that European grids have to be at least carbon-neutral, or even of negative emissions (to make space for developing countries), to keep the global temperature rise to within 2°C, the attainability of these climate change and renewables targets may not be as realistic with the current energy policy paradigm, transport and storage capacities in Europe.

One promising solution is to make use of the enormous potential for solar and wind power in North African and the Middle Eastern deserts. Scientists said just 0.3% of daylight there is sufficient to satisfy the electricity needs of the Mediterranean and the rest of Europe many times over. Nonetheless, the clean electricity generated there needs to be transmitted over vast distances back to European load centres. Transmission losses are so high that long-distance transport is unfeasible with the current AC system, even if the interconnection capacities were sufficient, which is not the case at present. Thanks to the high-voltage direct current (HVDC) technologies, it will underpin the proposed SSG by allowing long-distance transmission with minimum losses in an 'electricity highway' and, as researchers working under the EU CIRCE project believe, could solve both the fluctuation and instability problems of renewables generation. Commissioning of the first electricity highway is planned for 2020.

Intermittence of renewables

Conceivably the fatal weakness of renewable energy has been its intermittent nature which fails to provide a predictable, steady flow of 'base load' power to the grid. So merely creating renewable energy sources and plugging them into the grid in never a complete solution. But the wonder of nature lies in the fact that it is impossible for all sources, including solar, wind and tidal power, to be weak everywhere at any given time. Some European governments are embarking on a renewable energy master grid 'on a continental scale' – North Sea's Offshore Grid Initiative (NSOGI) – which is to couple different technologies in different environments to mitigate the natural ebb and flow of any one source. This means utility companies will no longer need to run back-up power, most often natural gas or coal, simultaneously in the event that the renewables cannot meet supply. As a result, real reductions in carbon emissions can be realised and renewable energy become more reliable and a better investment. (Caine, 2010)

NSOGI as a pioneer of Supergrid

Signed by nine countries around the North Sea in March this year, the North Sea's Offshore Grid Initiative could be regarded as a pioneer or simply a debut of the pan-European Supergrid. The UK, France, Germany, Belgium, Denmark, Netherland, Ireland, Luxembourg and Norway are planning a new high-voltage electricity network which links up the world's longest subsea power cable in the North Sea in order to expand the use of renewables such as offshore wind, solar and hydro-power. This €30-billion project will connect the 'super-nodes' of power generated by wind turbines in the UK and Germany, tidal power stations in Belgium and Denmark, hydro-power in Norway (30 coal-fired plants equivalent) and solar and geothermal power in the rest of Europe, forming a large battery of renewables.

With NSOGI in place, not only does the combination of power sources raise the likelihood of a more steady flow of clean energy, but also Norway's large supply of hydro-electric facilities can provide 30GW of energy storage to further secure the system's reliability. For instance, surplus wind energy produced off Britain's coast (when electricity demand in the UK is low, but wind speed is high) could be exported to Norway and used to pump water in its hydro-power stations. Electricity generated by hydropower could then be sent to Britain at times of high demand when the wind is not blowing.

Opportunities for renewables

Higher security of supply of renewables-generated electricity means energy prices can become less volatile and an integrative, single electricity market a reality in Europe. As an international infrastructural investment, the undertaking of the Supergrid is likely to generate thousands of jobs along with further ratification of other renewable energy projects in the region, including the huge expansion planned in offshore wind energy. (Reuters, 2010) The Supergrid will create another global opportunity for European companies to export sustainable energy technologies. (GEC, 2011) A new generation of electrical grids is a cornerstone of the development of renewables in Europe, bringing new opportunities for energy trading amongst European states.

Opportunity does not end with the completion of the SSG project because it can be 'unlimited'. Once the Supergrid is in service, it will become a tool continuously utilised and expanded to accommodate more and more capacities, even beyond the pan-European region. In theory, the Supergrid system could be of potential use to link efficiency to consumer system on smaller scales. If a troop of 'smart meters' could be combined with the appliances, cars and users of individual homes, it would help encourage conservation and balance grid load throughout the course of a day.

Challenges to overcome

Notwithstanding the number of benefits that the Supergrid project will bring to Europe, nothing will go ahead until the huge financing problem is solved amongst the international players. For example, at today's costs initial investments for thermal solar plants in North Africa would be up to three times higher than for similar capacity increases with conventional fossil fuel plants in Europe. (Tournemille, 2009) The European Commission estimate that €1 trillion investment will be needed by 2020 for the entire EU energy system (including network expansion, promotion of renewable energies, and measures to increase energy efficiency). In the shadow of current sovereign debt crisis, who is going to foot the bill? This is an important issue for wider discussions.

Other than huge investment required, the factors which governments and energy investors will also need to consider include: the profitability of these investments dependent on renewable support mechanisms; uncertainty of future carbon prices; suitability of bilateral renewable support mechanisms; whether large-scale imports from North Africa to Europe are coupled with efforts to meet increasing local energy demand there; and, most importantly, the availability of a supporting, red tape-free, regime to obtain thousands of permissions from various authorities, etc. After all, it is always the political motivation that counts. This Supergrid model, if successful, will also be a role model for the rest of the world, especially the world's largest polluter, China and potentially India.

References

1. BBC News. (2009, May 18). Electricity to power 'smart grid'. *BBC News*.

2. Caine, T. (2010, January 25). A New European Supergrid for Renewable Energy. *Intercon*.

3. GEC. (2011). *Supergrid, Clean Power for Europe*. Retrieved July 10, 2011, from Green Economy Coalition: http://www.greeneconomycoalition.org/node/25

4. Prodi, V. (. (2011). *Smart and Super Grids: vision for a future European energy infrastructure*. Strasbourg: The Secretariat of the Intergroup on "Climate Change, Biodiversity and

Sustainable Development".

5. Reuters. (2010, March 8). Europe 'supergrid' hopefuls cast fate to wind. *CNET News* .

6. Tournemille, H. (2009, June 8). *Europe's Super Smart Grid: Bad Name for an Ambitious Idea*. Retrieved July 10, 2011, from Energy Boom: http://www.energyboom.com/europes-super-smart-grid-bad-name-ambitious-idea

5.7 €1tn investment for Pan-European super smart grid

Winston Ka-Ming Mak

I believe we need to achieve a 20-30% emission cut by 2020?

To do so, experts agree that our grids must become at least carbon-neutral. Last December, the European Commission unveiled its plan for a Super Smart Grid joining up the electricity networks of the EU and North Africa by 2050 to bring low-cost, low-carbon electricity and better investment opportunities in renewable energies. But it estimates that all infrastructural upgrades will need €1 trillion investment. So, the Pan-European Supergrid can't go ahead unless the financing arrangement is sorted out soon.

In the current debt crisis, our government won't have much money to spare to foot this bill. Hundreds of billions of private funding will have to be mobilised through either the user-pays principle or nationwide electricity retail tariff.

Some propose a European Network Fund, funded by a fixed and additional tariff charged to consumers, and guaranteed by European Investment Bank (EIB). However, tariff levels set by other national regulators tend not to sufficiently consider cross-border priorities. Also, the investment risks of high-cost infrastructures that coexist with uncertain profits distributed over decades cannot be insured by a bond insurer (so-called 'monoliner') since the outbreak of Eurozone crisis.

To offer private investors partial risk transfers, "project bonds" 20-30% guaranteed by EIB or our Green Investment Bank should be more feasible. A project company financing, implementing and operating an infrastructural project would be more attractive to investors as even government bonds look insecure under the current debt crisis. Thus, investors can distribute their risks among various projects.

Noteworthy is that EIB guarantees should only be used for trans-European network projects, not for those limited to one member state.

Chapter 6. Green Economics in Government

6.1 Managing the economy :Creating Green Economies in Sub National Jurisdictions

Meredith Hunter MLA

Whilst some national governments are stepping into this space, until now it has been primarily left to sub national jurisdictions to start the economic shift away from fossil fuels and towards new low emissions technologies. Around the world there have been many very successful schemes and mechanisms used to encourage innovation and industries that will be the key to reducing emissions while protecting the current economic prosperity. The Australian Capital Territory has begun to implement a range of measures that will reduce emissions and make the economy more sustainable. The section attempts to explain some of those initiatives and highlight areas where more could be done to make the shift to a sustainable green economy.

With some exceptions national governments have been reluctant to tackle climate change and create the necessary settings for green economies to flourish.(1) Many sub national and particularly smaller economies have been victims not only to inaction but also national schemes that swallow up or otherwise negate their own initiatives.(2) In spite of national reticence there is much that smaller jurisdictions can be doing even when their federal colleagues continue to resist. The Australian Capital Territory (ACT)(3) is an example of one such jurisdiction where initiatives have begun to deliver outcomes and better position the economy and community for future climate change challenges.

This is not to in any way overstate what the ACT has done; or to pretend that there still isn't a long way to go. All too often good initiatives still aren't adopted because we haven't managed to overcome the established economic orthodoxy that fails to see the longer term picture. The challenge now is to move beyond stand alone discrete initiatives to a more integrated approach that provides the right settings across the whole economy to adequately respond to the scope of the task.

The basis for a timely shift to a green economy in the ACT is set out in the *Climate Change and Greenhouse Gas Reduction Act 2010*. The Act requires the ACT to reduce its emissions by 40% by 2020 and 80% by 2050.(4) The Act also provides for the creation of renewable energy and energy efficiency targets.(5) Unfortunately the renewable energy target that has been set by the Government is not as ambitious as the emissions reductions target suggests it should be.(6) Whilst it must be noted that there is some debate about the effectiveness of renewable energy targets in the context of more effective emission trading schemes, they have proven to effectively promote additional energy generation and support renewable technologies in the shorter term. The renewable energy target issue is also a good example of where overlap between national and sub national initiatives creates difficulties.(7)

More positively the ACT Government has committed to developing a green economy strategy by April 2012. In 2010 an initial study on the framework for the green economy within the ACT was undertaken by the University of Canberra.(8) The discussion identifies the issues and potential for the ACT across a range of industries and found that. 'the ACT has an unrivalled opportunity to take a lead position in Australia in relation to 'being green'. High levels of education, high levels of income, high levels of R&D and a relatively small physical footprint give Canberra a significant advantage'.(9)

Whilst it is accepted that economies need to shift to low emission technologies and that this is ultimately the more prudent economic path,(10) too often the very immediate economic dollars per unit of output cost remains detached from the broader and accepted necessity of a large range of responses. This is not to suggest that we should be lackadaisical in our assessment of anything you can pin a green badge to; rather that we need economists to find ways of quantifying these benefits and improving the quality of the economic debate to reduce the space needed for environmental and social arguments.

The ACT Feed-in-Tariff is a good illustration of this point. The scheme is often criticised as a costly mitigation program in terms of dollars per tonne of CO_2 without considering the economic benefits of new sustainable jobs, the security of a fixed price for electricity generation for the next 20 years, the cost savings from not having to upgrade the grid infrastructure because of decentralised generation or the increase in stamp duty revenue because of increased property values.

Probably the key areas that sub national governments can and should be addressing to create a green economy in their jurisdiction are the taxation settings (including government charges and other revenue mechanisms), land use and planning, transport networks and the phase out of wasteful or unsustainable technologies in favour of investment in new sustainable industries. Importantly there is a connection between each of these areas and the ACT probably has made more progress in relation to taxation and land use and new technologies so I will briefly look at each of these.

The Taxation System and Land Use Planning.

The taxation system, together with other government charges, has an enormous capacity to influence sustainability outcomes and support the green economy.(11) Even in countries such as Australia where the majority of tax is paid to the federal government there are significant measures that can be adopted to stimulate positive and discourage negative outcomes. This applies particularly to land use which accounts for a significant proportion of all own source revenue in all Australian states. Ensuring that the right housing is built in the right place is something that all jurisdictions have to grapple with and it will form an important part of the green economy in many if not most jurisdictions across the world.

One difficulty in Australia is that the constitution provides that excise taxes may only be levied by the federal government.(12) This means that state governments are restricted in their ability to impose duties or charges for environmentally damaging activities or behaviour. Consequently it is generally easier for state governments to provide financial incentives for positive action rather than imposing additional charges as disincentives. It should be noted that the political reality is that it may well be easier to make tax expenditures than to fund programmes, or introduce new taxes through a government budget.(13) Again this is particularly relevant to land use issues.

Although we have not seen outcomes yet, the recently enacted *Planning and Development (Lease Variation Charge) Amendment ACT 2011* is perhaps the best example of ACT tax expenditure on sustainability outcomes. The changes revised the existing betterment tax system and ensure that the lever created by the increased charges is used to encourage more sustainable development. Specific exemptions were created for developments that achieve minimum energy efficiency ratings, are located in appropriate places such as transport corridors or that achieve other community purposes.(14)

Currently transaction based taxes provide a significant disincentive to the reallocation of land resources as well as contributing to a range of other negative environmental outcomes.(15) Broad based land taxes that tax the value of land would ensure that land and housing is more efficiently allocated.(16)

Currently many governments including in the ACT offer stamp duty concessions based on the value of a property. These schemes could be significantly improved by including concessions for energy efficiency to encourage owners to make the capital investment in efficiency measures and make their properties more attractive to the market. It should also be noted that the ACT was the first jurisdiction to mandate the disclosure of energy efficiency ratings for houses and that it has been shown that the market attaches real value to energy efficiency.(17)

Wasteful technologies and new sustainable industries
While progress has been made in Australia on improving the availability of information to consumers,(18) less progress has been made on prohibiting particularly wasteful or unsustainable technologies. Last year the ACT banned the use of polyethylene plastic bags.(19) This measure was first adopted in Australia by South Australia, which has also banned the sale of inefficient air-conditioning systems,(20) and has since also been implemented by the Northern Territory.(21)

The ACT *Building Act 2004* provides that the Minister must create sustainability guidelines for materials to be used in buildings in the ACT and prohibits the use of materials in contravention of the guidelines.(22) Unfortunately the guidelines have not been forthcoming and no progress has been made on this issue in the last 7 years. Whilst it hasn't been implemented this is a good example where wasteful or unsustainable materials could be prohibited and market would be created for more sustainable technologies.

Capital investment, both public and private will of course be essential in assisting new technology to develop. The ACT Greens tabled an exposure draft of the *Financial Management (Ethical Investment) Legislation Amendment Bill 2010* that is now being considered by the Public Accounts Committee.(23) The Bill not only prohibits certain investments it requires the ACT sovereign fund to invest in environmentally and socially responsible endeavours. The Government has indicated in their response to the committee inquiry that while they do not agree with the bill as a whole, in principle they do think it would be appropriate to set aside a portion of the fund for private equity investments in clean technologies.(24)

This is an example where the government and the community get both a direct and an indirect economic return. No longer would the government be investing in harmful practices and technologies instead they would be providing the capital for the development of the green economy.

Like many other jurisdictions the ACT Feed-in-Tariff has been a very effective mechanism for encouraging private capital investment in renewable energy technology. The ACT has a gross feed in tariff system that provides renewable energy producers with a fixed price for 20 years.(25) The scheme creates categories of installation with commensurate tariffs and a further strength is that it allows those who don't have a suitable house or aren't the occupier of the premises to also participate.(26)

The ACT has also a range of initiatives for retrofitting homes for energy efficiency. The 2011/12 ACT budget allocated $4 million to improve the energy efficiency of public housing. This initiative reduces greenhouse gases, reduces utility bills, provides a more comfortable living environment, for those least able to afford the associated costs and supports small businesses. The ACT will also be one of the first cities across the world to roll out the Better Place electric vehicle network. (27)

Conclusion

While nation and ultimately international emissions trading schemes will be the most effective means of addressing climate change and creating green economies there is much that sub national jurisdictions can do in the interim that will ultimately ensure that their citizens are in a much better position to deal with the economic reality of climate change. It should also be noted that the most effective mechanisms have not been direct subsidies but rather systemic responses that recognise the otherwise external costs and reward enterprise and initiative.

Notes and references

1 * Note that the Australian Government announced its carbon tax package on 10/7/11, details are available at http://www.climatechange.gov.au/.

2 See for example the Australian Government's proposed Carbon Pollution Reduction Scheme Bill 2010.

3 The ACT is a small jurisdiction with a population of about 368,000 and a gross state product of $27,773,000,000 in 2009-2010.

4 Climate Change and Greenhouse Gas Reduction Act 2010 (ACT) s 7.

5 Climate Change and Greenhouse Gas Reduction Act 2010 (ACT) ss 9 and 10.

6 http://www.legislation.act.gov.au/di/2011-81/default.asp.

7 In Australia state based renewable energy targets have typically operated outside the national scheme to ensure that renewable energy generation was in addition to the national minimum. See for example Victorian Renewable Energy Act 2006. The ACT target effectively includes the national target and therefore offers little guarantee of increased renewable energy production.

8 University of Canberra, Framework for an ACT Clean Economy Strategy: Economic Environmental and Social Perspective, (September 2010) p iv, available   at http://www.business.act.gov.au/functions/2010_business_news _articles/clean_economy_strategy.

9 University of Canberra, Framework for an ACT Clean Economy Strategy: Economic Environmental and Social Perspective, (September 2010) p42.

10 See generally Stern, N. Stern Review: The Economics of Climate Change (2006) p vii; Garnaut, R. The Garnaut Climate Change Review: Final Report (2008).

11 See generally Mann, R. 'Back to the Future: Recommendations and Predictions for Greener Tax Policy', Oregon Law Review [2009] Vol. 88, 355.

12 Australian Constitution Section 90 available at http://www.comlaw.gov.au/Details/C2004C00469/Download.

13 U.S. Government Accountability Office, Government Performance and Accountability: Tax Expenditures Represent a Substantial Federal Commitment and Need to be Reexamined (2005) p18, Available at http://www.gao.gov/new.items/d05690.pdf

14 Planning and Development Act 2008 (ACT) ss 278- 278F.

15 See Australia's future tax system; Report to the Treasurer (December 2009) p 255 available at www.taxreview.treasury.gov.au.

16 See Australia's future tax system; Report to the Treasurer (December 2009) pp 247 – 257 available at www.taxreview.treasury.gov.au.

17 In 2006 this was 1.91% for each energy efficiency star. Energy Efficiency Rating and House Price in the ACT, Australian Government Department of Environment, Water, Heritage and the Arts (2008), available at http://www.nathers.gov.au/about/publications/pubs/eer-house-price-act.pdf

18 Larger electrical appliances and all passenger motor vehicles must disclose their electricity or fuel use.

19 Plastic Shopping Bags Ban Act 2010 (ACT).

20 Electrical Products Regulations 2001 (SA).

21 Plastic Shopping Bags (Waste Avoidance) Act 2008 (SA); Environment Protection (Beverage Containers and Plastic Bags) Act 2011 (NT).

22 Building Act 2004 (ACT) s143.

23 See http://www.parliament.act.gov.au/committees/index1.asp?committee=116&inquiry=991.

24 ACT Government submission to the Public Accounts Committee, ACT Legislative Assembly, Canberra, 2011, pp 5 and 31, available at http://www.parliament.act.gov.au/downloads/submissions/No.%205%20-%20ACT%20Government.pdf.

25 Electricity Feed-in (Renewable Energy Premium) Act 2008 (ACT).

26 Electricity Feed-in (Renewable Energy Premium) Act 2008 (ACT) s 5F.

27 See http://australia.betterplace.com/.

6. 2 China is Getting Greener

Wei Lu and Wenjun Wang

A huge population size, large economy size, rapid industrialization and urbanization, none of these facts in China are favourable for its blueprint to get greener. Energy consumption and associated CO_2 emissions in this developing country are large in scale and growing rapidly. It is a tough challenge for China to balance the needs of economic development and environment protection. However, the challenges are viewed as opportunities to push the country's economy and social infrastructure to become greener. So far, the country has witnessed both policies and actions to achieve its energy conservation and emission reduction goals.

The 2010 Chinese government work report released in March 2010 made the statement that:

-- China will work hard to develop low-carbon technologies;

-- China will endeavour to build an industrial system and consumption pattern with low carbon emissions;

-- China will participate in international cooperation to address climate change and work for further progress in the global fight against climate change;

--Focusing on industry, transportation and construction industry, China will give great impetus to energy conservation and to improving energy efficiency. The energy-saving capacity will be increased by the equivalent of 80 million tons of standard coal.

2010 is the last year for China in its 11th Five-Year Plan period. The Plan has the binding target that during the five years of 2006-2010 the energy consumption per unit of GDP and total emission of major pollutants will reach a 20% and 10% reduction respectively (compared to year 2005). In the first four years, the energy consumption per unit of GDP has reduced 14.38%, the emission of chemical oxygen demand and sulfur dioxide has reduced 9.66% and 13.14% respectively.

In November 2010, China Climate Change Policies and Actions −2010 Report was released by the National Development and Reform Commission (NDRC). According to the report, China has adopted all kinds of policies and actions since 2009, dealing with climate change and persisting in both energy saving and energy efficiency improvement, developing low-carbon energy, increasing forest carbon sinks, initiating experiments of national low-carbon provinces and cities, and setting up the industrial system and consuming mode characterized in low-carbon and less-emissions. China has unveiled a series of policies in various fields, including agriculture, water resource, marine resource, health, and climate, to be adaptable in climate change. China has also promoted irrigation projects in rural areas, constructed several flood prevention projects, enhanced marine climate precaution and ecosystem conservation and recovery, etc. China is endeavouring to strengthen infrastructure and information systems that will enhance awareness of public participation in the community.

The emphasis on energy conservation and emission reductions can be seen everywhere in China. On the central government level, amounts of policies have been released only in 2010.

In April, the Ministry of Industry and Information Technology (MIIT) released Guidelines on Enhancing the Energy Conservation and Emission Reduction in Small- and Middle-Sized Enterprises (SMEs), calling for raising the level of energy conservation and emission reduction in SMEs and announcing that the government will provide more financial support and promote the establishment of financing mechanisms for energy conservation and emission reduction in SMEs.

In the same month, National Development and Reform Committee (NDRC), Ministry of Finance(MOF), People's Bank of China (PBC) and State Administration of Taxation (SAT) jointly released the Advice on Speeding up the Implementation of Energy Management Contract to Promote Energy Saving Service Industry Development and called for the recognition of the significance of developing energy saving service industry. In June, MOF and NDRC released Provisional Regulations on the Management of Financial Subsidies for Energy Management Contract. In 2010, 1.24 billion RMB (about 0.2 billion US dollars) government subsidies will be granted to energy saving service companies that adopted energy management contracts to provide energy conservation modification services.

In September, the Executive Meeting of State Council passed the Decision on Accelerating the Fostering and Development of New Strategic Industries. Three of the seven new strategic industries are related with energy conservation and emission reduction, namely energy conservation and environment protection, new energy and new energy vehicles. These new strategic industries will be granted preferential financial support and policy support. In 2010, the government assistance and support to new energy vehicle has been continuously strengthened. The MIIT has set out the Plan for the Development of Energy Conservation and New Energy Vehicle Industry (2011-2020) and the government will provide a large amount of fund to promote the development of the technology as well as financial subsidies for individuals who buy and use new energy vehicle and participate in battery recycling. At the same time, the National Bureau of Quality Supervision is launching research projects on formulating a standard system for car energy conservation and new energy vehicle. In 2010, 75 public charge stations and 6209 charge poles will be built.

In the same month, the State Council Information Office announced on its press conference that during 11th Five-Year Plan period, the national technology program has arranged a grand total of more than 10 billion Yuan (about 1.5 billion US dollars) for the R&D projects of energy conservation and emission reduction.

Economics measures such as green taxation are also being utilized to serve as financial incentives for companies to participate in energy conservation and emission reduction. Firms doing business in energy saving and emissions reductions can benefit financially from the preferential provision in terms of value-added tax, consumption tax, business income tax and resources tax. Individuals buying low-emission cars will benefit from favourable vehicle purchase taxation policies.

Market-based means are also on the way. In August 2010, NDRC has selected a series of pilot carbon cities as a way of addressing the nation's carbon emissions issues, including five provinces, Guangdong, Hubei, Liaoning, Shaanxi and Yunnan, as well as eight cities, including Tianjin, Chongqing, Hangzhou, Xiamen, Shenzhen, Guiyang, Nanchang and Baoding. Each area is required to draft its own plan to reduce carbon emissions and develop a green economy for the nation's 12th Five Year Plan (2011-2015). For example, Liaoning province, a traditionally heavy industrial base in north-eastern China, has vowed to reduce its 2010 energy consumption by 20 percent and cut carbon emission by 100 million tons before 2015. Lin Boqiang, director of China Center for Energy Economics Research at Xiamen University, said the pilot projects are the central government's response to global pressure over China's huge carbon emissions and demonstrate the government's commitment to going green.

The local governments are taking actions too. On September 30 2010, Northwest China's Qinghai became the first province to establish a regulation that holds local governments and state-owned enterprises responsible in coping with climate change. Called Qinghai's Regulations of Coping with Climate Change, issued by the provincial government and scheduled to take effect on October 1, the regulations will cover the Qinghai-Tibet Plateau, which has one of the most fragile ecological systems in the world. The regulation stipulates that, energy savings, emissions reductions, water resource conservation and other works related to climate change will be considered when evaluating senior officials of governments and state-owned enterprises administered by Qinghai. The regulation is a landmark in China's creation of a legal framework in curbing climate change as it stresses and specifies local government's responsibility on climate change.

NGOs and grassroots organizations are also actively painting the country a greener picture. NGOs have made a significant contribution to preventing deterioration in the environment and they have facilitated the development of environmental policies. The first environmental NGO in China was formally registered on March 31, 1994. This was the Academy for Green Culture, affiliated to the non-governmental Academy for Chinese Culture. It is now called Friends of Nature (FON) for short. Liang Congjie, a descendant of Liang Qichao (a prominent reformer of the late Qing Dynasty) and a member of the Chinese People's Political Consultative Conference (CPPCC), is the President of this organization. More environmental NGOs have now been set up. These have included Global Village of Beijing and Green Home which were set up around 1996. Together with Friends of Nature, they have become China's three main pioneering environmental NGOs. Up to October 2008, there are 3539 environmental protection NGOs in China, 1309 of which founded by the government, 1382 from universities, 508 grassroots and the remaining 90 the branches of international NGOs. At present, the focus of Chinese environmental NGOs is in three main areas. They seek to educate and guide the public, to promote public involvement and to lobby government on issues of environmental protection policy. They also monitor what is happening in the field of environmental protection and help enterprises develop a greater concern for environmental issues.

At the same time as actively moving forward to a greener country, due to the anxiety and ambitious, China has witnessed some unreasonable steps in achieving the emission reduction targets. At the beginning of November, in a hurry to meet their regional targets assigned by the central government, many local governments chose the blackout method for enterprises in the remaining two months. This method quickly spread to many provinces around China. In Wenzhou city of Zhejiang Province, with China's most prosperous private economy, power supplies for some enterprises will be cut for two to four days following one day with electricity. However, the blackouts have apparently led to the linking effect of the diesel shortage. Long queues of cars and even "Sold-out" signs at gas stations are increasingly common scenes in many cities.

Now China is looking forward into its 12th Five-Year Plan period (2011-2015). On November 24, 2010, on China International Green Industry Forum, Xie Zhenhua, deputy director of the National Development and

Reform Commission (NDRC), said China will make energy savings increasingly compulsory for enterprises, instead of simply persuading them to do so. Strict evaluation systems must be established and laws must be enforced to make enterprises accountable to goals of energy saving and emission reduction. The country will continue the effort to push forward the industrialization of energy saving technologies in the 12th Five-Year Plan period. At the same forum, Wu Xiaoqing, vice minister of the Ministry of Environmental Protection (MEP), forecasted that in the next 5 years China may double its investment in environmental protection from the 11th Five-Year Plan period to 3 trillion yuan (450 billion U.S. Dollars).

Chapter 7: Re-integrating the Formal & Informal Economies: A Green Economics Perspective

Miriam Kennet and David Amos

This chapter argues for a Green Economics perspective on the reintegration of the informal economy into mainstream economics.

The informal economy consists of all work except for the paid, official or contractual variety. Yet mainstream economics has not recognised or made best use of the potential contributions of the informal economy. It has also over-emphasised the formal economy, leading to crises of environmental and social justice. Therefore, this section urges a recalibration of economics, re-evaluating the worth of the informal economy, and questioning the endless emphasis on the formal economy.

The chapter first introduces the current problems created by this misfocusing of economics. It then assesses the characteristics of mainstream economics and some of its foundational aims and ideas - in particular, the way in which economic growth treats the informal economy. Green Economics is contrasted as an inherently pluralist and heterodox approach. As they are central concepts to this section, definitions of pluralism and justice are also discussed. Upon the above theoretical framework, a number of ways forward that apply the Green Economics perspective are proposed. These include examples of policies and practical approaches that recognise and encourage the input of the informal sector. The ambitious scope of Green Economics, not least in its aim to mesh environmental and social justice (ends regarded by many as contradictory), necessitates using such applications to simultaneously resolve environmental justice and social justice.

2.   Introduction

This chapter argues for a Green Economics perspective on the reintegration of the informal economy into mainstream economics. The informal economy consists of all work except for the paid, official or contractual variety. Yet mainstream economics has not recognised or made best use of the potential contributions of the informal economy (e.g. Tokman, 1978). It has also over-emphasised the formal economy, leading to crises of environmental and social justice. Therefore, this section urges a recalibration of economics, re-evaluating the worth of the informal economy, and questioning the endless emphasis on the formal economy.

Heinemann (2007) strongly believes this to be a progressive approach, which the literature defines as one which builds on older learning and re-invents ways of understanding and explaining findings from older schools. Economics generally is different in this respect from other sciences, in that it does not have a natural tendency to disregard previous learning from its own discipline in the longer term.

This progressive approach has two constituent parts: (a) the green or ecological part, being simultaneously concerned with natural sciences, and (b) the economics part which is predicated on social theory and social justice, with an approach to economics which is multidisciplinary, borrowing heavily from philosophy and anthropology. The section first introduces the problems of today and explains their importance. It then assesses the characteristics of mainstream economics and some of its foundational aims and ideas. Green Economics is contrasted as an inherently pluralist and heterodox approach. As it is a central concept to this section, pluralism is also defined and justified. Since Green Economics is predicated on the concept of social justice, it shall prove useful to understand this concept in its philosophical historical context (shedding light on the origins of part (b) above). Upon this theoretical framework, a number of ways forward that apply the pluralist perspective are proposed. Since Green Economics has such ambitious scope, not least in its aim to mesh environmental and social justice (ends regarded by many as contradictory), these solutions shall target the dilemmas inherent within a green social analysis and practice.

3. The Pressing Problems of Today

The Millennium Ecosystem Assessment Synthesis Report (2001) states that, *"Any progress achieved in addressing the goals of poverty and hunger eradication, improved health and environmental protection is unlikely to be sustained if most of the eco-system services on which humanity relies continue to be degraded"* (quoted in Spicer, 2006: 154). Thus it is clear that an approach dealing with solely one aspect of social or environmental justice is actually doomed to failure. Only a pluralist and composite approach is now believed to be likely to work.

Green Economics is such an attempt to provide an economic framework for environmental and social justice for all, including all people, all species, and the whole planet. In so doing, it acknowledges that the economy (as currently constructed) does not even conceptualise these parties. Rather it factors them out together with reality from its scope using the *ceteris paribus* (*'all other things being equal'*) condition in its quest for promoting and creating economic growth.

In fact, on the ground, the reality of what the economic system has so far constructed looks rather different from real economic progress and development. Today's pressing problems are highlighted in some of the recent environmental and poverty statistics.

177

Giradet (2007) advises that Britain had its wettest winter in 270 years of record keeping. In 2001, northern China suffered from blizzards in which the best part of 100,000 herders starved, 40 people died in Pakistan in a heat wave and 92 hurricane events were recorded. In 2003, 1400 people died from heat in India and Pakistan, and 35,000 people in Europe died from the heat. This was all on top of the catastrophe in New Orleans, which hit the poorest sections of the population. One quarter of species are predicted to not survive the century (Stern, 2006; IPCC, 2007) and in a report in New Scientist (2007) one quarter of UK species are heading north due to being unable to cope with the new climatic conditions (Berry, 2008). Claussen (2003: 430) reveals that the interaction between components of the climate system is non-linear, with multiple equilibria involved. These issues are caused by potential velocity patterns, atmospheric flow, and the Hadley walker circulation shifts to the west. There is albedo-induced aridification, plus changes in surface conditions directly influencing vertical motion and flow in the tropics (but not in high latitudes). Additionally, there are influences proposed from atmosphere vegetation sea ice systems in high northern latitudes (Claussen, 2003: 420). All this illustrates how Hahn (1908) considered the climate as *"a sum of meteorological phenomena which characterise the mean state of the atmosphere, at any point of the earth's surface".*

Its components consist of the abiotic world, or physical climate system, and the living world called the biosphere. The physical system is further subdivided into open systems namely the atmosphere, the hydrosphere, the cryosphere (ice), the pedosphere, the soils, the lithosphere (the Earth's crust) and the mantle (Claussen, 2003: 432). Their interaction affects the climate and thus influences economic resources and potential. For example, changes in land surface temperature give rise to an additional warming of some 4% at regions north of 60N in spring and 1% in other seasons (Claussen, 2003: 424). The additional warming is mainly caused by a reduction of snow and sea–ice volume by nearly 40% which in turn reduced the surface albedo in the artic region by nearly 40% on 1996 levels. There is also the taiga-tundra feedback, for instance, which is a problem of vegetation, snow and albedo that enhanced summer warming on average over northern hemispheres continents by 1.7 degrees C in summer in the past, and now by 2.2 degrees C, but is increased by 2.5 % by synergism of taiga-tundra feedback and artic sea ice albedo feedback. It is this synergism which enhances winter warming –so here studying one mechanism in isolation failed to reveal the answer- only a composite plural question produced the predictions that made the model fit the evidence (Claussen, 2003: 426).

Importantly for a Green Economics analysis, including the biosphere and planetary systems in our economics calculations can begin to factor in resources available and also impacts at each level. This is of course an integral part of economic responsibility, as well as social and environmental justice. Economics now needs to be far more mature and complex than current mainstream allows for. How can one unique equilibrium theory (largely that of Walras) encompass even just the interactions merely outlined above? Consider, as a further example, abrupt transitions in vegetation structure, as happened around 3500 years ago. One sees that such changes are not gradual but in steps, and faster in some areas than in others. Some are quite abrupt as in the Eastern Sahara 5500 years ago (according to drilled marine cores). Such changes are amplified by biophysical feedbacks, leading to abrupt aridification, and there was a very a fall in precipitation reflected in an abrupt shift in terrigenous material. A complete simulation of Holocene climate changes requires inclusion of biochemical models. This is being done to include terrestrial and oceanic carbon cycles into a climate model (as in the New Scientist, for example). *This requires information about oceanic biochemistry, and detailed apleobotanic reconstruction of Holocene carbon pools as well as oceanic biochemistry* (Claussen, 2003: 434). This is completely beyond the scope of mainstream economics - but it is one of the few ways to predict the future of local, regional and global agricultural economic production.

How can we rely solely on neo classical economics to provide the impetus we need? All it leaves the vulnerable with are incongruent facts, such as how sub-Saharan Africa's share of world exports has fallen from 1.0 to 0.3 percent between 1960 and 2002 (Wallis, 2007: 160). Meanwhile, the average Sunday lunch had travelled 20,000 miles (Wallis, 2007: 161), using up resources and contributing to these problems of global environmental and social justice. So invisible have these problems been within economics, that even some of Oxfam's wristbands for its 'Make Poverty History' campaign were manufactured using indentured labour (Richardson, 2005). Supply chains have been subtly hidden and have misunderstood the implications of today's economy for social and environmental justice and its mechanisms (Kennet and Heinemann, 2006).

The Royal Economics Society published an analysis of poverty and social and environmental justice in April 2007 (Collier 2007). The figures show that mainstream economics has not delivered on either the global elimination of poverty or on environmental justice (Kennet, 2007; Kennet and Heinemann, 2006). Although globalisation is powering growth for the middle four billion, it is not working for the bottom billion. Indeed the very success of the four billion might have made it harder for the bottom billion to get started. Collier (2007) suggests that a critical mass of educated people must be retained, and also that war is more likely in those countries to set up a cycle of deprivation. He further suggests that returns from valuable natural resources leads to the undermining of governance, and impoverishes the country (this is a pattern he finds repeated often). He proposes peacekeeping, security guarantees, and trade policy, advocating neither protectionism nor fair trade, but temporary start up protection from more advanced start ups and other direct competitors in European markets, as well as international standards and codes of conduct and governance.

Furthermore, the Stern Report, Millennium Ecosystem Report and IPCC (Kennet 2007) have all published worrying findings about species extinction. In addition to over a quarter of species being under threat by the end of the century, climate instability and warming by up to 5 degrees centigrade may mean farming is only viable in the polar regions (not to mention all the other numerous economic disruptions).

The climate is very unstable and our economy which depends on it - as well as our civilisation - is currently threatened with conditions of species extinction and climate conditions never experienced in the 10,000 years since our civilisation began.
This leads to a conclusion that either we must urgently reform the economics system which was the justification of these developments, or we must adapt our civilisation and our economy to these new conditions (if that is possible). Indeed, we probably are going to have to do both.

Mainstream Economics Versus Green Economics

3.1.   Reconceptualising Economics

However the mainstream economy that has led us to this position is narrowly focused on profit maximising behaviour - *"pleasure and pain are the ultimate objects of the calculus of economics"* (Jeevons, 1871). Wicksteed (1910) described economics as *"the psychology of the choice between two alternatives, and not constructed to be able to provide wide, complex, non mathematical inter and multidisciplinary decision making"*. Mill saw it *"as imaginary and not an exact science, and political economy is concerned with him who desires to possess wealth, and who is capable of judging of the comparative efficiency of that end."* (Mill in Udehn, 2003: 144).

Therefore a more pluralistic approach is urgently required (e.g. Davis, 2006 and Soderbaum, 2008 forthcoming), involving natural science data for its modelling and an analysis which includes information from other disciplines. This is the only way that economics can adapt to meet its changing requirements and to meet the needs of a much wider group of its own stakeholders - which green economics now defines as the planet, and its physical systems, the biosphere, and all people everywhere, not only rational economic man.

According to Bronfenbrenner (1971) (in Negushi, 1989: 3), outmoded ideas are never definitively displaced in economics. *"Advances in economics tend to be major accretions without rejecting existing paradigm"* Negishi, (1989:3). This makes economics a special case and incompatible with Kuhn's catastrophe theory of scientific revolutions. Outmodedness is only defined in relation to other paradigms, making the study of economic history especially pertinent. This also makes economics unusual as a 'science' as the need to promote environmental and social justice could use tools in existence previously, instead re-orientating their outcomes, ends and means. This is in part what Green Economics attempts to do (Anderson, 2006).

Latakos suggests that the history of science is a history of competing research programmes. Such research programmes in economics could be considered to include (though not exhaustively): Marxian and non Marxian economics, Mercantilism, Malthus, underconsumptionists, overproduction and deficiency of effective demand, Monetarism and quantity theory of money, Neo-classical traditions such as neo–Walrasian and the neo-Austrians, the Ricardian research programme, Neo-Ricardianism, the German historical school and institutionalism (its American equivalent). Veblen argued that economics should be an evolutionary science which examines the emergence and modification through time of economic instructions, divided into production or acquisition. He suggested that there exists a tension between engineers and businessmen, or the makers of money or the makers of goods.

According to Lipietz (2000), there is another altogether more profound difference. The green paradigm, while certainly politically *progressive*, it is not *'progressivist'*. Its vision of history is not a tale of progress. In fact, it is far from a linear historical vision. If history did have an inner dynamic, it would, if anything, be governed by the second law of thermodynamics: a history of an inexorable rise of entropy, a history of decay. Only a reflexively critical human consciousness can slow or reverse this decline. Political ecology thus defines progress only as a tendency - defined in terms of certain ethical or aesthetic values (solidarity, independence, responsibility, democracy, harmony). There is no real guarantee that the world will actually move in this direction (as through the "socialization of the productive forces"). The historical and dialectical materialism of the greens is non-teleological, then, even rather pessimistic.

"That state, organization, and place of economics are argued to be undergoing change as a result of contemporary historical forces. This implies that the meaning and character of pluralism in economics is also changing, and that the nature of pluralism in economics (and in heterodox economics) needs to be re-conceived accordingly" (Davis, 2007, abstract accessed on web, May 2007). A pluralist approach today has no meaning unless it addresses the foundations of all economic transactions, the social and environmental context (without which it would not exist at all and in which it is actually firmly embedded). Yet this context has been denied under the *ceteris paribus* condition and the marginal revolution for two hundred years. The costs of climate instability alone, quite apart from other social and environmental dilemmas, will start to overtake neo-classical economic forecasts. For example, up to 25% of species would be extinct by the end of the century (Stern, 2006) and this will affect the global economy which depends on other species to a large extent, not least to provide agriculture and food and also to provide a gas balance to maintain climatic conditions favourable to mainstream economic growth. This kind of aim and

understanding requires consideration of economic assessments to be complex, specific in time and place, and can no longer be one dimensional and easy to represent on a graph or simple model.

Profit maximisation to meet short term economic goals is no longer enough. For example, how can it be reconciled with sea level rise which may submerge the trading entity or its host or home town? The economic assessment simply has to have a more complex set of considerations and data included in it, and these must include natural resources, as well as the social conditions governing its inputs and acceptability of its outcomes from a moral perspective. However, all these issues are dependent on the power situation of economic actors and so this must be factored back into economic discussions. A Green Economics assessment is therefore predicated on 4 very practical areas of influence in most decision making - Politics, Business, Academia and Campaigning. This helps form its pluralist character. Such writers as Tony Lawson (Cambridge University) argue that *"For I am indeed convinced that a pluralistic orientation is desirable, not least because it seems essential both to human flourishing in general and to knowledge advance in particular"*.

There are particular challenges and contradictions which occur when social and environmental justice are joined at the core of such a literature (Dobson, 2000). Having economic aims which explicitly define beneficiaries as all people everywhere, non human species, nature, the planet and the biosphere immediately comes into conflict with mainstream economics. This is because mainstream economics takes a more anthropocentric view and a more 'first world' view, which Foucaultian discourse might argue presents a perspective of white, male, western-educated, middle-class MBA graduates, rather than a discourse concerned with the voices of the other half of the human population (women), or nature, which has no legal standing of its own with which to express 'economic preferences' (Mies, 2007). Green economics is also influenced greatly by anthropology which has sought to explore other voices and look at societies from the outside. Such an approach is influenced by such writers as Mauss, Polyani, and Sahlins all of whom sought to find other meanings in economic transactions and to inform themselves about previous economic systems and other societies.

The discipline of Green Economics operates within a pluralist and non-orthodox framework. It links social sciences, using information from philosophy, history, archaeology, economics and psychology, with natural processes and biology found in natural science. Its practitioners, in general, are multidisciplinary at the highest level, with many reaching professor status in one field and realising that the answers to social and environmental equity and justice elude them when they reach the pinnacle of a single academic discipline. Therefore, they seek a pluralist approach through using green economics methodology which does not bound the learning, questioning or knowledge applied to specific economics dilemmas. It does not bind itself unyieldingly to concepts of equilibrium (Walras and Marshall, in Turner and Roth, 2003). Green Economics aims not on price per se, but rather on needs, requirements and rights - benefits for all with strong foundational concepts of sharing out nature's bounties and boundaries.

3.2. Reconceptualising Economic Growth

On the one hand, traditional mainstream development theory is based around models such as Rostow's (1990) - an evolving model of economies working through his five stages towards mass high consumption from indigenous economies. Green Economics, on the other hand, does not regard a "man in a business suit" as the pinnacle of all the stages of economic growth. Quite the contrary – it is now known that this over consumption is one of the main factors harming the planet, using up resources and creating greater poverty (Kennet and Heinemann (2006). Consider that one fifth of human kind is still in life threatening poverty, and that Britain, although fifth in the GDP league, has the most unhappy children and young people of any industrialised nation (UNICEF, 2007; Alderson, 2008). Such findings begin to reveal the fundamental flaws in mainstream economics focus and analysis.

Indeed, Kennet & Heineman's (2006) argument for a green economics brings with it the need for a new measurement of economic growth. Economic growth is most commonly measured by Gross Domestic Product (GDP) - and this often makes rather inaccurate assessments on society. For instance, GDP recognises none of the value of housework. Yet even in 1991, UK estimates of hypothetical remuneration of all housework reached £739 billion (Grint, 1991). If society is to change so that it appreciates the work of the informal sector, its value shall have to be included in the goals that (for better or for worse) shape our society. This means incorporating valuations of informal sector work in GDP. After all, if it was practical to value its contribution in the form of housework, all the way back in 1991, there must be all the more accurate and advanced techniques to do so now.

"Increase in the GDP of a country is not described as growth or progress by Green Economics, if many of its people remain hungry, its resources are removed or its women trafficked and forced into prostitution." (Kennet & Heineman, 2006). Green Economics recognises the value of all forms of work, especially those that fall outside of the boundaries of officially measured economic growth. So Green Economics should aim to develop more methods of including other forms of informal work, such as voluntary third sector work or domestic care of incapacitated relatives. This is a major opportunity for Green Economists, where they can facilitate a far more equitable and just appraisal of work.

4.   Pluralism in Theory

A heterodox pluralist approach enables green economics to meet the challenges and conflicts involved in trying to provide social and environmental justice. It therefore includes unlimited learning from other disciplines and from life and from reality outside academia. The Green Economics Institute is predicated on four pillars for the scope of its activity, business, academia, campaigning, and policy, with an overarching moral/social framework. Its early work on procurement activity investigates the effects of such activity on stakeholders and examines real situations in an attempt to factor reality back into economics and to remind economists of the effects of their actions on people, the planet, and the biosphere.

There have been many particular attempts at pluralism in the history of thought. Pluralism has a chequered history, and is a term which needs to be used with extreme caution. It has been used to justify illogical parallel existences or truths, as in cultural pluralism, and to justify activities of extreme racism. According to this alternative pluralism, there is no one absolute truth. Therefore this way of thinking is forced to condone views such as extreme racism, as it cannot say they are any less true or valid than any other view. This form of pluralism simply does not hold up to scrutiny - how can this view, one that believes there is no absolute truth, itself be true?

In contrast, Green Economics requires a stance of inclusiveness and diversity as two of its most important drivers. This is completely at odds with the above use of the word 'pluralist'. Here pluralism is instead the usage and inclusion of a number of sources of information about one same reality. Where two of these sources present two inherently conflicting pieces of information, one must recall that they cannot both be true. To say otherwise would be to subscribe to the earlier form of pluralism. Rather, a Green Economics pluralism honestly appraises both and compares them to determine which one is an accurate depiction of reality, and which is not. It is with this framework that Green Economics is able to pick out the contradictions of mainstream economics, and instead integrate more accurate insights from other social and natural sciences.

In general, Green Economics refers to an inter-, trans-, or multi-disciplinary approach. This legitimises its use of data and progressive learning from economic analyses of past and other schools put together in a new way. This occurs through the lens of the search for environmental and social justice, but also much more the search from other disciplines and the real world, in order to assess economic imperatives and to make judgements about likely overall impacts. In this respect the discipline is part of the pluralist school of economists, although in general the inter-, trans-, and multi-disciplinary descriptions are used. There is even the possibility that Green Economics can spread its multi disciplinary or pluralist analysis to influence the mainstream economics accounts to become pluralist, and there is already some evidence that this may be beginning to occur (from economists such as Lawson).

5. A Multidisciplinary Approach to Social and Environmental Justice

It is thus useful to investigate the inherent difficulties with the concepts of social and environmental justice and the need to have them work together. This is in spite of the perceived contradictions of less poverty leading to more consumerism and more poverty leading to more environmental degradation (Potter et al, 2004).

Therefore, an important further research agenda is to establish what social justice entails, following the tradition of Sen, Rawls et al (Sayer, 2006), and to establish its meaning within the context of economics and within green economics in particular. It is important to establish and understand the complexities of social justice in the real world and in implementation as an ends and also as a means. For example, learned discussions about poverty often do not include the issue that more people in poverty are women or that in the UK only 3 economics professors are women. It is not surprising that by practically excluding half the population from top economic decision and theory making, the 'solutions' it produces all too often continue to exclude women in practice (Jacobs, 2006, Royal Economics Society Journal Newsletter). This is also a good example of Foucault's deconstruction of power, that institutions (even those promoting justice) reflect and promote the values and power systems found in the society to which they belong. After all, there is no evidence that women are not as good at economics as men. Yet within academia in the UK, most women are earning 40% less than equivalent male counterparts according to a recent survey. As usual, pluralism and its counterpart, diversity, lead to a different result.

The term "social justice" was coined by the Jesuit Luigi Taparelli in the 1840s, based on the teachings of Thomas Aquinas. He wrote extensively in his journal *Civiltà Cattolica*, engaging both capitalist and socialist theories from a Catholic natural law viewpoint. He stated that society should be based on cooperation and not class conflict and competition, and that can only be achieved if people are just. He considered it the principle that all persons are entitled to "basic human needs", regardless of "differences such as economic disparity, class, gender, race, ethnicity, citizenship, religion, age, sexual orientation, disability, or health". This includes "the eradication of poverty and illiteracy, the establishment of sound environmental policy, and equality of opportunity for healthy personal and social development."

The political philosopher John Rawls (1921-2002) draws on the utilitarian insights of Bentham and Mill, the social contract ideas of Locke, and the categorical imperative ideas of Kant. His first statement of principle was made in *A Theory of Justice* (1971: 3), where he proposed that, "Each person possesses an inviolability founded on justice that even the welfare of society as a whole cannot override. For this reason justice denies that the loss of freedom for some is made right by a greater good shared by others". This is a deontological proposition that echoes Kant in framing the moral good of justice in absolutist terms. His views are definitively restated in *Political Liberalism* (1993: 14), where society is seen, "as a fair system of co-operation over time, from one generation to the next".

If economics is examined as currently constructed we find an orthodox rigidity predicated on mathematical models employing positivist data, on rational choice assumptions. These assumptions are on the part of those engaged in what has been termed a commodified world which tends to exclude all other aspects of society and non-commodified economy and of reality. Rational choice theory, game theory, etc. are all ways of understanding purchase decision-making on the part of 'rational economic men', in a perfect market when they have power and assets to make unfettered choices in the absence of limiting institutional or regulatory presence. It does not address the access to this universal market for other players who lack the ability or resources to enter it.

Most importantly, it does not address the non-commodified market activity that Williams (2005) sees as far larger and more important. It does not address any of the impacts of such transactions on the global stakeholders, other people, the biosphere or the planet. He cites this as including subsistence work (see Mies, 2007), self-provisioning, self-servicing, housework, domestic work, and also where goods and services are exchanged but no money changes hands such as unpaid community work or voluntary work or community self help where the profit motive is absent. He states that some writers argue that every human transaction is being transformed into transient market exchange with the near complete penetration of the market into our lives. However, Williams argues that there is no evidence for this at all, although it is a widely accepted thesis (Williams, 2005: 14).

The Green Economics approach aims to create a methodology for achieving social and environmental justice as equal ends and means. If these two factors are borne together in all conceptualisation and reasoning then there is some hope of turning economics round to become a discipline which can help establish what we ought to do in a normative way. It may then be able to explore effects and implications of our activities, helping us to provision for and take into account everyone and everything on the planet.

However, in order to do this, it has to be accepted that economics as a narrow and focused discipline has had its day. This type of economics arose at a given time in response to the success of the physical sciences. It was an attempt to move away from its earlier more pluralist beginnings as an art of provisioning, with a strong moral and transformative character under Adam Smith and Mill, to becoming a "toy for boys in sandpits" (McCloksky) enabling modelling, mathematics and physics envy to be conducted well away from reality. Ietto Gillies' theories about the actual impact of the firm, for instance, should underscore the need for returning reality into economics. Considering that most modern justifications for environmental degradation are given as economic, and most justifications for enduring poverty are so as not to inconvenience or limit the market from allowing others to become wealthy so that they may provision for the poor, then we must re-evaluate the whole hypothesis and factor reality straight back in to economics for a completely different result.

Social and environmental justice are often split so the cause of one is advanced in preference to the other, in the belief that they contradict and cannot occur together. This is a view advanced in mainstream economics (Guardian 26th May 2007). A most recent example was the 'need' to expand Stansted Airport at the expense of the Hatfield Forest and to the discomfort of local residents, as it was claimed that the economy would benefit by a total of £16 billion if UK airport expansion plans proceeded. Stewart (2006: 193) suggests *"that the argument is that the expansion of aviation is generally an effective way to boost the performance of a mature economy, and in general it actually caters for the leisure market, and as such there is emerging evidence that it actually takes out more money than it puts back in, investment in other industries not subsidized the way aviation is could bring more benefit to the economy. ... Artificially cheap aviation is a major component of the globalised economy transporting people and goods across the globe. As such it hinders the development of economic localisation underpinned by equity."* He concludes *"that the evidence suggests that not only is cheap subsidized air travel causing real problems for today's economy, but it is a positive hindrance to the development of a greener more equitable and more localised economy."* This is partly due to the fact that in the UK only 11% of people who fly come from socio-economic classes D and E and the poorest 10 % hardly ever fly. This makes a mockery of rational choice theory, as constraints of power and access to assets are in fact the biggest determinants of the fundamentals of economic decision making.

6.   Green Economics in Practice

1.   Green Economics in The Primary Sector

A pluralist multidisciplinary approach is the only way to realise the project of a socially and environmentally just economics. For instance, there has been reported a noticable decline in the UK population of bees over the past few years. A mainstream economic perspective cannot provide a comprehensive economic view on such biological phenomena - a holistic understanding of the economics of such problems must integrate biological insights with economic analysis. It turns out this phenomenon is related to the effects of mobile phone radiation, which also need to be integrated, as does the role of bees in pollination. Only then, finally, can its overall contribution to provisioning of our food and crops and the economy (perhaps the least important of these spheres) also be fully understood. However, the need for mobile phones is an economic assessment too - do we really need to them and do corporations really need to sell them? And if so do we need to allow the corporations to sell them more than we need the bees to continue to pollinate crops? Therefore, we need to work to understand the theory of the firm and why it needs to sell phones, as well as the institutional decisions which allow for transmitters to be placed on schools for income, even though the health implications of this economic transaction contravene the precautionary principle. Also, perhaps most importantly, we must integrate into the analysis the supply chain of the mobile phone, which allows for mining of coltan in the Congo, in turn allowing for wars, murder and child mining in order to obtain this precious component for 85% of mobile phones. These are the economic questions to answer, rather than whether or not some 'rational economic man' decides to buy a phone or not and at what market price or monetary value.

Is there not so much more to economic decision-making than rational economic man's decision to buy at a particular price from a particular supplier? For instance, Goldsmith describes the current state of world climate and food production, showing how we need to tackle this in a non-traditional economic way. Goldsmith argues for including ideas of equity, justice and science (of climate change), as well as non-economically based agriculture, as the purpose can no longer be to make money for the grower but to feed people and to help people to feed themselves locally (Goldsmith 2007).

Costs in a mobile phone transaction according to a Green Economics Analysis (Kennet (2007)		
Layers of effects of a transaction	**Costs**	**Green Economics using a pluralist approach**
Society, people, biosphere planet effects of transaction	External social and environmental justice effects and costs of transaction	-Costs to society of use of good. -Opportunity costs of local economy displaced by global production (Hines) -Costs to indegenous peoples in area of resources exploitation land used for exploitation of resources which could be used for food or water - power structures replaced in areas with focus on foreign market Foucault
Health effect of siting a repeater on a school to enable reception in use	External costs of use of product (Pigou)	Social and environmental costs of transaction
Health effects of transaction	Longer term	Cost to actors of use of good

	transaction costs	Increase in brain Tumours
and use on actors		
Effects on biodiversity or dissapearence of bees For pollination of other products- eg crop reduction which is food production (Goldsmith 2007)	Biosphere reduction costs	(New Scientist)
Effects on labour and social effects of corporate activity		(Ietto Gilies 2006)
Transaction takes place and immediate costs are paid	TRANSACTION COSTS (Coase)	Market cordinates buyer and seller and price
Transaction takes place between two actors	Rational choice theory	
Price is decided	Just price theory	
Supply chain for the good (Bridger) (Kennet 2006) (New)	Resources used for production of goods	Environmental and social Costs of supply chain
Production and health effects( )		Social and environmental costs of production
Effects of work on people alienated by it	Mellor Mies Robertson	
Labour conditions in colonies	Mies, Shiva Klein	
Raw materials for the good (Coltan in the Congo) supply chain vulnerability (Fenwick 2006)	Market cost of raw material	Social and environmental cost of resources obtained from Congo

Goldsmith argues that traditional and local agriculture is much more energy efficient and in fact the only viable solution, as proposed by Pretty (1999). Pretty shows that to produce a ton of cereals or vegetables by means of modern agriculture requires 6-10 times more energy than it does by using non-mechanised agricultural systems and sustainable agricultural methods (Goldsmith, 2007: 61). He suggests that in economic terms governments and international agencies are keen to prevent traditional agriculture being practiced as this stops economic development, making it difficult to introduce new crops and large scale production for export. He says that small scale farmers are outstanding managers of their own resources, land, fertiliser, and water but according to the World Bank, this prevents economic development. The new developments such as GM crops perhaps reached the limit of what people wanted from large scale business, as people began to understand the difference between crops and products solely for profit and those for use to meet needs of purchasers and consumers - for the first time these two ideas were seen to be clearly divergent. Similarly with global supply chains the unnecessary movement of goods round the planet is using up resources at an alarming rate and contributing to greenhouse gas production just at a time we desperately need to reduce it.

Overall, Green Economics provides a more holistic understanding of all manner of processes and linkages in the primary sector, as demonstrated by the above examples concerning agriculture and mining. Understanding these linkages allows for the design of more socially and environmentally just production systems.

2.   Green Economics in Policy

⅄   The Moral Economy

Sayer (1997) makes interesting observations on this point, and argues that a *"commodity can be valued for its intrinsic use value but to the seller it is unequivocally a means to an end, to the achievement of the external goal of making a profit and if it is unlikely to make a profit it will not be offered for sale"* (in Williams, 2005: 16). So here lies the interest of Green Economics: How do we return to an economics which includes in its scope the consideration, provisioning and producing of goods and services which people need, rather than those which can be bought and sold?

Sayer (2006: 150) further argues that what he calls *"a moral economy is a way of thinking about economic matter for the point of view of social justice and well–being"*. Note that up to now this has not necessarily included environmental justice, but Sayer is working within Green Economics in order to add this dimension to his work. He draws attention to the fact that economic relations between people have ethical implications because they affect their well being. He argues that moral economy and green economics should be compatible and that current forms of economic relation alienate us from both nature and society. He suggests that economic inequalities are largely undeserved, cause suffering and weaken social cohesion and frustrate the achievement of the green economy. Instead he advocates a steeply progressive income tax justifiable on both social and environmental grounds. He proposes that the *"point of economic action is to enable us to live well and to do sustainably"* (Sayer, 2007: 150). He suggests that unalienated economic practices should be governed by reason, justifications, and deliberative democracy, all three grounds on which capitalism fails. He suggests that capitalism if modified could provide these, if adequately regulated, as an advanced economy requires that we are dependent on others through the market mechanism, whilst acknowledging our dependence on nature and a deep social division of labour.

He suggests that high income lifestyles are contrary to a green lifestyle in general and since they are often undeserved, there is no moral reason why a steeper tax system could not remove the inequalities which he claims are largely generated by pure luck and a game won by the smart, and that people earn what they are worth. After all, rewarding people for their intellect in large part rewards luck (not least genes). None of these he says actually can be justified and therefore our basic assumptions about economic rights in the market may be overturned in the search for environmental and social justice and more progressive taxes introduced.

⅄ Basic Income Schemes

Lord (1999) defines the Citizen's Income, or Basic Income, as "an automatic weekly payment sufficient to cover all the basic needs". Its automatic status, would negate the need for application. It would be paid ex ante, i.e. prior to and independent of other income. Therefore, it would be a purely universal benefit. A Basic Income would replace other social security benefits (except those for specific needs, e.g. Disability Living Allowance).

The Basic Income is one example of a pluralist policy, because only a pluralist perspective grasps what many see as its main attraction - its ability to promote sustainability. Non-sustainable practice may be as much a result of a lack of basic security as anything else. Its preponents often present the removal of material insecurity as the chief argument for a Basic Income. As Lord (1999) explains, one cannot expect a citizen to care for the long-term when they fear for their basic needs in the short-term. Material insecurity, they argue, leads to desperate competition for scarce resources, which eventually leads to resource degradation (Kennet, 2007). Some may also conside material security to be a human right (Werner, 2007). Either way, this core rationale of the Basic Income is a reminder that social justice can in fact help pave the way for environmental justice.

The Basic Income is thought by its advocates to hold several economic advantages over means-testing (the current system that it would replace). Being a universal benefit (paid to all, without conditions), it may be far cheaper to administer. Kay & King (1990) estimated means-testing to be ten times as costly to administer as a universal benefit of the same overall value. Means-testing also requires the applicant to negotiate bureaucracy and form-filling, meaning a lower take-up rate compared with a Basic Income. In addition, means-testing generates a 'marginal tax rate' for the unemployed or low-paid. This refers to the withdrawal of benefits as income rises or a job is taken, disincentivising work, since what workers earn is offset by loss of benefits. In contrast, being independent of income, Basic Income imposes no marginal tax rate.

As Robertson (1999) points out, a Basic Income may be considered as part of a wider green overhaul of the tax and benefit system. Some, such as Lord, propose ending National Insurance Contributions, and possibly Income and Corporation Tax too. These revenues would be replaced with land, energy and resource taxes - a shift from taxing 'goods' to 'bads'. Therefore, for many of its supporters, the Basic Income is not simply a replacement for Income Support, but is instead considered as part of a complete restructuring of taxes and benefits.

One outcome particularly relevant to the aim of recognising and encouraging non-monetary forms of work is that other forms of work may become viable. This would include casual labour, volunteering and internships. Such a viability would especially facilitate the growth of the third sector, which is heavily dependant on the latter two forms of work. The idea of a Basic Income is also increasingly relevant to the current credit crisis. This is because it finds a way to address two urgent needs created by the current economic downturn. First is the need to support those whose work is reduced or withdrawn, as a Basic Income would boost household provision. The other need is to discourage hysterisis (where short-term unemployment becomes long-term and systemic) resulting from the credit crunch, as the Basic Income removes marginal tax rates on the unemployed.

It is too early for observable results of BI to emerge. However, in the UK, the most similar benefit to the BI has been the Child Tax Credit, since it is also unconditional on income. From 1998 to 2004 this benefit helped achieve a 17.2% fall in child poverty (Brewer et al, 2006) - its fastest fall in UK history. Meanwhile, the Irish, Finnish and Dutch governments are already discussing the idea of a BI.

It must be borne in mind that it is not the purpose of this section to argue for one particular sort of policy response over another. Rather, the Basic Income is simply presented as an example of one of many sets of ideas that proceed from a pluralistic perspective on global problems.

⋏   Non-market social-democratic thought

This involves the development of non-commodified work as an alternative to the commodified realm (Mayo, 1996). Non-market social democrats, including Gorz (1999) and Sachs (1984), find profit-motivated exchanges stultifying and alienating. The workplace is regarded as almost a place of social disintegration. Overall, profit-motivated exchanges reduce self-esteem, social respect, self-identity and companionship. Beck (2000: 58) says that *"the idea that social identity and status depend only on a person's occupation and career must be taken apart and abandoned so that social esteem and security are really uncoupled from paid employment"*. Capitalism makes the two synonymous according to Gorz (1999: 72).

Furthermore, people need to work to provide corporate profit even though the goods produced are not economically indispensable and do not respond to the needs of the consumer. Friedman (1982) found that only 35% of the population is engaged in indispensable production. Employment should not be seen as an end in itself, but as a means to achieving a better quality of life. There has also been a devaluation of non-commodified work or socially-embedded economic activity and Polyani argues for assigning non-commodified work a crucial role in the future of work and welfare. They argue to reduce heteronomous work and those productive activities over which individuals have little or no control.

⅄ Post-development discourse

This discourse questions the binary western idea of paid commodified work, and reattaches a value to non-paid forms of work. It recognises interdependencies between the two. Identifying obstacles to growth and prescribing development pathways has in effect violently subjected individuals and regions and entire countries to the powers and agencies of the development apparatus. The vision of the good society comes with commodification as the only story. With western commodification both the referent and the context, the plural economies of other nations have been deemed to have a problem of backwardness that needs to be resolved. This policy perspective argues that, using commodification as a benchmark, these supposedly backward nations have been subjected to 'development' and 'progress'.

Plural activities are described by Beck (2000) as commodified employment alongside parental work, work for oneself, voluntary work or political activity. In the economic sphere, commodified work retains its status as the only form of work of any true worth. To rectify this we must revalue work in the other spheres where people are fully engaged in society, to meet their needs. Williams proposes examples of how to overcome institutional barriers to build social capital, time capital and human capital, as well as economic capital.

There is a ready supply of practical ideas which implement the above principles. These include time banks, 'negative' income tax as a mechanism for benefits, Elderplan, mutual aid contracts, full engagement of community service with tax credits, local economic trading schemes, and many more. There is no space here for any in-depth treatment of these ideas - rather this article serves as a theoretically focused prompt for further study of these practical implementations. Hopefully the above policy ideas will be used as starting points for future research.

7.   Beyond Traditional Supply and Demand

An illustration of the need to depart from the neo-classical perspective is the practice of procurement, which forms a large part of international and European trade. At present there is a move towards standardisation, with large companies keen to promote their brand of environmental and social justice using corporate social responsibility and higher environmental standards. One way of doing this is to partner up with other companies like themselves whose products they know meet certain standards. However, the very act of doing this creates huge and insurmountable barriers for new, smaller, local suppliers, as one of the criterions for such partnerships with 'greener' companies is that the other firm has a global reach, thereby eliminating true competition. This alone ensures that diversity and local criteria, both essential elements in true environmental and social justice in a supply chain, are completely lost.

The input of Green Economics proves vital here, as it observes how economics has divided itself off from other disciplines and other aspects of life, forsaking a pluralist view that would retain these essential elements. This exclusivity has enabled economics to test outcomes on a model or a graph, but not against true implementation in reality. Instead, Green Economics factors reality back in, with specificity in time and place and above all outcomes. It attempts to assess the effects international corporate activities, using models such as those advocated by Ietto Gillies (2005).

The forgotten importance of the supply chain (Bridger, 2006, 2007; Kennet, 2006; Fenwick, 2006), one of the most influential and practical areas of economics which heavily influences social justice must be factored back into the equation. New concepts and developments, such as air freighting food from countries with very high levels of starvation and lack of social justice, and net outpourings of luxury food for trade with western nations, must be restored to centrality in economics. For too long, "supply-side" economics has been too content with glossing over the realities of the supply chain. Such recent developments involve the use of vast sums of capital which could be used to feed local people and to provide social justice. The unravelling of the role of supply chains in social and environmental justice, especially their increasing use of cheap aviation, is a feature of the writing of such authors as Bridger (2007).

Demand stimulation is now as in demand as it ever has been. It is seen as the solution to the oncoming recession and current financial crisis (although in reality this crisis is rather overshadowed by the wider natural crisis (Sukdev, 2008)). However, this approach on its own does not appreciate the true causes of the current financial crisis. These causes centre on an over-stimulation of demand, fuelled by a nonsensical availability of credit, and a system that over-stimulated risk-taking by financiers in the pursuit of growth.

A longer-term solution will involve refocusing demand, rather than simply stimulating it. There is more than one way to grow spending so that job losses are minimised. Government spending on climate change mitigation and adaptation, and species conservation, is one such alternative way. Indeed, these projects are so demanding that they shall necessitate continuous and substantial government spending, which would cushion the latest fallout from traditional demand stimulation. Demand, if not carefully managed, inevitably leads to over-consumption. The same system that precipitated this financial crisis is also precipitating an ongoing natural crisis. This latter crisis, if not averted, will eventually constitute the unavoidable brakes on consumer demand and economic growth (Daly, 1974). Therefore, it is much wiser to manage demand downwards now, and reorientate it from 'unnecessaries' to 'necessaries'. Keynesianism has always featured a fatal flaw - that its demand management failed to recognise the eventual futility of demand in the face of ecological limits.

This Green Economics assessment of supply chains should not be restricted to 'visible' goods. Credit, an 'invisible' good, also needs tough supply chain management to keep track of where it has come from. The public purchase of bank ownership is an opportunity to exercise influence over how and where banks source their credit. This credit then facilitates supply chains for practically all other goods. A Green Economics supply chain assessment would reassert the responsibility of lenders for facilitating the projects that they lend to. One example would be holding lenders to account for embedded emissions in lending to carbon-intensive projects (see, for example, Smith, 2008). The current credit crunch has created a level of support for tighter regulation unseen since the 1929 crash. Green Economics should take advantage of this to redress the balance of corporate and government power.

As the credit crunch tightens its throttlehold on ordinary households, there is urgent need for a pluralistic Green Economics perspective on its causes and cures. The hallmark of such a perspective is a broader appreciation of the interests and systemic failures that crushed the availability of credit to households and in particular small businesses that depend on it. The wider shift in power from governments to corporations is one such overarching cause. Consider that the main UK corporation tax rate fell from 52% in 1973 to 28% in 2008 (HMRC, 2008). This illustrates the historical backdrop to the now-recognised need for greater regulation. As well as encouraging greater responsibility in the demand-side, governments must take more responsibility for the supply-side.

8.   Conclusion

In conclusion, Green Economists, who regard economics as comprising aspects of moral and societal transformation and the alleviation of suffering and poverty, are proposing a truly radical and pluralistic school of economics. This school is well on the way to establishing itself as a useful methodology and development in economics, Reardon (2007) and Lawson (2007). Its twin roots in Green thought (meaning social and environmental justice meshed together simultaneously) and economic thought (in the sense of its Greek root *oikia*, meaning the household in the fullest possible sense, including nature, and the biosphere) make this one of most relevant disciplines of the moment. It is one which can naturally take economics into a more pluralistic mode of theory, operation and practice. It can only ever exist in a historically and geographically specific context, and comprises more than a little anthropology and psychology. Moreover, in this new discipline, economics' traditional envy of physics is not sated by equilibrium theory models far removed from reality, but rather the natural science of the world around us.

This green economics is able to serve a far wider set of interests. A pluralist perspective would allow economics to address all forms of work, both formal and informal. If it is to be logically consistent and morally justified, this economics must employ the concept of pluralism with the greatest care, avoiding any amoral or nihilist use of the term. Instead, its right usage allows for a thorough inclusiveness of alternative insights, producing a more accurate economics, fit for purpose in such critical times for the pursuit of justice. In this way, Green Economics has real potential to achieve the complex, intertwined imperatives of social and environmental justice.

This green economics is no longer measured by destruction of natural assets and through-put of resource depletion. Rather, it is measured by the well-being of humankind, the biosphere and the Earth's physical systems. Above all, it promotes and creates the alleviation of poverty and inequality, as the means and the ends, replacing the short-sighted profit-maximising choices of rational economic man.

This green economics is able to blur the previous distinctions between the formal and informal economy. It does so by usurping the agenda that ignores the value of informal work, instead integrating it into new policy aims and approaches. It is able to restore balance to economics, by shifting focus from a single-minded emphasis on the formal economy to a more holistic appreciation of all forms of work, as well as the natural environment on which they depend.

9.   References

Alderson, P. (2008) 'Economic Alternatives and childhood poverty', *International Journal of Green Economics*, vol. 2, no. 1, pp. 77-94

Anderson, V. (2006) 'Turning economics inside out', *International Journal of Green Economics*, vol. 1, no. 1/2, pp. 11-22

Berry, P. (forthcoming) 'Biodiversity and habitat', *International Journal of Green Economics*

Brewer, M., Goodman, A., Shaw, J. & Sibieta, L. (2006) *Poverty and Inequality in Britain: 2006*, Institute for Fiscal Studies, available at: http://www.ifs.org.uk/comms/comm101.pdf

Bridger, R. (2006) 'Redefining efficiency in food supply chains', *Conference Proceedings of 2006 Green Economics Institute Annual Conference*, Oxford

University, 8th April 2006

Bridger, R. (2007) 'The Chill-Chain in the Sky: Air freight's fastest growing sector', *Conference Proceedings of 2007 Green Economics Institute Annual Conference*, Oxford University, April 07

Bronfenbrenner, M. (1971), 'The structure of revolution in economic thought', *History of Political Economy*, 3, pp. 136-151

Claussen, M. (2003) 'Simulation of Holocene Climate Change Using Climate Systems Models in Global Change in the Holocene', in Mackay, A., Batterbee R., Birks J., Oldfield F. (Eds.) (2003) *Global change in the Holocene*, Hodder Arnold

Collier, P. (2007) 'The Bottom Billion', Royal Economics Society, Newsletter no 137 RES Annual Public Lecture

Daly, H. (1974) 'The economics of the steady state', *American Economic Review*, May 1974, vol. 64, no.2, pp. 15-21

Davis, J. (2006) 'The Turn in Economics: Neoclassical Dominance to Mainstream Pluralism?', *Journal of Institutional Economics*, vol. 2, no. 1, pp. 1-20.

Dobson, A. (2000) *Green Political thought*, Abingdon: Routledge

Freeman, R. (1984) Strategic Management: A stakeholder approach, Boston: Pitman

Girardet, H. (ed.) (2007) *Surviving the Century: Facing Climate Chaos & Other Global Challenges*, London: Earthscan

Goldsmith E. (2007) *Feeding People in an age of climate change*, in Girardet, H. (ed.) (2007) *Surviving the Century: Facing Climate Chaos & Other Global Challenges*, London: Earthscan

Grint, K. (1991) *The Sociology of Work: An Introduction*, Cambridge: Polity Press

Heinemann, V. (2007) 'Current developments in international trade – an opportunity for a new progressive approach in economic policies', *International Journal of Green Economics*, vol. 1, no. 3/4, pp. 351-373

HM Revenue & Customs (2008) *'Table A6: Rates of Corporation Tax'*, available at: http://www.hmrc.gov.uk/stats/corporate_tax/rates-of-tax.pdf

Ietto Gillies, G. (2005) *Transnational Firms and International Production:*

Concepts, Theories and Effects, Cheltenham: Edward Elgar

Intergovernmental Panel on Climate Change (2007) *Climate Change 2007: Synthesis Report*, available at: http://www.ipcc.ch/pdf/assessment-report/ar4/syr/ar4_syr.pdf

Jevons, W.S. (1871) *The Theory of Political Economy*, London: Macmillan

Kay, J. & King. M. (1990) *The British Tax System, 5th ed.*, Oxford: Oxford University Press

Kennet, M. (2007) 'Editorial: progress in Green Economics: ontology, concepts and philosophy. Civilisation and the lost factor of reality in social and environmental justice', *International Journal of Green Economics*, vol. 1, no. 3/4, pp. 225-249

Kennet, M. & Heinemann, V. (2006) 'Green Economics: setting the scene. Aims, context, and philosophical underpinning of the distinctive new solutions offered by Green Economics', *International Journal of Green Economics*, vol. 1, no. 1/2, pp.68–102

Lawson, T (2007) 'An orientation for Green Economics', *International Journal of Green Economics*, vol. 1, no. 3/4, pp. 250-267

Lipietz, A. (2000) 'Political Ecology and the Future of Marxism', *Capitalism Nature Socialism*, March, Translated by K.P. Moseley & C. Rodriguez, available at: http://lipietz.club.fr/MET/MET_MarxismCNS.htm

Lord, C. (1999) *An Introduction to Citizens' Income*, Chapter 9 in Scott Cato, M. & Kennet, M. (1999) *Green Economics: Beyond Supply and Demand to Meeting People's Needs*, Green Audit Books

Mies, M. (2007) 'Patriarchy and accumulation on a world scale – revisited', *International Journal of Green Economics*, vol. 1, no. 3/4, pp. 268-275

Millennium Ecosystem Assessment Synthesis Report (2001) *Ecosystems and Human Well-Being*, available at: http://www.millenniumassessment.org/documents/document.356.aspx.pdf

Negishi, T. (1989) History of economic thought (Advanced textbooks in economics) North-Holland, Netherlands

Polyani, K. (1944) *The great transformation*, Beacon Press

Potter, R. et al (2004) *Geographies of development*, Pearson

Rawls, J. (1971) *A Theory of Justice*, Harvard University Press

Rawls, J. (1993) *Political Liberalism*, Columbia University Press

Reardon, (2007) 'How green are principles texts? An investigation into how mainstream economics educates students pertaining to energy, the environment and green economics', *International Journal of Green Economics*, vol. 1, no. 3/4, pp. 381-393

Richardson, L. (2005) 'Charity Wristbands Made in Sweatshop Factories', The Scotsman, available at: http://www.corpwatch.org/article.php? id=12464

Robertson, J. (1999) *A Green Taxation and Benefits System*, Chapter 6 in Scott Cato, M. & Kennet, M. (1999) *Green Economics: Beyond Supply and Demand to Meeting People's Needs*, Green Audit Books

Rostow, W. (1990) *Theorists of economic growth from David Hume to the present*, Oxford University Press

Smith, K. (2008) *Cashing in on Coal: RBS, UK Banks and the Global Coal Industry*, PLATFORM, available at: http://www.oyalbankofscotland.com/cioc/pdf/cashinginoncoal.pdf

Soderbaum, P. (2008) 'Only pluralism in economics research and education is compatible with a democratic society', *International Journal of Green Economics*, vol. 2, no. 1, pp. 45-64

Spicer, J. (2006) *Biodiversity: A Beginner's Guide*, Oneworld Books, Oxford

Stern, N. (2006) *The Stern Review on the Economics of Climate Change*, available at: http://62.164.176.164/6520.htm

Sukhdev, P. (2008) *Interim Report on the Economics of Ecosystems & Biodiversity*, available at: http://ec.europa.eu/environment/nature/biodiversity/economics/index_en. htm

Tokman, V. E. (1978) 'An exploration into the nature of the informal-formal sector relationship', *World Development*, vol. 6, no. 9/10, pp. 1065-1075

Turner, S. and Roth, P. (2003) *The Blackwell Guide to Continental Philosophy*, Blackwell Publishing

UNICEF (2007) *Child Poverty in Perspective: An overview of child well-being in rich countries*, Innocenti Report Card 7, UNICEF Innocenti Research Centre, Florence

Wallis, S (2007) 'A radical new vision for the world trading system in surviving the century', in Girardet, H. (ed.) (2007) *Surviving the Century:*

Facing Climate Chaos & Other Global Challenges, London: Earthscan

Werner, G. (2007) *Einkommen für Alle (Income for all)*, Kiepenheuer & Witsch

Wicksteed (1910) *The Common Sense of Political Economy*, London: Macmillan

Williams, C. (2005) *A Commodified World? Mapping the Limits of Capitalism*, Zed Books

Chapter 8 Social justice

8.1. Social-ecological Transformation and Green Economics: New perspectives for solutions to the most pressing problems of today.

Miriam Kennet

Introduction

This chapter will examine why we need a socio- ecological transformation and introduce some of the global scale problems we are facing. These include climate change, species extinction and threats to the natural systems upon which we depend.

It then discusses neo – classical economics roots and causes of this situation, and what kind of economics transformations are needed. The contributions of Rosa Luxemburg are discussed including her work on international production, consumption, property rights and enclosure of the commons which are important elements today.

Finally there is a discussion of the characteristics of an economics which could produce such a socio – ecological transformation, which the chapter suggests could be a Green Economics with different attitudes to nature, inclusive of feminist perspectives and compatible with modern science, with a long term perspective. A focus on equity is in keeping with sharing the planet's resources with each other and with other species. This would also provide for wider involvement in economics.

Why we need a socio-ecological transformation in order to solve the most pressing problems of today

The world is currently experiencing crises of a magnitude and a type unseen in the 10,000 years of "civilisation." Our "civilisation" arose after the last ice age and was founded upon the particular climactic conditions of the Quaternary interglacial period. We now have the challenges of human induced climate change with sea level rise, and millions of environmental refugees predicted Lohachara Island was the world's first populated island, to be lost to climate change 5 years ago and left 7,000 people homeless. Sagar the largest island, houses 20,000 refugees from other islands along with many rare species and is also disappearing fast. This illustrates how people, planet and biosphere are intricately connected.

One fifth of humankind is in life threatening poverty, and three quarters of mammal species are predicted to be extinct by the end of this century, according to the IUCN Red List report (Barker 2007). There has never been a more pressing need for a simultaneous social and ecological transformation, which needs to now take on board that poverty is an environmental issue and the environment is a poverty issue.

Dr Rajendra Pachauri, the chair of the Intergovernmental Panel on Climate Change, warns that " the very survival of the human species is at risk," (Lean, 2005).

The polar ice caps are contracting and sea level rise could permanently displace up to 200 million people, (Stern 2006). With predicted global warming of between +2 to +4.5 % or up to + 6C by 2100, (Lynas 2007), extinctions, desertification and reduction in agricultural yields are anticipated. The Millennium Ecosystem Services Assessment, (2005) found that ecosystem services are being degraded and an increase in 'non-linear events' brings increased disease, collapse of fisheries and other threats, in particular to fragile ecosystems which are also hosts to rapidly growing human populations.

These changes make our task urgent and compelling. Further, our current economic system perpetuates poverty, inequality and social injustice. The economic system fails to meet even many wealthy people's needs. A UNICEF report, (2007) about the well –being of young people in the UK, shows that a country which has the fifth largest economy in the world, simultaneously has the worst rankings among the 25 richest nations, in terms of the well- being and happiness of its young people when analysing indicators such as relative poverty and deprivation, relationships with family and peers, health and safety and feelings of well being. The report raises significant questions about how the pursuit of economic wealth, as current attained and measured, may actually detract from broader measures of well being. Seventy per cent of the world's 1.2 billion people in life threatening poverty, according to a UN Report, (UN 2006) are women and children. Every day 6,000 children in developing countries die for lack of acess to clean water (Sullivan 2000, Crisis in water). Only 1 per cent of the world's titled land belongs to women,(Firth ,2006).

Gendered domestic violence is the single largest global cause of female morbidity, more than war, traffic accidents, and cancer (Smith, 2006). It is therefore vital to redress the balance of poverty and power between men and women on the planet. Wangari Maathai, likens the things that matter in society to an African stool, *"The three legs represent three critical pillars of a just and stable society. The first leg stands for democratic space, where rights are respected, whether they are human rights, women's rights, children's rights, or environmental rights. The second represents sustainable and equitable management of resources. The third represents cultures of peace. The seat represents society and its prospects for development."*

These three pillars have got lost in the drive for global economic success defined as ever increasing profit, industrial productivity and trade flows which has brought the risk of destruction of much of our habitat.

Neo – classical economics roots and causes of this situation and what kind of economic transformation do we need?

Today's economics discourse has become almost unrecognisable from its origins as provisioning for the needs of the household or the estate. Its root is the word *oikia*, ancient Greek for a house. The root of the word, Eco-nomics is the same as that of eco-logy. Green Economics reverts it to its original and useful beginnings: the provisioning of needs for all of us and the biosphere within the household we all share, which is actually the earth.

Neo-classical economics has come to mean the exact opposite, which is, everything formal, mathematical and external to the household sphere which has assumed superiority over the earth believing itself to be some how outside its systems and limitations. Examining our resource needs and working out how to share them fairly among the people of the world is a major task. In 1890 Marshall described economics as "it examines the part of individual and social action which is most closely connected with the attainment and with the use of the material requisites of well-being." (2005:57.Hogdson). However Samuelson (1948) the father of neo-classical economics, argued that "economics is the allocation of scarce means between alterative uses, as a universal matter of choice for every individual in a world of scarcity. Instead of the whole system of production and allocation of the means of life, the choosing individual alone became the foundation stone of economic theory (2005:57) in Hogdson.

Economics which purports to be value free science, is in fact practised in the main by white middle class men and outside the home sphere. The discipline of economics has to some extent been subsumed by business schools which aim to "grow" companies. There are very few women economics professors, just 23 in the UK in 2003(RES Report: Humphries). Economics has become mathematically oriented and exclusive with a fixation on " economic growth" as the key indicator of progress, conceived as more important than indicators relating to the health of people, well being or ecosystem integrity.

Economics, the provisioning for needs, is done by all of us. Every creature and every ecosystem has an "economic" or resource need and impact. We need to broaden the scope of economics in order for it to helpful in solving today's socio – and ecological problems. The emerging discourse of Green Economics reclaims economics for all people everywhere, aiming for all people and the biosphere to be beneficiaries rather than inputs. Green Economics rejects the short term timescales of business cycles in favour of geological lengths of time as only archaeological and palaontological explanations can illuminate what is happening.

Green Economics has arisen from the need for an framework which can encompass social and environmental insights and does not factor out "life- world" evidence but instead embraces the complexities of people, nature and their dynamic inter-relationships. Green economics logic is built upon an interdisciplinary range of philosophies and methodologies from human learning, from the economics of Aristotle and Xenophon, through the enlightenment to post-modern illustrations of difference and power

203

relationships. Its world view is that everything happens within the earth's boundaries and so no longer theorises economics as being separate from but rather within the earth's systems. There are no resources which don't come from nature.

Socio- ecological transformations and Revolutions: The relevance of Rosa Luxemburg's analysis for today's solutions

Luxemburg made a number of analytical observations which are useful in starting us on the path to transformation. An updated environmental definition of such transformation is given by Olsson, Folke and Hahn (2004). They define it as resilience, in social – ecological systems, the ability to cope with environmental variability and disturbance events. Characteristics of such a system might include property rights, environmental ethics, public accountability and reciprocal exchange systems. These are all pertinent to learning to live with change and uncertainty and elements can be found in the ideology of indigenous peoples. The industrial revolution brought benefits according to mainstream economics definitions. However Luxemburg correctly predicted some of the drawbacks.

Enclosure and the transformation of property rights

Concurrent with the industrial revolution, the commons began to be enclosed for the benefit of the few who made money out of them and prevented the rest of humanity or other species from accessing them. This has been followed most recently by the enclosure of knowledge with intellectual property rights and patents. (Shiva in Biopiracy). Luxemburg argued that three things were aimed for: to coerce labour power into service, to impose a commodity economy and to separate agriculture and trade and drive farmers off the land and into towns. She showed how colonizers created a fiction that land had always belonged to the political ruler- rather than being owned in common.(Luxemburg 1913 :352.). These ideas have largely been implemented.

Everything has been commodified including, including land, knowledge and ecosystems services which are a new way of defining the role of nature.

Capitalism and the transformation of wealth and power

A new system of economics, capitalism, emerged, whereby the rich could increase their wealth or capital. In theory the poor would benefit as wealth trickled down. There was a theoretical justification for periods of enduring hardship with the Kuznets curve which showed that theoretically less developed countries could take off into an accelerated growth, after a period of hardship. The view that more development along capitalist lines will provide the socio-economic transformation required has pervaded development theories such as sustainable development. It became accepted

204

that the rich should enjoy so-called free trade with no constraints or trade barriers for the good of society, as the invisible hand of the market would ensure their decisions ultimately benefited everyone.

Corporations grew in this laissez faire environment into huge monoliths and many of them are larger and more powerful than governments. Luxemburg argued that it was the very dispossession of the peasants of their common land which provided both the property, and also the labour with which to keep this system going, and hence that poverty is part of the engine of the capitalist system. She foresaw that this system needed previously non industrialised areas, beyond the spatial scope of the capitalist consumption or democratic area, to provide cheap international production but that this would ultimately reach limits of expansion. Encroachment for international production is a little explored area but is extremely pertinent to the issue of democracy. Corporations find an area of potential cheap labour and then set about creating favourable market conditions before entry, being complicit in combinations of civil instability, displacement of people, regime change, economic instability and military action.

Luxemburg realised that expanding capitalism would need new markets, and that there was ultimately a limit to them. Advanced capitalism's requirement of ever expanding rich consumer markets for its products and lower and lower paid, poor workers for its production must eventually must reach a saturation of possibilities, including finite physical limits of resources. Consumption is a battle ground. People are manipulated to consume more by government including infrastructure for global trade corridors and demand is artificially stimulated by activities such as corporate advertising.

Transformations in attitudes to nature, civilisation and agriculture

Luxemburg identified a struggle against the natural economy. Just when humans thought they had tamed nature, largely by means of economics and technology, climate change has forced a rethink of our position in the universe and our role as stewards of nature. We are beginning to realise that rather than using science to control nature, we are going to have to use our knowledge to live within and respect it. The power of nature was pivotal to elements of early belief systems and religions which we can learn from.

Transforming the limits of civilisation- 10,000 years of town dwelling-An audit.

We need to assess the viability of agriculture, and urbanisation during this period of rapid global environmental change and to establish the best course of action. The issues of population growth, people displacement and scarce resources raise important economic questions. Agriculture enabled cities to develop, but the project of "civilisation" itself is under threat. Civilisation derives from *civis*, the Latin word for townsman or citizen, *civis*, adjectival, *civilis*, which implies urbanisation. Mega-cities surpass human-scale communities, their own local ecosystem services and the carrying capacity of their immediate hinterland. There is an urgent task, fundamental to Green Economics, to reanalyse "civilisation" and to develop strategies for how human living and economic patterns can adapt for survival.

Transforming the human habitat and ecosystem services crisis and the current mass extinction. This is affecting the ability of our habitat to sustain us all, as a species. It is becoming clear that our economics is running into limits of expansion and we need therefore to re-think the whole premise of our economics to limit further human induced global environmental damage. If the consumption rate of the rich countries continues and is adopted by poorer countries we would require the resource of three planets, so we have reached the limits of possible ecological footprints within this earth and the natural world.

Transformations in international production

The internationalisation of production in globalisation is little understood, but is one of the most pertinent phenomena identified by Luxemburg. Large TNCs outsource production across sectors, firms and countries, (Ietto – Gillies 2005 :48) and workers rights are eroded by casualisation. The arms trade has grown rapidly and everything and everyone is commoditized and a growing slave trade including even in children.

Three quarters of world trade originates with multinationals and over a third is internal to the firm precluding regulation or scrutiny or competition from other companies. (Ietto -Gillies UNCTAD 1996).

The globalisation of international production and effects on national and local economies has been described by Dicken (2007). "There has been a huge transformation in the nature and the degree of interconnection in the world economy, and especially in the speed with which such connectivity occurs, involving both the stretching and the intensification of economic relationships. There is today a deep integration organised primarily within and between geographically extensive and complex transnational production networks and through a diversity of mechanisms. There are changes are not so much in volume as in **composition**. There has been a huge increase in intraindustry and intra – firm trade. Both of which are indicators of a more functionally fragmented and geographically dispersed production processes. Dicken (2007: 7)

Flows of material and non material processes are organised into relational structures and processes in which the power relationships between key actors such as firms, states, individuals, and social groups are uneven. (Dicken 2007: 8). States, labour unions and even NGO's compete to attract TNC's. Vertical dimensions of transnational production networks, intersect with territorially defined political and economic systems and horizontal dimensions of territorial systems of different geographical scales. Firms have global reach according to Ohmae,in The end of the nation state. According to the World Trade Report (2005a) 4/5ths of global manufacturing and 2/3rds of agriculture are concentrated in 15 countries, and outward FDI is similarly concentrated with 30% emanating from the US and the UK.

The Surmounting of democracy and government by TNCs and the transformation of existing power structures

Gillies explains that *"transnational companies can and do play governments of different countries or regions against each other with the objective of raising the offer of financial incentives for the location of inward investment FDI . Thus the TNC has a strong element of bargaining power towards both governments and labour force in that it canrelocate to different countries with relatively low costs of change.".*(2005:293 Ietto-Gillies)

This is a concern as there are several countries where democracy is under serious threat. Large MNC's can influence government. For example Shell is widely suspected of this in Nigeria, and Burma Oil in Burma, both of which are repressive regimes. In many cases corporate regulations are created in the same department that ought to be regulating their activity. Regulation has become the subject of lobbying at extra national level in order to resist the impositions and limitations governments place on corporate activity.

Differing currency and taxation laws give firms the opportunity of developing location and intra firm transfer strategies that give them the benefit of transfer pricing manipulation and therefore higher profits. With outsourcing and the transfer of rules and regulations environmental dumping is facilitated.

New markets reflecting environmental and other concerns are hijacked by larger firms buying up more ethical trading houses, for example the Body Shop was bought by L'Oreal. Large family owned organic dairies are bought up by global firms who retain the family name and marketing.

Large firms use their market power to avoid complying with usual labour standards. Lidl has been investigated as a firm with geographical variation in working conditions. In the case of Lidl this affects workers' human dignity such as very limited toilet breaks and pressure on women not to have children to discouraging unions.

The economics system needs to be fed by increasing consumption, and according to Rostow the final state of economies must be a stage of "high mass consumption." Here it has come up against the limits to growth (Meadows et al) . Furthermore, production is oncentrated into large scale operations to create "efficiency," or " lean supply" with a consequent reduction in diversity of suppliers.

Inequalities are widening between and within countries, with key indicators of infant mortality and life expectancy becoming increasingly divergent. Dicken points out that the benefits of trade, are limited in the poorest countries. This is due to dependence on a narrow economics base and exacerbated by downward pressure and lack of stability in the price of traded goods. Combined with a market mechanism that fails to share the benefits equitably (Dicken 2007: 519) this has resulted in the terms of trade worsening considerably between 1990 and 2000.

The characteristics and scope of an economics for socio – ecological transformation

a) Moral and Spiritual aspects of economics for transformation

Satish Kumar, (2007) suggests that we need a transformation in our attitudes to each other, and to other living things on the Earth. He suggests that we have lost the idea of spirit and become wedded to materialism," identifying the roots of this in the views of Descartes and Newton who looked upon the Earth as an object of human dominance. He reminds us that Nature rights are equal to human rights, Kumar suggests we need a *"geo centric world view"*- which is in fact how green economics is constructed with the earth at the center or foot of all activity and observations. Kumar says that we cannot solve a problem in the mindset that caused the problem in the first place and "we need to realise the subservience of economics to ecology."(Kumar 2007:33).

Green Economics recognizes poverty as a moral issue, yet the application of neo-liberal logic appears to be making matters worse for the world's poor. Neo-classical economics views world poverty as offering opportunities for further exploitation as a vast untapped market offering cheap resources and labour for revenue growth (Prahalad and Hammond, 2003, p.1). In Green Economics wealth and power are recognised as inextricably intertwined, so an appropriate level of decision-making is encouraged, which allows access and transparency for everyone. New indicators, rather than just GDP (which only measures the activity, throughput and quantity as monetary value of goods exchanged) show what the social and environmental justice targets could be, analysing trends and identifying risks such as in education, work, consumption, relative distribution of wealth and health of people, species and ecosystems (Anderson, 1991) .

b) Eco – ecological/economic transformation

It is recognised that all these elements need to be reworked, and particularly that power structures need to be changed as economic power is often concentrated in the same hands as political power. Lack of democracy appears to be a factor in several parts of the world where there is unrest or extreme poverty where a small ruling class hold the economic power and control the government

c) Economics objectives for transformation

The objectives of Green Economics are indivisible from its methodoloy:
i) To create economic conditions where social and environmental justice thrives and benefits all people everywhere, non human species, the planet and its systems.
ii) To reform mainstream economics into a discipline which no longer supports or accepts that only a minority can be wealthy, but which works towards a fair and equitable society which lives within its means in all senses. Further Green Economics seeks to re-examine broader versions of

reality, beyond the views of the rich and powerful, rejecting the idea of rational economic man "homoeconomicus" as a benchmark in order to hear different voices, as proposed for example by feminist theory (Ghilligan,1982).

A key reason for mainstream economics' failure is its lack of influences and learning from other areas. Green Economics attempts to combine trans- and inter-disciplinary studies to counteract this narrow thinking, As Welford exhorts, *"if we were to emphasize moderation and sufficiency rather than maximisation of output, consumption, incomes and profits, this would have a radical and fundamental impact on the way we lead our lives and the way we treat the environment."* (Welford, 2007)

iii)To enable all people everywhere to participate in the economy with equal power, equal rights and with equal access to decision making. Green Economics methodology brings new perspectives to conventional economics tools and enables it to reveal the power relationships and vested interests in the global economy. It also reincorporates political economy and the moral and transformational aspects of the economics of Smith (1776). It offers new solutions to 'managing the commons', which has been restricted to theoretical models (von Neumann and Morgenstern), and exercises based on the prisoner's dilemma (Arrow, 1951) which perpetuate assumptions of self interest as the key motivation of human activity.

Learning from this broad range of wisdom is essential to enable our economic systems to adapt to operating within a 'carrying capacity' of the earth. Pegging the level of that capacity should be a pressing subject for economic debate. Green Economics re-embeds the economy within ecological and social structures. Economic growth, progress and development are measured by indicators that aim towards 'creation' mimicking the abundance of nature, not 'annihilation' of resources (Goldsmith, 2005). Profit, prices and markets are regarded as incidental, rather than drivers of the economic system. Green Economics treats people, the planet, nature, non-human species, and the biosphere as beneficiaries, not just resources or economic factors of production.

This new discipline operates on the principle that the needs of people and natural systems must be satisfied simultaneously. The purpose of economic activity is to satisfy needs, not to enhance the power of people, corporations or states. Global industrialism, according to Dobson (2000, p.27), is regarded with suspicion. The welfare value of products is questioned, as well as their transformation into forms of identity through marketing.

The concept of equilibrium is reclaimed from price concerns to encompass impacts and effects in political, social, moral and ecological terms reflecting concern for people, society, non-human species, nature and the biosphere as a holistic whole. In this way, Green Economics acts as a filter for other systems as it is does not seek to impose one system globally, as in capitalism or socialism, but rather advocates diversity using a Green Economics analysis for each situation. Many practitioners of conventional economics are critical of their own discipline, according to Medena and Samuels (1996) and Ormerod (1994). "The subject has become so obscure that even orthodox economists are bemoaning its intellectual poverty," says Kitson (2005). Mainstream economists observe that their work has little bearing on the real 'life-world' or on important concerns such as ending poverty (Kitson, 2005). However, disciplinary insurgence is rare because of the limited professional progress that usually follows. Unfortunately, many well-known economists, for example, Pasinetti (2005) continue to advocate a more intensified business as usual approach, fixated on growth, more profit, which entails increasing economic hegemony of global corporations and is framed by increasingly elaborate theory,. Green economists argue that these blinkered and alienating positivist dogmas cannot solve the problems of today.

d) Transformation in attitudes to economics and its relationship to science and earth science

Mainstream economics employs a set of positivist, modern tools to produce the desired simplified logic that is vital for the picture of the world that is its basis. It produces results that contradict insights from other sciences such as the urgency of human induced climate change. It is focused on an infinite growth assumption and supposedly innate individual preferences in our prescribed role as passive consumers.

Green Economics can integrate the world's big ideas, such as those presented by The Big Bang, Evolution, Quantum Mechanics, Risk Theory, New System Theory, Relativity and Climate Change. Green Economics incorporates the ideas of progress in scientific thinking and in scientific methodology such as natural science, ecology and social science rather than econometrics. reen

Economics therefore challenges the reductionism and supposed objectivity of mainstream economics which is based on the supremacy of unadjusted market solutions at the expense of people and the planet.

f) A Transformation from short termism to long termism

Green Economics takes a view that is much longer-term than the short business cycles of neoclassical and economics. Due to its consideration of the effects of a transaction on the 200 000th generation and beyond (Myers, 1985), Green Economics can draw from history, paleontology and archaeology. As a consequence, Green Economics does not simply discount the future. Intergenerational equity is investigated by such writers as Alderson (2006) who is greatly influenced by Chong (2006). Instead of mobilising the resources of the planet in support of human kind, we must surely mobilise the resources of human kind in support of the planet. This postulates a revision of our value systems, social paradigms and consumption culture (Myers, 1985).

g) An inclusive transformation including women and men together, using a feminist economics discourse

There are two realms of economic activity, that of competitive production and exchange in markets and that of direct production such as subsistence agriculture, care and reciprocity. Feminist economics contributes the notion that production does indeed occur in the home or 'okia'. Mies (1994) concentrates on methodology in economics and has been in integral influence on the development of green economics along with Mellor (1992) and Henderson (1983). Their approaches warn against theories that legitimise a single-gendered *homo economics* (rational economic man) version or 'story' of reality that excludes *gynaika oikonomika, (economic woman)* from the public economic sphere. Feminist methodologies allow us to dig into the foundations of a discipline and expose them as particular and contingent. It reveals the placing of boundaries in economics as an intensely political act.

Feminist economics has opened debate about the role of women in the global economy (Mies, 1994) and found evidence of patriarchy and exploitation. Women have provided unpaid, nonvalued, invisible work and the discipline of economics has excluded their experience. There has, been a recognition of the power of nature, due to human induced climate change and this has challenged the belief of man's domination over nature, which is embodied in patriarchal culture.

There is an urgent need to design an economics which helps to limit further ecological devastation, and to design an economics which can work under some of the radically changed environmental conditions predicted in some scenarios, such as agriculture being limited to smaller regions of the world. Major climatic and other shifts could bring a lack of availability and viability of natural resources impacting on our basic needs such as food and water and the likelihood of major displacement of people. Our economics must be able to deal with such severe problems and the inherent uncertaintyof climate change.

Conclusion
Humanity has come to a crossroads where we have reached the limits to the economic logic on which its agrarian, industrial, and technological revolutions were based. Economic growth sustained by resources in furtherance of this aim have been discovered to be finite. Yet supply chains have become more globalised and wasteful of resources. Furthermore, the natural world has turned out to be extremely complex and fragile whilst at the same time enjoying the ultimate power to wipe us out as along with many other species. In order to preserve a natural world which we could reasonably call home- and an economics based in that home- or oikia, we need to undertake a rapid socio-ecological transformation and to re-align our entire economics systems.

Luxemburg also pointed out the need for grassroots democracy and co-operation. Recent primate studies indicate that co-operation is an important aspect of society, De Wal (2005), contradicting economic theories like the prisoner's dilemma and the tragedy of the commons. De Waal suggests that reciprocity arose from sharing of food within the group, in prehistoric times. This, he suggests involves keeping a balance of good deeds which we expect them to be roughly equal and reciprocal.

Main stream neo classical economics has been based on inequalty between rich and poor, between men and women, between man and other species, between man and the planets natural systems. Our economic system has allowed for one fifth of humankind to go to bed hungry at night and there is no justification for this. If we want to call ourselves *civilised,* it's time to transform in a peaceful and positive way to a caring and sharing culture where everyone and everything counts, and into a Green Economics system of abundance and growth in nature shared by all and richly embedded in the natural world.

The ideas in this chapter were first published in German and in English by the Rosa Luxembourg Foundation in Germany in 2008, in a book edited by Kraus G. and Delheim J.

8.2 Social Aspects of Green Economics. Social and environmental Justice

Miriam Kennet

Green Economics aims to provide an economics paradigm which provides for simultaneous social and environmental justice for everyone and everything on the planet. One does not have to look very far to see how urgently this is required.

In the UK, the latest appointments to the panel of judges, after due consideration to increasing diversity using a new Independent Judicial Appointments Commission system, every single appointment was a white middle aged, middle class male. Of the entire judiciary in the high court only 10 are female out of 108, and one only is from an ethnic minority. (Dyer 2008) It is probably fair to say that worse than the selection being subject to "cloning" the entire system which got these men to eligibility is stacked against more diverse candidates. This would be just shocking if it didn't have implications for us all and especially in the context of today's discussions. The same situation is found in economics. " Homo economicus" forms the basis of today's mainstream micro economics. The supposedly innate preferences of white middle class male are deemed to be the most urgent requirements for economics to satisfy, hence possibly the growth of the car, arms and sex industries. Neo classical economics is built on expressed preference theory by Samuelson, which deduces value as a product of scarcity, rather than abundance. It ascribes importance and priority to the spending decisions of rational economic man, and then aggregates them to the entire global population. There is no room in such a theory for the analysis of power and lack of ability or capability to express such preference due to poverty which results from prevention of access to resources or ownership rights. It seeks economic growth, (calculated from overall activity – both destructive and constructive). However, economics started off as management and provisioning for the household, which now includes the earth. The last 10,000 years of " civilisation" have seen the rise of the monotheistic religions and agriculture. From earlier more balanced beginnings which are widely thought to have been more matrifocal, the last 10,000 years have produced a preponderance of literature and philosophy concerned with how to tame, and conquer and steward nature and to use the resources that are provided on the earth.

The problem is that in meeting the preferences in the most " efficient" way means an acceleration of global activity and growth. This means that the items that provide for this global economy are commoditized. White collar work is increasingly becoming commodified, and businesses have started outsourcing and off shoring their manufacturing activity, and shifting work to places where labour costs are a fraction of the price.

213

"When everything is the same and supply is plentiful, .. clients have too many choices, and no basis on which to make the right choice, And when this happens, you are a commodity. Freidman in Holmes (2008:xviiii). Commodification is no longer just about machinery, computers and plant. Nor is it just about, the odd industry or two. It is beginning to be about people, human capital, skills, and expertise, and it is spreading into those industries that have previously held up their margins, and kept out the competition. Two areas he cites are project management and the other is software application and management.(Holmes 2008:2).

The signs of a commoditized zone include increasing competition, prevalence of me too products and services, a belief that all suppliers are fundamentally the same, the decreasing desire on the customers part to look at new options or features, an increasing preference for customers to select on the basis of price and very little else, a reluctance for customers to pay for anything they consider unnecessary, and increasing pressures on margins.

There is pressure in a world of increasing competition to conform to this new trend or step out and risk being sidelined.

There are two main aspects of this trend that concern us here.

a) **Commodification of people: short term disembedded contracts:**

In more and more industries people are indeed become commoditized. Where the pay is high as in software industries then the comoditized person can pay to make up the shortfall in social security provision. However increasingly the commoditization of people has started to take on sinister tones.

The latest example is prostitution, now often referred to as 'sex work' which is a sanitised way to describe a larger and faster and increasingly cruel business which involves a global sex trade of people across borders. The other example which is also perhaps symbolic and ironically is a symbol of western manhood- is the football industry which now buys African players and keeps some of them in a modern slavery, remarkable parallels to the slavery trade of years ago. These players service the European first divisions for a brief period, with no papers or permission to stay. After their term, these players are often turned out on the streets and go into prostitution which tends to indicate that it's the supply chain structure itself that is causing the social degradation rather than individual industry structures. The logic of economics where increasing economies of scale as advocated by the neo- classical economist Krugman is played out in this fashion which makes perfect sense if modelling of economics reality is used without value or normative considerations.

b) **The commodification of social support structures: The Basic Income**

The other issue is that in such a world where there is no job security and social cohesion breaks down and the indigenous social security support from the community become absent as people are moved by globalisation, away from such support, a new deeper level of community support needs to provide that support in new ways. The evidence for the need for this is abundant. The new methods in a sense also reflect the culture of commodification and alienation from the community. For some the idea of basic income precisely appeals because it decouples the recipients from their identity as employee- wife mother, family person and the person receives benefits non means tested and calculated on the basis of them as an individual without ties.

The basic income in a sense therefore is a reflection of the times, and as such it is receiving much interest- a book about it achieving best seller status in Germany last year.

However there are mainly other benefits from a basic income scheme – and one is that potentially when pegged correctly, it is claimed in theory to provide for those very basic needs of the household originally that economics aimed to provision for, and it does not discriminate in favour of the most rich and powerful and therefore it is extremely important to begin to explore its potential and to debate related opportunities for change in the social structure.

Other issues of difference and diversity are a function of rapid demographic shifts in the age of the populations and in the spatial distributional changes in the abundance of workforces.

This section explores such issues and why a shift in our economics assumptions is urgently required.

The inequalities and social injustices in society: How social issues are linked to Green Issues

The inequalities are continuing to grow at an alarming rate- the gender pay gap in the UK alone is 17% in 2008, which is truly shocking. A report by the UN noted that women are generally under represented in the democratic process and that this affects their financial position too and makes them much more vulnerable to poverty as their needs are not catered for in the economics discussions. Before we make the assumption that this does not happen in the radical or alternative movement, it is certainly important to note that that poverty is a gendered issue, where only 1% of the entire world's resources are owned by women (Firth 2007). At the launch of the Green Fiscal Commission in January 2008, at Portcullis House, arguing for eco – taxes, not a single one of the 6 people on the speaking panel was a woman and not a single one was from an ethnic minority, in fact they were all white, middle class, middle aged men. So no change there- even in a purportedly radical environment. All the women who attended noticed it immediately and felt alienated- and none of the men commented. It has become so far ingrained in our perception of a current economist that its a white man in a suit that we don't question it. However with the current threat to biodiversity and climate stability we have to correct this, half the world is women and there is much diversity and we need to get a grip on inclusiveness before its too late. Ursula Barnett in a very useful article, The Greening of South Africa(Barnett 2006) is Basic to its Healing had the far sight to realise that social and environmental justice are two halves of the same dynamic, and cannot exist without the other.

215

We can address some of the issues. We can start by assuming that therefore in view of the above there is no level playing field today in terms of access to resources. Women do not have access to the same management or control of resources as men do -if we average this out over the globe, and the large corporations in the main are also run by white middle class men. The section addresses the results of this situation.

In a world of rapidly changing climate, sea level rise, and where one third of all species are Critically Endangered according to the latest IUCN Red List Report (Barker 2007), and inequality of wealth distribution within and between countries and also poverty is increasing every day, it is difficult to argue that neo classical economics methodologies have been successful. It is even harder to conclude that the Brundtland definition of Sustainable Development has been fulfilled or that future generations will inherit a bundle of economic resources even as plentiful of those the current generation inherited which will be able to protect their social well being.

Economics and the role of the market

In particular the way we apportion or earn our right to use those resources is an important consideration. There is a sense in which we do things or are things which Sayer believes makes us feel we deserve to earn or receive a certain amount. In particular we measure the overall well being of the economy in GDP increase and growth. However it is purely a measure of activity. Our economy needs to provide for everyone on the planet, not just the elites, or the national government.

The way we do this has been in recent years predicated on the capacity of the market to apportion fairly the resources that exist in the manner of Adam Smith. However Nicholas Stern has now explained that climate change cannot be solved by the market, also the smaller incremental changes- such as the need to stop using plastic bags or incandescent light bulbs where the market reward is too small for each preference based transaction will fail. The incentive in neo classical terms is simply not there. Therefore the role of the community or state in providing incentives or guidance or regulation is now very important. However at this time the role of the nation state has never been weaker- due to erosion by large multinational corporations – who believe, that due to their supreme power only they have the power to end poverty(by trading with the bottom fifth of the poverty pyramid) and to end the environmental crisis by voluntary corporate social responsibility. This attitude is also reflected in their assumption of guiding governments towards the particular trading regime or environment a state needs to provide to attract them. In the literature and in popular conceptions the health of an economy is now synonymous with how many corporations the state hosts in foreign direct investment. It is perceived that the more large global players in the country the more wealthy it is and them more jobs and poverty ending work is provided. One example of this is China, another is India, but the role of Brazil as the third part of the trade triangle providing agriculture does not feature in the same way in the literature.

The neo classical response to climate change – relying on the market to correct the situation

The resources of the earth underlay every single economics transaction and this is in some senses denied in main stream literature – as if the conquest of the earth is the aim and today- the achievement -that techno fixes can solve every possible problem. However it is the role of economics to ensure that they are protected and shared out fairly and appropriately.

There are two factors underlying the assumptions of main stream economics -perfect substitutability of natural capital and ignoring the constraints of thermodynamics according to Daly in Sullivan (2005) and that the destruction of natural capital is accounted for in income streams- ie growth rather than destruction which is what it really means.

In a new survey by Accenture (Brady 2008) Mark Spelman Head of global strategy discovered that only 5% of the global companies surveyed and not one in China regarded climate change as its main priority. They put other trading factors first. These concerns were sales growth, cost reduction, new product development, emerging markets, innovation, technology development, and after that climate change. This inspite of predicted sea level rise which will affect their entire surroundings as many big cities will go under water. Bush in the US argued that it was voluntary changes that global corporations want as a response but the survey found that in fact companies themselves want regulation by governments, not voluntary schemes as this gets prevents the free rider problem. The World Council for Business and Sustainable Development is predicated on the idea that it is business with its superior power, both political and economic that should sort out poverty and the environmental issues. However Mark Kember Policy Director at the Climate Group thinks otherwise" *These disappointing findings highlight the fact that carbon pricing mechanisms are not yet strong enough for business to incorporate climate change risks and opportunities into traditional business strategy.*"(Davis, Lean and Mesure 2008)

Green Economics links the different aspects holistically

Green Economics addresses the human, biosphere and the earth dimensions of economic questions and imperatives. It is important to treat the field holistically, and this section examines certain aspects and makes certain practical linkages. It is worth focusing on particular aspects which make up the overall picture.

In particular the rampant failure of neo classical economics to feed or to make provision for one fifth of human kind in an acceptable fashion is a particular concern. Since it is humans who construct the conceptualisation of the human part of the global economy, it is humans that need to sort out that aspect.

The social and environmental problem is linked as cause and effect. For example environmental degradation of several kinds in the New Orleans area, including mining as well as human induced climate change, are believed to have caused huge loss of life amongst some of the poorest in

America. However those are the people least able to defend themselves and they have now been shunted off their land in order to make way for a profitable development.

In certain parts of the world extreme poverty leads to women having many more children and too many children is the only insurance policy open to the very poor, this lack of access to resources, environmental and otherwise leads to more children and more environmental degradation as well as a lack of ability to mitigate its effects.

Increasing inequalities and poverty : the need for social justice to be included in economics

In particular the inequalities within societies are increasing -as the ravages of large global economics corporate players injects a dual economy of global players and non global players side by side so that some in a society have and some have not. Local businesses are sucked in and destroyed in the competition with the larger companies. This is leading to an acceleration in relative poverty, and the factors combine to cause an acceleration in absolute poverty. 9Sullivan).

1100 million people don't have access to water and 2400 million don't have access to sanitation. (Sullivan) as Sullivan says there are more than 10 kinds of descriptions of poverty in the literature but all agree there is too much poverty. Indicators of poverty include the poverty line the headcount index and the poverty gap. In addition to being national and ignoring regional differences they also ignore household and caring work that is mainly done by women, non monetary well being and depreciation of natural capital (Sullivan 2006). Sullivan has suggested a water poverty index, (Sullivan 2002). The World Bank considers someone to be in absolute poverty if they are living on less than $1 dollar a day a level at which more than 1000 million people exist on today.

However the term absolute poverty has been criticised as being based on the assumptions of experts about what might be peoples basic needs, (2006 Sullivan).

However the inequalities within poor countries as with others is very high, having both some of the richest people on the planet, and also some of the very poorest.

Women and debt: women's problems assumed to be overconsumption – in fact its unequal pay

In 2000 the UN noted that most of the world's poor are women. 70 per cent of the world's illiterates are women. 75 per cent of the world's refugees are women. Some 585,000 women - one every minute - die each year from pregnancy related causes. Most of these deaths are preventable.

Of the eight Millennium Development Goals, Goal 3 calls for empowering women and promoting gender equality, specifically setting targets to eliminate gender disparity in all levels of education by 2015, with additional indicators on employment of women and the proportion of women in parliaments. However, it is widely felt that gender equality is an essential cross-cutting component for meeting all the targets. (UNDP 2003)

Also we find the argument that The <u>United Nations Fourth World Conference on Women in Beijing</u> in 1995 identified *environment* as one of twelve critical areas for women. Section K of the Beijing Platform for Action, on women and the environment, asserted that "*women have an essential role to play in the development of sustainable and ecologically sound consumption and production patterns and approaches to natural resource management*" (paragraph 246).

2000s.This means that women share the burden to produce sustainable development but do not reap the benefits. However there is now a commitment reaffirmed in 2002 that more representation of women must accompany all the work of the UN DP. The benefits of sustainable development are now aimed to be for women, no longer from women; the elimination of violence and discrimination; access to health services; access to land and other resources (particularly in Africa); the enhancement of the role of women in resources management; education for all; participation of women; gender mainstreaming; and gender specific information and data.

Women experience difficulties with debt such as being behind on one or more bills, including rent, utilities, loans or credit agreements with 13% in arrears compared to 7% of men in the same age group. There is a wide-spread image that young women's with debt are due to 'frivolous' spending, in particular on clothes. Although the pressure to maintain social status through consumer spending is likely to play a factor in young women's debt. The group believes the image of young women as being irresponsible with money has been overplayed, since our research found that similar numbers of young women and young men have credit or store cards, that young women are also slightly more likely to be saving than young men and that women are more likely to be using forms of credit that are associated with poverty. (Fawcett 2007)

Other factors in the gap between young women's and men's to cope with debt are:

- Young women have lower incomes than young men; the gap is small at first, but grows to 15% by age 25 (Fawcett 2007)
- Young women's debt is more likely to be associated with poverty than young men's

It is important for the government to take action to close the pay gaps and to prevent debt problems and the drops in income women are more likely to experience when having children or when a relationship breaks down. There needs to be more access to affordable credit: Ensure young women can access affordable credit and loans. There needs to be easily accessible money and debt advice for women after they leave education too.

Jenny Westaway of Fawcett wants to correct the idea that young women struggling with debt are just irresponsible and unable to resist handbags. "*In fact our picture is of many women struggling to make ends meet on lower incomes than their male counterparts*". (Fawcett 2007)

The meaning of work

The meaning of work and what it is for and what is acceptable is coming to the fore as a serious question. As work for useless purpose also destroys the environment and can create more poverty as it uses up resources. The nature of the organisation of work is also a subject scrutiny, as if there are huge discrepancies between rich and poor many of the poor work simply to satisfy the whims of the rich and in particular in the sex trade. Trafficking update from independent -supply chain of footballers and trafficking of babies and children is a modern slavery, using people as commodities.

The skewing of activities in the economy towards the benefit of certain groups and elites who also relate to the corporations or in particular enable them to maintain their position with regard to the state and controlling it – mean that democracy is reduced.

The role of the state and the identity of the individual today are undergoing change. Are we individuals and citizens or are we employees, are we wives mothers, or are we people in our own right? The role of the trade union movement protects the workers but actually we are more than workers. There is a need to reconceptualising who we are and the nature of the human role in the economy- both as a contributor to it and as a beneficiary to whom provision for needs is also an important part. There are also discussions about the meaning of work and its boundaries, both informal and informal as a description for overall activities and contributions to society. This fits with feminist discourses and other questioning of how we account for such activity and the role of GNP and GDP and therefore the need for a " growth economy" as a central driver. There is thus a framework for questioning the issue of China's phenomenal economic growth and whether this fits with goals of "sustainable development" or " sustainable growth" concepts, when pollution is reaching unacceptable levels and inequality is increasing to levels which threaten stability overall.

The role and nature of work is also changing with temporary work and insecure contracts becoming a feature of the global economy- so that there is no longer job security which led the French to riot for example. The integration of the supply chain and increasingly international production – affects the environment and the workers.

The ultimate change is the change to commodification of goods and services and ecosytem services where we can argue that the citizens income also makes us into commodities- removed from family and social structure.

The ultimate commodification is that of the body in prostitution and trafficking of people in the revival of the classical slave trade.

Examples:

Trafficking a symbol of the logic of an economics predicated on economies of scale and commodification

Supply chain integration and international commoditisation is illustrated very well in the example of the trafficking of young potential African footballers. Described below by McDougall (2008)

Charities and NGOs across West Africa are now voicing their concern about the activities of illegal football academies. This new 'slave trade' is leaving a tragic legacy of homeless young footballing hopefuls across Europe. 'The motivation for these children joining these footballing schools and being trafficked out of the country is purely about money and that is not surprising as these families are incredibly poor. Quite often we find it's the parents who send their children to the West or take their children out of school and force them to concentrate on becoming footballers because they want the youngsters to earn more money for the family.'

Middlemen, haggle over the best players, signing some as young as seven on tightly binding pre-contracts - effectively buying them from their families - with the hope of making thousands of dollars selling the boys on to clubs in Europe. Many take the deeds on houses and even family jewellery in return for their services. This process of exploitation is raising alarm among West Africa-based NGOs including Save the Children and Caritas. Tony Baffoe, the former Ghana captain, now an ambassador for this year's African Nations Cup, admits that 'the trafficking of children to play football is a reality we must all face as they are exploited by illegal academies. 'Families should be questioning these coaches, not putting all their hopes and life savings into the relationship they have with them.'

Last year Sepp Blatter, president of Fifa, football's world governing body, accused Europe's richest clubs of 'despicable' behaviour and engaging in 'social and economic rape' as they scour the developing world for talent. But in many ways the problems for Africa begin at home. n diplomatic circles, passports for young players are regularly bought and sold. Marie-George Buffet, a former French Sports Minister, recently claimed that many French-run academies, both in France and in Africa, were corrupt and run by unlicensed agents who needed controlling.(McDougall 2008)

Trafficking of children and babies is now big business (Harrisson 2008) Babies are offered for sale by desperately poor parents who believe the children will get a better life in more developed countries. This globalisation and commodification of children as workers in industries from football, to the sex trade or as domestics is nothing new. However the scale is probably on a larger scale and in normative terms it is impossible to justify as the middle men are fully aware of the hardship they are imposing.330 children were trafficked to Britain in the last year, something we need to take responsibility for. Traffickers use transit cities to bring in the children illegally with false papers. This trade is a supply chain which reflects other supply chain structures. People are reduced to commodities to satisfy any market expressed preference. Adam Smith tended towards the view that the market would provide an environment where individual buying decisions would benefit the whole community. This trade shows that this logic is certainly imperfect or even has had its day and needs market correction through regulation or a complete new paradigm which includes community, human dignity and social cohesion and social justice and diversity at its core. This is the role of Green Economics. These externalities do matter and because much of this trade is illegal its social costs are not picked up by society.

In some senses it can be argued that a basic income does capture the social externalities and ensures that needs are met, rather than relying on the person receiving the costs to prove they require compensation. It could possibly be regarded as a more efficient social system therefore.

Basic income

German drugstore owner Goetz Werner's book Einkommen für Alle, ('Income for all') climbed to number 13 in the best sellers' list of Der Spiegel this year. You might think this an unlikely contribution to the Citizen's Income debate, but the idea of a Citizen's Income has re-emerged from the centre-right of European politics as a response to the social costs of unemployment.

According to Werner, people should be provided with a tax-financed basic income that would free people from the need to earn money, rather than trying to create jobs for the many Germans who are still unemployed, an idea that Green Party members have been proposing for the last thirty years – the Citizen's Income. As such the division of benefits is changing and the basic income is one debate currently extremely interesting as it is opening up the whole concept of our conceptualisation as a worker and as a family and towards the individual as a person with needs and responsibilities towards society and what society owes to the individual.

The principle feature of a basic or citizen's income is that it is paid irrespective of any income from other sources and it is paid without requiring the performance of any work or the willingness to accept a job if offered.

Society can fulfil its needs without full employment, Werner said, and it would be better off if it did.

"The work that we are compelled to do can also be done by machines and methods," he said. "Where we have a great potential is work that focuses on people: social work, cultural work."

Ridding people of the burden of work would allow them to devote time to things they actually want to do, whether volunteering at an old folks' home, pursuing dreams of an artistic career or spending more time with their families. And it would relieve millions of people from the stigma of not having a job.

In Werner's scenario, every man, woman and child would receive a monthly allowance that would cover the costs of living, plus a little bit more. The state would finance the new system through a high consumption tax that would replace all current taxes and could be gradually introduced over 20 to 30 years. The non-wage labor costs, such as social welfare and pension contributions, that add to the high cost of German jobs, would be a thing of the past as would the bureaucracies that administer them.

Werner's ideas are supported by Thomas Straubhaar, head of an influential think tank in Hamburg, who proposes that the system could be financed by a combination of high consumption tax, 25% for example, and direct taxes of the same level on income from work, rentals, investments, dividends and speculation.

In fact in Germany (Sinn 2006) There is simply no popular majority in favor of liberal reforms, because in the near term such reforms would create too many losers. Germany's extensive welfare system spends 31 percent of the country's GDP for entitlement programs operated by the government sector. No less than 41 percent of the voting-age adult population lives primarily on government transfers such as state pensions, full-scale public stipends, unemployment benefits, disability benefits, and social assistance. (In East Germany, the figure is 47 percent. (Sinn 2006) Among those adults who actually vote, recipients of public transfers form a clear majority. Indeed, the upper 10 percent of income recipients pay more than 50 percent of aggregate income tax revenue, and the upper 20 percent pays about 80 percent, while 40 percent of income recipients pay no income taxes whatsoever. Small wonder that a huge majority of the population -- and even a slight majority of CDU voters -- prefer a strengthening of the welfare state to a more market-oriented system.

In Finland, where the greens are in a coalition government, the Prime Minister Matti Vanhanen of the Centre Party has suggested that such a basic income could be pegged at about 600 Euros a month while in Ireland the government is producing a green paper on basic income. This current interest is being driven by a perceived need to reform social insurance systems. One aim is to reduce the cost of job creation by shifting the social contributions for health and other benefits away from taxes on employment onto taxes on other production factors such as capital and land. Eco-taxes could also be used to generate the required revenue for such a shift. A Citizen's Income creates new possibilities for how an economy could be run and could change its overall character. For example, at present low taxation on materials and high taxation on labour makes it cheaper to throw away a broken toaster than to get it fixed. If we removed the tax on labour – halving labour costs say, and increased the taxes on materials and energy, we might end up with an economy where it was cheaper to repair an item than throw it away and buy a new one. One of the additional key green benefits of an increase in the labour intensity of production processes would be a reduction in the need for ever increased growth in order to maintain employment levels. The Green Economics Institute (GEI), suggests a comprehensive reform of the tax system where revenues for a Citizen's Income could be raised by taxing economic or environmental bads much more heavily than at present. There is an increased focus on making an even more fundamental change to social security systems: basing them on human rights, rather than on 'paid contributions'. Its important not just to discuss Citizen's Income in general terms but had modelled the effects of changing the social security system on productivity, labour supply and the properties of such a system for people on low or no income within their own national systems.

A pan European tax system could reduce the destructive activity of corporations by preventing them from escaping taxation by cross border repatriation as is currently the case.

The true social and environmental costs could be met using eco taxes combined with a comprehensive citizens income

A radical green approach to taxation could both reduce bureaucracy and help save the environment. Robertson (1999). Prices could reflect true costs, rather than the artificially low value currently placed on non-renewable natural resources which completely ignore external costs – to the air, the water, the soil, to future generations, to workers' health, and these costs are 'externalized' and society picks them up as Pigou found.. Prices need to include real costs including especially the human costs.

Green taxes have developed from initially discouraging people from damaging the environment by making them pay for using natural resources, to evolving into a wider restructuring of taxation – Eco-tax reform – to providing for better economic performance, more jobs and greater economic justice within and between nations. They effectively could tax away undesirable social and environmental 'bads' instead of 'goods'. However in particular the taxation of the use of common resources is designed to correct the market failure that was identified by Garret Hardin. This can help to shift the balance between the use of human resources (now under-employed) and natural resources (now over-employed).

However, critics charge that green taxes are regressive because they hit poorer people relatively harder than richer. For example, if a tax on household energy raised the cost of heating, cooking and lighting, poor people would find it harder to pay and harder to invest in energy efficiency to reduce the higher rates. Especially if green taxes replaced taxes on incomes and profits – which many poorer people never had to pay in the first place. The Green Party of England and Wales wants to replace VAT with eco taxes. For economists, the function of green taxes is to 'internalize' present and future costs which are currently 'externalized'. Costs of company activities would in theory be met at source, instead of being allowed to impose them on other people, including other parts of the world and future generations. Ideally, green taxes should be set at rates that reflect these 'true' costs. However it is very difficult often to identify who or what or where a problem is arising from, for example with water pollution it is notoriously difficult to find and prove the source. As with Basic income , eco-tax reform helps to shift the balance from resource-intensive, environmentally-damaging production to people-centred activities.

An example quoted by Robertson (1999) is that of a global tax on each nation's chemical emissions would encourage the North to reduce the burden it now puts on the planet's capacity to absorb atmospheric pollution. A significant part of the revenue might be distributed to all nations on a per capita basis – as an international 'citizen's income' recognizing everyone's rightful share of common global resources. In that way, financial transfers now seen as aid would be transformed into 'rental' payments, received as of right by the peoples of the South from the high-consuming, high-polluting peoples of the North for the higher-than-average use we make of common global resources.

Conclusions

There is a renewed sense of urgency for finding tools, and methodological frameworks with which to meet these challenges. It is no longer enough to find perfect and scientific theories if they lead to human misery, and it is therefore important to investigate the effect of economics paradigms in real situations and if it is failing the needs of one fifth of people and endangering the future of three quarters of mammals and other species- it is time to reconstruct the basis of assumptions made.The Green Economics school aims to factor in the missing data from poverty, climate change and earth sciences at its core, and so is evolving to provide a philosophical and practical methodology. There are increasingly obvious links and interdependencies between social and environmental problems and their solutions.

In particular there is interest in social solutions and new ways of meeting social requirements within the economy, with new emphasis developing throughout Europe on such schemes as the Basic Income or in decoupling work and employment from benefits and pensions, and pensions from a person's position in a family and towards the economic rights and responsibilities of the individual in society. This is also related to the role of people as consumers of natural resources, in the current economy. The current socio- economic system requires and delivers over- consumption and wasteful consumption in order to keep it fuelled and strong enough to provide enough jobs to maintain it.

There is a pressing need now for all economics discourses and business planning to include social and environmental justice in all calculations and planning. It is clear that the evidence is that firms are not even beginning to do this and neither are governments. The result is increasing social and environmental injustice, and intense and cruel comodification of the most vulnerable people. Therefore a green economics predicated on social and environmental justice needs to be the next development in economics discourse.

References
Barnett U.(2006) The Greening of South Africa is central to its healing.International Journal of Green Economics. Volume I issue 1/ 2 Inderscience.
Brady B (2008) Only three sustainable homes built in the Uk this year. Independent 27.01.2008
Barker (2007) The IUCN Red List Report
Davies TH. Lean G. and Mesure S.,(2008) Big Business says address climate

change " rates very low on agenda". Independent 27th January 2008.
Dyer C.(2008)Independent Committee under fire for white male
appointments.First 10 High Court Judges under new diversity rules. Sunday
January 6, 2008 The Observer http://football.gw Biodiversity Rules. The
Guardian. 28.01.2008 . Fawcett's new research reveals women and debt
paradox (29/08/07)http://www.fawcettsociety.org.uk/index.asp?
PageID=513
Women and Debt Fawcett society august 2007 report
http://www.fawcettsociety.org.uk/documents/Women%20and
%20debt(1).pdf
Harrison D. (2008) Children for sale, The new slave trade to Britain.
Trafficking of children and babies. The Sunday Telegraph. 26.01.2008
Firth M. ,(2006) UN Report women denied representation : making the war
on poverty hard to win, Independent,. 8th March p.2.
Holmes A.,(2008) Commoditisation, the strategic response. Gower. Kennet
M.,(2007)Income for all, The Basic Income Scheme, Greenworld No. 58
http://www.greenworld.org.uk/page55/page57/page57.html accessed
27.01.2008
McDougall D., (2008) The Scandal of Africa's trafficked players. Sunday
January 6, 2008 The Observer http://football.gw Biodiversity Rules. The
Guardian. 28.01.2008 .
uardian.co.uk/News Story/0,,2234283,00.html accessed
27.01.2008uardian.co.uk/News Story/0,,2234283,00.html accessed
27.01.2008
Robertson J. (1999) A green benefits and tax system in Scot Cato and
Kennet Green Economics

Sinn H. -W.,(2006) 3.09.2006Merkel's reforms drift toward dead end
accessed web Jan 27th 2008
The Japan Times On line

Stern N (2006)Stern Review on the Economics of climate change .HM
Treasury, Cambridge University.30 October.

Sullivan C. (2005) Do investment and policy interventions reach the poor?
Centre for Ecology and Hydrology. Wallingford UK Cortina-13. Tex.209.
2005. 11.2 p.221

Photo Miriam Kennet:Fly in a flower

Green Economics enables us to practise sustainable economics for all people everywhere, nature, other species the planet, and its systems and to create an abundance of resources for each other and for future generations.

Chapter 9: Green Economics, Young People and Education

9.1 Green Economics Pedagogy

Miriam Kennet and edited by Professor Jack Reardon

Green economics is fast emerging as *the* economics story. And the one story of hope and optimism on an otherwise rather bleak economics landscape. The first shoots of this wave was around the time of The European Business Summit in February 2008 when it told industry leaders, including leaders of Shell and Lufthansa, that the only hope for the European economy was to go green. In October 2008, green economics made the front cover of *Newsweek*. In the UK, government officials were told that mainstream economics is so fragile that it should be considered radical – and that the only way forward from now on was to use green economics, the only robust methodology. Ban Ki-moon, leader of the United Nations, declared "*we are in an age of global transformation – an age of green economics*" (Dickey and McNicoll 2008).

More and more people began to realise that human kind is at a crossroads: we can either save or destroy ourselves and the planet. Either way, the choice is ours. Unfortunately, economics has long been out of balance with the environment, and the hegemony of orthodox economics remains a formidable stumbling block: the two are on a collision course (Anderson 1999). If disaster is to be avoided, they have to become mutually compatible – the voice of the earth has to be heard. Voice comes through diversity, but at present we only have, thanks again to the hegemony of orthodoxy, "monocultures of the mind" which alienate people by precluding other voices from being heard, in turn depleting the strength of the whole. Green economics, on the other hand, has a strong subjective element and is more concerned with life narratives and outcomes than theoretical prescriptions, monoculture or grand narratives. It respects and empowers diversity and other voices. Green economics combines earth voices, green issues, and a practical, real approach characterized by fairness and respect for the environment; it is economics with access for all.

Green economics is by its nature multi-, inter-, and trans-disciplinary: It builds on ideas of ecologism, conservation, socialism, feminism, political economy, civil society and counter hegemony, as well as all aspects and limits of natural science. These areas are indivisible – not one of them can be simply a social or positivist science. They are an indivisible unit, which must now be explored in a holistic manner. (Kennet and Heinemann 2006a: 3)

This chapter recalls some of the first attempts to discuss the challenges of teaching green economics. Green economics is interactive – it is economics by doing. The *means* are as important as the *ends* and the ends are as important as the means, so, for example, achieving an equitable distribution of resources without including
women or minorities in the decision-making process contravenes the modus operandi of green economics, which includes diversity of methodology and of practitioners within its core. Green economics does not impose one system on the world; we work and create the spaces to allow diversity to flourish.

This chapter will first discuss the core concepts and principles of green economics. The principles of green economics, including the all-important dictum that the means are inseparable from the ends, provides a recipe for teaching: trans-disciplinary, providing access for all. Teaching pluralistically is intrinsic to green economics and completely intertwined with its main principles.

The core principles of green economics
The core challenge for green economics is that rather than imposing a grand narrative we must ensure economic systems meet minimum requirements for social and environmental justice while also incorporating local needs. Unlike traditional economics, which filters out awkward elements as externalities, green economics recognizes the ultimate interdependence of economic justice and the environment.

Three main objectives of green economics are:
1. To create economic conditions where social and environmental justice thrives, benefiting all people everywhere, along with non-human species, nature and the planet;

2. To re-examine new and broader versions of reality, beyond the vested interests, to listen to different voices. Green economics jettisons ceteris paribus as a limitation of scope and rejects "rational economic man" as a benchmark; instead listening and incorporating the voices of all;

3. To establish new thinking in order to provide the means for all people everywhere to participate in the economy with equal power, equal rights, and equal access to decision making. Green economics provides "out of the box" thinking while combining trans- and inter-disciplinary studies to counteract the myopic thinking of orthodoxy. "The world needs a new economics more than it needs a new anything else" (Anderson 1999: 6). Green economics requires that economic models reflect the complexity of the real world; it does not tolerate simplistic economics, which factors out the facts.

The key to uniting the three objectives is factoring nature back into economic theory. Just when people assumed they had completely tamed nature, climate change has forced rethinking of our position in the universe and our role as stewards of the earth. Rather than use science to control nature, we need to use our knowledge to live within nature and respect it. Green economics argues that nature has its own intrinsic value, which it extends to animals (Singer 1985).

Green economics extends this to all life forms. Arne Naess (1973) argued for the preservation of the biosphere, geological and biological systems, and all life forms for their own sake, not only for human benefit. Green economics is highly critical of anthropocentric ethics and the "shallow anthropocentric technocratic environmental movement," concerned primarily with pollution, resource depletion, and the health and affluence of people in developed countries (Sessions 1995: xii).

Since its inception, orthodoxy has assumed nature as an expendable and plentiful given resource, while only valuing scarce resources. It is, however, palpable that nature and the economy are mutually dependent, with the former becoming more fragile and scarce. Georgescu-Roegen (1966) highlighted the continuous mutual influence between economic processes and the natural world, long ignored by orthodoxy. In addition, White (1967) criticized Western attitudes to nature and attributed them to the influence of Christianity on the development of technology and assumption of human mastery through the taming of the natural world. He argued that Christianity has desacralized nature, encouraged its exploitation, and promoted a world view in which humans are superior to the rest of nature.

In order to address these topics and revisions, new and critical ways of thinking are needed that include questioning the scope and meanings of economics, facts, evidence, and reality in positivist economics, as well as so-called "rational and reasonable choices." Green economics welcomes the insights from sister social sciences (Kennet and Heinemann 2006b) as well as Eastern spiritual traditions of questioning the assumed virtues of competition rather than cooperation, and exploitation rather than engagement.

Wall (2005) argues that reciprocity arose from sharing of meat and is strongest in capuchin monkeys, chimpanzees, and people. Confucius asked if there was a single word to sum one's life, responded, "reciprocity: don't do to others what you would not want yourself" (Wall 2005). Aristotle argued that reciprocity may not be adequate to account for corrective and distributive justice; thus we need to introduce an exchange bond and exchange justice which provides and governs reciprocity (Meikle 1995: 10). Thus, in reconceptualizing "value," we need further to consider how each individual decision based on value would be assessed in the light of absolute boundaries to consumption that might be imposed by ecological restrictions to human activity.

Despite and probably because of the popularity of green economics, our message has been usurped and distorted for myriads of reasons. Sometimes, what passes for green is more greenwashing – passed off as green but without merit, existing for the most popposite of purposes. It is easier to comprehend the confusing array of policy outcomes when they are viewed as a continuum. Central is the ambivalent relationship between green economics and the multi-faceted and multi-layered term "sustainable development," defined by Brundtland (1987) as meeting "the needs of the present without sacrificing the ability of the future to meet its standards." The approach argues for a more enlightened globalization to reach these standards and to resolve environmental degradation. Sustainable development has been eagerly adopted by such groups as the World Business Council of Sustainable Development and it nicely comports with Corporate Social Responsibility and stakeholder theory. Acknowledging that many nation states are weaker than global corporations, sustainable development argues for the corporation to be the agent of change. In contrast, many green economists regard corporations as agents of hegemony; and as undemocratic, unelected, lacking in transparency, and the fundamental cause of the problem. Green economics seriously questions how it can be in a corporation's short-term interest to implement equity and environmental justice through the managerial "environmentalist" approach of sustainable development. Dobson (2000) and Springett and Foster (2005) criticize short-term techno fixes which on the one hand remain within the confines of traditional economics and, on the other, hijack environmentalism and the language of "sustainability" (Welford and Gouldson 1993).

Sustainable development is regarded by green economists as an oxymoron, often in reality counteracting existing community economic patterns. Greens instead seek to reverse the trends of neo-colonialism
and corporate destruction of local assets, replacing them with new subsistence, local self-determination and community control (Norberge-Hodge 1991; Mies and Shiva 1993). In addition, gigantism, monopoly, and oligopoly contravene green economics arguments for "small, appropriate and diverse production" developed by Schumacher (1976),. Nevertheless, given the inexorable complexity of the environmental crisis, there is a growing realization within the business world that business as usual is no longer a choice An ongoing task among green economists is to analyze the growing,

231

complex, and multi-faceted role of the corporation (Reardon 2007b). Needless to say, the nineteenth-century orthodox firm, assumed to maximize profits and externalize any environmental concerns, must be replaced by a more complex and realistic model.

Even within the Green Economy literature there are competing narratives. A green economy policy (United Nations)for example focuses on the three Fs: fuel, food, and the financial crisis. Just as Roosevelt's New Deal set the stage for the biggest economic growth the world has seen, Stern argues that this will get us out of our current predicament with more and accelerated growth in the coming 50 years to pay for environmental improvements. Green economics argues today for more radical vision of the economy, confined more by the limits growth, and more interested in moving to the next stage of human evolution. Rather than worrying about fuel it is concerned to reconceptualise planning and transport concepts and public amenities to make them fit for purpose in the 21st century. Rather than jump-start consumption to aid an ailing economy, however, green economics seeks conversion to greener technologies to enable greener lifestyles so we can live within our means and that of the planet. Accelerating this transition is at the core of the green economy initiative and is the best bet for global sustainable wealth and employment generation for the world's 1.3 billion poor.

A formidable barrier to this transition is the myopic vision of traditional economics, which has been instrumental in the commodification of nature and perpetuation of poverty. Central to green economics is the incorporation of knowledge from other disciplines, particularly the sciences, which helps to circumscribe the forms and extent of economic activity within realistic environmental parameters.

Postmodern ideas are absent from traditional economics and from a green perspective this misses important developments in human thought. In particular, the prevalence of the Western-dominated, white, middle-class, "homo economicus" ignores the experience of most of the world's people. Derrida (1978) rejects single narratives and investigates whether reality is fact, truth, myth, interpretation, or one person's view of events. Derrida analyzes binary oppositions and dualisms such as West and East, feminine and masculine, light and dark, civilized and primitive, them and us, to criticize the power structures in which they are embedded.

Green economics and pedagogy
I tend to think of green economics as a slippery eel – if you catch it and think you have understood its imperatives, something else arises and you need to conceptualize more deeply or in another dimension in order to capture its meaning. Green economics continues to evolve, provoke, and question. So how to teach
this evolving slippery eel? Perhaps it is best to reflect on what it is trying to achieve, which is interaction, responsibility, and accessibility. This suggests that its classroom and lecture hall are very different places from the usual

conventional lecture as solution provider. Green economics looks for a new mode of working and empowerment as well as a two-way process.

The ambitious aims of green economics to start a new discipline and to change the paradigm of economics to one which creates social and environmental equity means taking the practice of economics beyond the classroom, i.e. making it economics by doing. This means more instruction on site, which differentiates green economics from its sister social sciences. Green economics is holistic, pluralist, and progressive; thus its pedagogy has to reflect its nature. This is one discipline which cannot be amended to the usual macro/micro stuff with a small portion of the lesson looking at the costs of energy. Green economics is different and its foundational concepts are different and this must be reflected in the entire approach of teachers, trainers, and lecturers. A rewarding aspect of green economics is that because it supports diversity and means/ends approaches, it is not country specific. Thus, teaching green economics has to appeal to all kinds of cultures.

Should we equip a new generation of students to learn only the reformed version of greener economics or should we teach our students enough about the mainstream to enable them to cogently critique it? I feel it is important to map previous developments in economics, especially those concerned with nature and social equity, and to provide students with enough knowledge to enable them to understand and respect differences between schools of thought and their modus operandi. This is especially necessary in order to provide students with the tools to begin investigation of newly evolving issue for themselves. Green economics is equally relevant to the very young and the very old, so the Green Economics Institute has been experimenting with teaching the very young and very old together, as the enforced separation of one group has been a disabling factor, similar to segregating different racial groups or disabled and not disabled groups.

In conclusion, based on the discussion of the core principles of green economics, the following are central elements in the pedagogy of green economics:

1. Incorporate scientific evidence on the environment and how it adapts and changes. This can easily be incorporated into the circular flow diagram usually given on opening day (Reardon 2007a). Throughout the course, additional scientific data can be incorporated, particularly regarding interest rates, externalities, economies of scale, public goods, and the role of government. This will teach students that no one discipline has a unique solution to global problems, and the necessity for pluralist, integrated thinking.

2. Continuously discuss the value-laden concepts of economics, such as freedom, the market, externalities, etc. Is, for example, reliance on the continuous, competitive pressure of the market to force people to behave in a

certain way antithetical to the classical economists' demand for more freedom from an obtrusive state? Whether markets enable or disengage and whether markets are congruent with the environmental demands is fundamental to green economics.

3. Understand the historical evolution of economics, particularly the visions of classical economics and how they sharply differ from traditional economics, which jettisoned political and social concerns in favor of an ostensibly neutral, scientific and value-free economics (Dowd 2004). I place economic theories and concepts in their intellectual and historical background, discussing all available information about the economists – their backgrounds, their looks and hairstyles, etc. This provides a vivid, lively, personal account, previously discouraged as hearsay, but which nevertheless elucidates how and why a theory/concept was developed.

4. Emphasize students as the greatest ambassadors for our ideas. As teachers, we should regard each learning experience as a moment in the learning chain which extends into the past and hopefully well into the future, to be handed down like the verbal stories of the ancient world.

5. Teachers must engage in outreach – speaking/lecturing in nonacademic settings – as well as in in-reach – inviting others to participate in class. If you are passionate about your subject (especially given a rapidly dwindling window of opportunity), in addition to lecturing to traditional students it is incumbent to lecture and teach to potential students, idea makers, policy-makers, and activists. My most successful courses are those where former students continue their presence in my life, where former student and teacher continuously learn from each other. Teaching green economics breaks past assumptions and conceptions of the world. The next generation is witnessing real climate change, species extinction, and festering poverty and inequality. We can no longer assume all problems will be solved by technology and economic growth; but we need a more realistic assessment of human capabilities and the mutual dependency between humans and the environment. And we can no longer assume that the teacher has all the answers; any solutions will be forged in a continuous and ongoing dialogue. 6 We must listen to other voices, from the South, from special needs, voices of older people, younger people, voices of women, and the economically disenfranchised, and engage with them in both outreach and inreach. We need to provision in a more precarious world. We as teachers have to pave (rather than lead) the way forward.

Conclusion

These ideas describe the learning landscape possible within the new paradigm of green economics. These ideas set the scene for the development of a new way of doing economics. While the roots of green economics are extremely eclectic and diverse, its scope is truly global, its methods innovative and its context long term and holistic. It aims to re establish true "planetary equilibrium" between individuals, peoples, communities, nations, genders, and nonhuman species and the planet. As civilization enters a new phase, the need for innovation in economics education and the requirement for innovative and engaging teaching is paramount.

References

Anderson, V. (1999) "Can There Be a Sensible Economics?," in S. Cato and M. Kennet (eds) *Green Economics – Beyond Supply and Demand to Meeting People's Needs*. Aberystwyth, UK: Green Audit Press.

Brundtland, G.H. (1987) *Our Common Future: World Commission on Environment and Development*. Online: http://www.un-documents.net/wced-ocf.htm.

Derrida, J. (1978) *Writing and Difference*. Chicago: University of Chicago Press.

Dickey, C and McNicoll, T. (2008) "The Green Rescue," *Newsweek*, 3 November, www.newsweek.com.

Dobson, A. (2000) *Green Political Thought*. Abingdon, UK: Routledge.

Dowd, Douglas (2004) *Capitalism and Its Economics – A Critical History*. London: Pluto Press.

Georgescu-Roegen, N. (1966) "The Entropy Law and the Economic Problem," in H.E. Daly and K. Townsend (eds) *Valuing the Earth: Economics, Ecology, Ethics*. Cambridge, Mass.: MIT Press.

Goldsmith, E. (2005) *Rewriting Economics*, www. greeneconomics.org.uk (accessed 17 January, 2006).

Kennet, M. and Heinemann, V. (2006a) "Foreword," *International Journal of Green Economics* 1: 1–10.

—— (2006b) "Green Economics: Setting the Scene," *International Journal of Green Economics* 1: 68–102. Indersciece

Meikle, Scott (1995) *Aristotle's Economic Thought*. New York: Oxford University Press.

Mies, M. and Shiva, V. (1993) *Ecofeminism*. London: Zed Books.

Naess, A. (1973) "The Shallow and the Deep, Long-Range Ecology Movement," *Inquiry*, 16: 95–100.

Norberge-Hodge, H. (1991) *Ancient Futures Learning from Ladakh*. San Francisco: Sierra Club Books.

Reardon, J. (2007a) "How Green Are Principles Texts? An Investigation Into How Mainstream

Economics Educates Students Pertaining to Energy, the Environment and Green

Economics," *International Journal of Green Economics* 1: 381–393.

—— (2007b) "Comments on Green Economics Setting the Scene," *International Journal of Green Economics* 1: 532–538.

Sessions, G. (1995) *Deep Ecology for the 21st Century*. Boston: Shambhala.

Schumacher, E.F., (1976) *Small is Beautiful*. London: Sphere
Singer, Peter (1985) *The Animal Liberation Movement: Its Philosophy, Achievements, and Its Future*. Abingdon, UK: Routledge.

Springett, D. and Foster, B. (2005) "Whom Is Sustainable Development for? Deliberative Democracy and the Role of Unions," *Sustainable Development* 13: 271–281.

Welford, R. and Gouldson, A. (1993) *Environmental Management and Business Strategy*. London: Pitman.
White, L. (1967) "The Historical Roots of our Ecological Crisis," *Science* 155: 1203–1207.

9.2 Green Economics for the Young People

Miriam Kennet

This article appeared in Eco Sprinter the magazine of the European Young Greens in Spring 2009

Our challenge to main stream economic orthodoxy is gaining ground globally, in the corridors of power for solving today's and tomorrow's pressing problems such as climate change, financial downturns, poverty and biodiversity losses.

It is about reclaiming the practices and policies of economics, for all people everywhere, nature, other species, the planet and its systems, provisioning for the needs, impacts, effects and responsibilities, for everyone and everything on the planet.

Mainstream economics argues that "Trade offs" or conflicts of interest, occur between Ecology and the Economy, and hides behind economics as an excuse for inaction. Green Economics reminds us that Economics only exists as part of Ecology and factors this forgotten Factor "Reality", back into the centre of economics. The root of "Eco- nomics" is the word "Oikia" or house, exactly the same as " Eco-logy". However the two have become so separated, so opposite, that economics now excludes the household, caring and home work from GDP.

Mainstream economics has come to refer to profit, growth and price, as expressed by the buying preferences of *"homo economicus, "* rational economic man. It claims to represent therefore less than half of humanity, that is those with the power to be able to make consumption choices. Green Economics is heavily influenced by feminist theory, which urges us to listen and to be inclusive, diverse and to act for other voices, all voices, the voices of the quiet, older people, younger people, people with disabilities, minorities,the colonised and all the voices of the weak or powerless, to enable them to flourish and have their say. Many of the worlds poor are women, many women are poor and many farmers are women!

One fifth of humanity, 1.3 billion people, live in life threatening poverty and a further 900 million starve as a result of land competition between food for the poor, and land use for company profits from bio- fuels. Mainstream Economics uses quantitative price and growth in GDP considerations rather than equity, and chooses adaptation and mitigation of effects, instead of prevention of global environmental change, and a sustainable economic path for the future. It discounts future generations, who it selfishly   assumes need fewer resources than we do!

Many green economists are also scientists, physicists, ecologists or archaeologists, and they take a longer term view, more informed by physical realities than simply short term company balance sheets or political cycles. They know that a 5 degree rise in the climate is extremely dangerous and that agriculture, as we know it, won't survive under such conditions.

Green Economists, knowing that there is no economy without the planet, and so ensure their solutions work within the resources on offer from nature. They also seek solutions for all people everywhere, the planet and its systems to benefit from economics transactions. Mainstream economics discards them as throwaway inputs for a temporary product or service, and ignores long term costs and impacts from disposal or use (Externalities).

We are living the world's sixth ever Mass Extinction of species, with ¼ of all mammals on the seriously endangered list for example. The incredible costs of rapid biodiversity loss are estimated initially at over 7 times as much as catastrophic climate change. In China – expensive hand pollination of crops is necessary, as the honey bees are threatened. Main stream economics calculates that human capital and natural capital are "substitutes" and can be interchanged whenever we like! Greens argue that we have to live within the boundaries of nature and the planet, rather than thinking we can steward it, manage it, or rip off all its treasures.

Most main stream economics is concerned with "use value" – market values of goods and services and commodification and markets for clean air, water and also trees. But there is value in a tree for itself. Intrinsic value, and we need the trees, to go about their tree business, unhindered, for lots of reasons...e.g. as a habitat for other species, for oxygen and as a soil fixer, and water absorber.

In 2008, the world woke up to the benefits of Green Economics, and we launched the Greening the Economy Initiative with UNEP. The European Business Summit and even Obama, Sarkozy, Ban Ki Moon, the ILO and others are using Greening the Economy, Green Economics and green jobs to kick start the economy.

Old gas guzzling car companies no longer make sense, and desperately seek support financing as their businesses become more obsolete, too long ignoring the needs of most people on earth in favour of homo economicus. Even Ford Motor's, "Fordism,"was the bedrock of main stream 20th century industry and economics and based on wasteful mainstream economics policies of high mass consumption, commodification and outsourcing which wrecked the planet and particularly the climate and squandered resources. Newer more efficient smaller vehicles and public transport will replace them.

In the Congo, fighting over supply chain inputs, for larger companies, for western luxury goods such as mobile phones, requires that we reflect on our own role in this- as every single one of us, participates in this mainstream folly.

We must share our resources, manage them well, and recognise the consequences of our own actions.
Green Economics enables us to practise sustainable economics for all people everywhere, nature, other species the planet, and its systems and to create an abundance of resources for each other and for future generations.

9.3. Youth's Struggle for Change

Eleni Courea

Introduction

In one of J. M. Barrie's lesser known plays, Ernest Crichton announces teasingly: "I am not young enough to know everything." And perhaps youth does know everything – or else it likes to think so. In a different context, George Bernard Shaw declares: "Youth is a wonderful thing. What a crime to waste it on children."

Indeed, the power of young people is often forgotten. Our unfaltering confidence in our opinions is dismissed as arrogance. We are deemed temperamental, inexperienced and ignorant until we reach our thirties, at least. It is important, therefore, to realise not only what green economics can do for young people, but what young people can do for green economics.

As always, the world is plagued with problems. The international economy is flailing under the Great Recession—considered by many to be the worst financial crisis since the Wall Street Crash—which led to the crises in Portugal, Ireland, Greece and Spain. In the Middle East, we have witnessed the uprising of thousands of people against the oppressive dictatorial regimes which have governed the nations of Egypt, Tunisia, Libya, Yemen and Syria (among others) for decades. With these affairs in mind, many do not seem to realise the role young people have played, and how we are affected more than anyone else.

Financial Crisis

Within the last 60 years, the proportion of 16-to-19-year-olds with regular jobs remained consistent at around 40%. This figure even rose to a relatively high 45% in the year 2000. As a result, almost 7.3 million teenagers were employed, full- or part-time.

But at the turn of the 21st century, something changed. The number of teenagers employed began dropping dramatically, with young people being expelled from the workforce. And although from 2000 to early 2008 overall employment rose by about 10 million jobs, teen employment dropped by more than 1.5 million. In this day and age, the job market is difficult for everyone, but the youngest workers are by far the hardest-hit. Half the young people aged 16 to 24 now seeking a job cannot find one. "The numbers are incredible," according to Andrew Sum, a US expert on teen employment,

"Proportionally, more kids have lost jobs in the last few years that the entire country lost in the Great Depression." Even darker is the revelation that, in the United States, there has been a sharp rise in youth suicide as a result of the recession.

Arab Spring

In this bleak financial situation, is it any wonder that the public—and especially youth—is discontented with the government? In the Middle East, financial hardship in combination with oppressive dictatorships set off the large-scale and ongoing revolution. It's no coincidence that the revolution was initiated by countries with little oil revenue (Egypt, Tunisia) and was most successful there, when compared with the struggle in oil-rich countries. In Libya, for example, Gaddafi can afford to bribe supporters and pay troops with money from his sources of "black gold".

What is surprising about the uprising is that it all began from one of the smallest Arab countries, Tunisia. Even more incredible is how—in essence— the entire uprising was sparked by one young man, a 26-year-old street vendor named Mohamed Bouazizi, who set himself on fire in protest of police corruption and ill-treatment. This set off multiple demonstrations which evolved into the Tunisian Revolution, and consequently the Arab Spring.

With the expulsion of President Ben Ali from Tunisia and President Mubarak from Egypt came the spread of the revolution throughout the Middle East. It is common knowledge that none of this would have been made possible without the internet and the emergence of modern-day social networks. It is wrong, however, to cite such websites as the reason why the revolution has spread—a gun does not fire a bullet of its own accord. It is young people in the Middle East who took the initiative and used Facebook, Twitter and Youtube as their medium to spread the fight for liberty and justice to neighbouring countries.

It is now undoubtable that youth played the key role in the Arab Spring. From 26-year-old Mohamed Bouazizi, the first man to turn against the authorities, to the rapidly growing and disproportionately large population of young people (the "youth bulge") in the Arab world, it is the youngsters who are at the frontline of the fight for democracy.

Where Green Economics Comes In

Clearly, however cliched the phrase has become, young people are the future. We are hungry for change and we are the ones full of energy and determination to create a better world for ourselves and future generations to live in. What we need is a medium to help us make these changes, something beyond the biases of politics and the media. This is where Green Economics comes in. It can be used to tackle issues which conventional economics has so far failed to address. It could even find a solution to the major woes of the sovereign debt crisis, the depleting sources of fossil fuels, the rise of nuclear energy. It brings in a fresh perspective, seemingly providing us with a view of our planet through brand new eyes.

Likewise, Green Economics itself needs someone to advocate it, someone to use the means it provides us with to build a better future. Within the very first years of a new millennium, conventional economics has failed us. We can see with our own eyes the corruption and poverty which is widespread throughout the third world, crippling the entire continents of Africa, Asia and South America, and threatening to spread to formerly prosperous countries such as Greece. The injustice is clear, with a gaping development gap which is only growing wider, with dictators in some countries basking in their riches while their own people are scavenging for food. Huge expanses of rainforests continue to be cleared incessantly; oil and toxic waste is constantly spewed into our oceans, polluting our water, the very essence of life. The time has come for green economics to make a stand: and young people are the ones who can initiate it.

Conclusion

Our generation was first defined by a more peaceful revolution: *Generation Z*, hit by a technological revolution which brought us modern touch-screen mobile phones, laptops and all sorts of gadgets, the newest of which all revolve around Internet access and Social Networking. This recent wave of young people has been heavily criticised for being fixated with technology, for doing nothing but sit at home in front of a wide-screen TV, for spending hour after hour surfing the net, for never going out to change the world. But we have become the first to achieve a revolutionary change without leaving the house.

Thus today's youth will be able to take pride in its actions and tell it's children: "When I was your age, I found a job during the recession because of my knowledge with computers." "When I was your age, I created my own website from scratch and ended up earning thousands." "When I was your age, we used the internet to start a revolution."

References
The Admirable Crichton – J.M. Barrie
http://books.google.co.uk/books?
lr=&ei=5eYnTqnMG4PoUOC_gJkN&client=firefox-
a&cd=1&as_brr=0&as_drrb_is=b&as_minm_is=0&as_miny_is=1800&as

maxm_is=0&as_maxy_is=1920&id=ulpJAAAAMAAJ&dq=
%22not+young+enough+to+know+everything
The Arab Spring
http://www.guardian.co.uk/world/interactive/2011/mar/22/middle-east-
protest-interactive-timeline
http://www.usip.org/publications/youth-and-the-arab-spring
http://www.lemonde.fr/cgi-bin/ACHATS/acheter.cgi?
offre=ARCHIVES&type_item=ART_ARCH_30J&objet_id=1151265&clef=A
RC-TRK-D_01

The Arab Spring and Social Networks
http://www.miller-mccune.com/politics/the-cascading-effects-of-the-arab-
spring-28575/
http://www.newsweek.com/2011/01/27/inside-egypt-s-facebook-
revolt.html
http://www.fastcompany.com/1720692/egypt-protests-mubarak-twitter-
youtube-facebook-twitpic

Generation Z
http://www.smh.com.au/news/parenting/children-of-the-tech-
revolution/2008/07/15/1215887601694.html

George Bernard Shaw Quote
http://www.quotationspage.com/quote/30143.html
http://quotationsbook.com/quote/45094/
http://www.1-famous-quotes.com/quote/7528

Great Recession
http://www.guardian.co.uk/business/2009/jan/26/road-ruin-recession-
individuals-economy
http://www.mcclatchydc.com/2009/01/27/60822/congressional-budget-
office-compares.html

Mohamed Bouazizi
http://www.nytimes.com/2011/01/23/weekinreview/23worth.html?
_r=1&src=twrhp

Young People in Great Recession
http://www.time.com/time/magazine/article/0,9171,1952331,00.html
http://www.frumforum.com/how-will-great-recession-shape-youth
http://www.huliq.com/10282/recession-wake-finds-more-youth-suicide-
and-others-putting-life-hold

Photo Miriam Kennet 2010. The Economics of Biodiversity: Green Week in Brussels 2010: Our team of women economists

Photos: The Economics of Climate Change: Some of the Green Economics Institute Delegation Team members Michele Gale D'Oliveira and Katie Black inside the COP16 Kyoto Climate Change Conference in Cancun. Just prior to the agreement in December 2010

Chapter 10: Green Jobs and green careers and Green IT
10.1 Beyond Green Jobs

Enrico Tezza

Introduction

The debate on Green Jobs seems polarized between two extremes: Efficient Growth and Social Justice. In the Efficient Growth scenario, human and natural resource are seeing as means rather than end while the managerial approach is prevailing. On the contrary, the Social Justice scenario highlights the key role of a partnership approach to development, opposite to free market imperative, whereas nature and people are ends in themselves: intrinsic value rather than instrumental goal to material accumulation and financial profit.

The 2011 ILO Director General report on Social Justice provides evidence in favour with Just transition and a new development paradigm based on a decent work for all.

A just transition can not be confined to the greening of economies. A just transition is needed both for those affected by the shift to a green economy and for those facing poverty. When the equation green jobs = decent jobs is stated, then the managerial vision of growth is prevailing to stress efficiency without reducing inequality. I shall explain steps towards a statistical definition of green jobs, and then highlight an alternative link between jobs and development, one that identifies a "sufficiency economy" as the development framework in which "good jobs" (green + decent) replace green jobs, inspiring a social and ecological transition. In the words of the ILO DG, "good jobs" should be the key objective of International institutions to meet the societies' needs.

A statistical definition of green jobs

Different disciplines have looked at green jobs, including "pollution economics" (Roberts, 1995), "environmental economics" (Daly, 1997) and "ecological economics" (Livingstone, 1998). However, only "green economics" has brought together the two dimensions of green jobs (environmental degradation and poverty). Green economics scholars, recalling the "good life" theory, deny the equation consumption = identity, and decry the concept of sustainable development as a "managerialist" construct that supports a free-market ideology. Green economics questions the conventional assumption that the route to more employment and public contentment is via the acceptance of globalisation and restructuring in the name of international competitiveness. The concept of green jobs reflects this tension between a managerialist approach to development (see Limit to Growth, Meadows 1972, 1987, 1992, 2004) and an ethical discourse on "good development". The ILO definition of green jobs follows previous attempts to produce a   new concept, such those describing jobs protecting the environment (UN World Commission on Environment and Development, 1983) green-collar jobs (During, 1999) and green jobs (Pinderhughes, 2004). From 2007 to 2009, the ILO and UNEP defined green jobs as jobs that reduce   negative   environmental   impacts,   ultimately   leading   to environmentally, economically and socially sustainable enterprises and economies. In practical terms, green jobs contribute to less consumption of energy and raw materials, fewer greenhouse gas emissions, minimisation of waste and pollution, and protection of ecosystems. This emblem of a more sustainable society does not correspond to the real world, even though its intent seems practical. To find a useful operational definition, a statistical one has been sought, going back to the European Commission definition of "eco jobs" (European Commission, Eurostat, 1999). "Eco jobs" are jobs in "eco industries": activities which produce goods and services that measure, prevent, limit or minimise environmental damage to water, air and soil, or deal with problems related to waste, noise and ecosystems (Eurostat, 1999). In 1999, eco industries earned around 200 billion euros, split between pollution management and cleaner technology (127 billion) and resource management (70 billion). Eco industries provided over 2 million jobs (1.5 million jobs fighting pollution and 650,000 in resource management). In 2002, Canada's Institute of Statistics defined the environmental industry in the same way, adding a definition of environmental goods and services (goods and services that are used to measure, prevent or limit environmental damage to water, air and soil) and a definition of environmental employment as jobs in at least one of the following sectors: environmental protection; conservation and preservation of natural resources; or environmental sustainability, concerning education, policy or legislation (Statistics Canada, 2002). The American Engineering Association specified green jobs as work in a renewable or energy-efficient industry, including "indirect jobs" such as accountancy, computer analysis or truck driving. In 2010, the US Department of Commerce distinguished the green economy (the clean and energy-efficient economy) from green products and services (energy conservation and pollution). In the face of so many interpretations of green jobs, the Bureau of Labour Statistics clarified the classification and its coverage by adding a long list of criteria. Nuclear power and hydrogen are excluded; carbon capture and sequestration are included; equipment manufacture for transport is included; the entire production chain of green goods is excluded. As a result, green jobs, in the US financial year 2011 are *"either jobs in business that produce goods or provide services that benefit the environment or conserve natural resources (output approach), or jobs in which workers' duties involve making their establishment's production process more environmentally friendly or use fewer natural resources*

247

(process approach). Groups of green goods and green services, as well as groups of technologies or practices used by workers, are added. Apart from methodological debate among statisticians and measurement bias (respondent bias, green firm and not green jobs survey, self-employment not measured, reliability of information about green connotations, etc.), what is relevant here is the "constitutive nature" of green jobs and their difference from decent jobs, defined by the ILO in terms of working time, work intensity, employment contract, occupational safety and health, social security, contingency (unemployment benefits, sickness, maternity, pension), rights at work (minimum wage, child labour) and discrimination at work. If green jobs are needed to sustain the current development model based on deregulation, privatisation and structural adjustment, then the "business as usual" principle is followed and green jobs will expand green vulnerability.

What development approach is required for decent green jobs? Sustainable development? Perhaps so, but the word "sustainability" invokes the paradox of sustaining current practices whilst changing to better ways of living, which is arguably a contradiction in terms (Packard, 2009). Rather than looking at the rhetoric of sustainable development, which recaps concepts moulded by Bretton Woods institutions, it is worth looking instead at a sufficiency economy.

A sufficiency economy

According to the sufficiency economy theory (Thailand National Economic and Social Development Board, 2000) the land is divided into four parts in a ratio of 30-30-30-10.
30% of the land is organized for pond and fish culture, 30% for cultivation, 30% for growing fruit and perennial trees, and the remaining 10% for housing, raising animals and other activities, including manufacturing. Decency in living conditions, cooperation and building up connections are the interaction principles of the sufficiency economy theory.
Living a decent life at a self-sufficiency level entails cooperation as a group in order to handle production, distribution and consumption. For a community, the sufficiency economy theory emphasizes education, welfare and health, and urges building up connections with different groups so as to expand cooperation between the public and the private sphere.
Its economic model is based on progressive stages of development, starting from basic needs.
Moderation, knowledge and self-reliance are the pillars of the sufficiency economy. It draws on the following factors: a) state of mind (good consciousness, honesty, integrity, perseverance, prudence and the sharing of wisdom); b) ethical business (decent work and social justice); c) natural resources and environmental management (a low-carbon society, protection of biodiversity); d) appropriate technology (linked to human needs).
A sufficiency economy is based on local needs and the demand side, rather than the supply side and the power of the market. Its structure, technology

and environment are contingent or dependent upon the context and needs (Hodge, 1996). Moderation in consumption, reasonableness in desire, and endogenous development are the main components of a sufficiency economy.

Its principles are related to human development towards a good life and correct interaction among humans and between humans and other beings (biodiversity) and natural resources. The pattern of interaction shapes the sufficiency economy. According to Venkatraman (1989), the concept of interaction is used in the decision-making process. First, the degree of specificity of relationships is chosen among local people (how strategy and organisational structure fit together). Second, at community level, people themselves decide whether a certain criterion is applied to the concept of fit, which is achieved through mediation and matching.

The philosophy of the sufficiency economy is linked to happiness, in terms of improving both the human mind (self) and local development (community and environment). Happiness starts from the ability to become self-dependent (taught by the education system) and to satisfy one's own needs ("capability" is Sen's word) within a long-term perspective of development.

Attention is given to public policy, public resource management and ethics in resource utilization and allocation: "the public-minded attitude" in Keynes' words, rather than consumerist or liberalist practice. Globalisation, trade and capitalism are replaced by people's participation, national security and local control of production factors.

The different approach to human development proposed by the sufficiency economy is reflected in its learning perspective. The process of happiness development starts at the basic level and is rooted in ethics, because training of the mind is linked to moral behaviour, kindness, compassion, justice and honesty. The continuous knowledge-generation process at local level embodies this collective learning along the path towards the good life. Self-capability and local connectivity forge development and the achievement of happiness.

Because moderation promotes social networks, mutual trust and shared values, priority is given to "relational goods" rather than consumer goods. At a basic level, the principle of moderation provides guidance on how to become self-reliant by generating income or resources, namely by cutting unnecessary expense, by developing social capital and networks of people who can help, share and work together for local and endogenous development. Less consumption and greater demand for more "relational" goods and services teach people to become less self-centred and more community-oriented.

The "sharing and giving" principle helps others to help themselves, a sort of kindness not expecting return, free from attachments and focused on relational happiness.

The sufficiency economy puts into practice the principle of "doing well by doing good" (Kaemthong Indaratna, 2008), with happiness as the ultimate goal.

Einstein's oft-quoted "the problems of today cannot be solved with the thinking that created them" raises the question of what sort of economics is required for current generations to be able to deal with the magnitude of current problems. Rational thinking to solve problems in a scientific way is seen as the most relevant tool by western institutions. However, eastern economics could help the connection between our heads and our hearts. The real shift is when community relationships are built by the connection between head and heart. This vital link helps with suspending judgment, practising inclusiveness, sharing insights and developing a community of dialogue which fosters human and societal development.

In this framework, labour is the crucial dimension at various levels of happiness. At basic levels, labour leads to subsistence, while at higher levels it helps social participation, creativity, identity and capability. Labour makes it possible to get resources for a decent life, and it is itself a resource that can be used to move to further levels of happiness. Because it is not a commodity, as stated in the ILO Constitution, labour is a vital part of human life. As a result, employment is the key component of a sufficiency economy and should be considered an independent variable in development algorithms.

There is a universal agreement on labour as the source of wealth. In mainstream economics, labour in considered a cost by both employers and workers. For employers, it must be reduced to a minimum, if it can not be eliminated. For workers, it is a sacrifice of one's leisure time for some kind of compensation (wages). For Buddhist economics, work has three functions: a chance to develop human competency, a means to join other people in common tasks and to obtain goods with which to live. Extremes are rejected: labour exploitation and striving for leisure (the Buddhist "middle way"). The emphasis shifts from the products of work to the workers themselves (people are more important than goods) and full employment is the primary purpose of the economy (maximisation of employment, not of production). Liberation from consumerism stems from opposition to the mainstream economic assumption that a person consuming more is better off than a person consuming less. Since consumption is merely a means to human well-being, the imperative is the maximisation of well-being with the minimum of consumption. That is the opposite of mainstream economics, in which labour is exploited to obtain optimal patterns of production and capital is used towards the optimal pattern of consumption.

In the sufficiency economy, a new meaning for green jobs is given: the social dimension is entrenched in the environmental and economic dimensions, forging a holistic perspective of good employment (green + decent).

Conclusion

"What is wrong with green jobs?" is a recurrent question that green economics scholars ask (Douthwaite, 1999). Our discussion has brought out some answers. While growth seems desirable, not all growth is good. Just as the wrong form of cell growth, cancer, can be damaging and even fatal, so, too, can the wrong sort of economic growth. In the words of the Economist in 1989, a country that cut down all its trees, sold them as wood chips and then gambled the money away playing tiddlywinks would appear from its national accounts to have got richer. The development idea here is quite different. It follows an economic approach based on relational goods and a just transition to good development.

This path highlights personal transformation as the key issue in good development. In the words of Sivaraksa:

"We have more than enough programmes, organisations, parties and strategies, but we still put all our faith in the power of action alone to alleviate suffering and injustice. Activists and intellectuals tend to see all malevolence as being caused by others, or the system, without appreciating how these negative factors also operate within themselves. Those who want to change society must understand the inner dimension of change".

This inner dimension is the vital resource that can lead us towards good development.

References

M. Kennet, Green Economics 1999.

C. E. Lunn, The role of green economics in achieving realistic policies and programmes for sustainability, International Journal of Green Economics, Vol.1, No. 1, 2006

K. Nitnitiphrut, The Concept of Happiness, 2008.

F. Eyraud, D. Vaughan-Whitehead, The evolving world of work in the enlarged EU, 2007.

The Gross National Happiness Abridged Survey, 2006

R. A. Easterlin, Does Economic Growth Improve the Human Lot? Essay in Honor of Moses Abramovitz, NY Academic Press, 1974.

B. J. Hodge, Organisational theory, Prentice Hall, 1996.

K. Venkatraman The concept of fit, Academic of Management Review, Vol 14, No. 3 1989.

Kaemthong Indaratna, Sufficiency Economy, 2008.

P. Dasgupta, Human Well-Being and the Natural Environment, Oxford University Press, 2001.

A. Packard, Cultivating the future: integrating idealism and rationality, 2009.

E. Schumacher, Small is Beautiful, 1973.

K. Nitnitiphrut, The Concept of happiness, 2008.

10.2 The role of Decent work CONDITIONS in greening the urban environment

Dr. Edmundo Werna & Mr. Abdul Saboor Atrafi[1]
International Labour Organization

Introduction

The existing literature extensively explores the impact of urban areas on the natural environment. At macro level, under the umbrella term sustainable development, it also lays out the roles of economic, social, and environmental policies in addressing climate change and promoting green urban development practices. However, it is equally important to understand the situation and challenges faced by the very actors who deliver the necessary goods and services (i.e., workers and enterprises) to improve the urban environment and highlight the importance of better labour conditions in ensuring green or environmentally sustainable urban areas. If workers and enterprises are not properly trained or face unfavourable working conditions, the improvement of the urban environment in a socially inclusive manner will be far from achievable. This section analyses challenges faced by workers and enterprises in both conventional and green urban development scenarios using the broad concept of decent work. It argues that greening urban environments and improving labour conditions can be mutually beneficial, and makes suggestions about good practices that could be explored, analyzed, and mainstreamed in ensuring better labour conditions and greener urban areas. In particular, it emphasizes the importance of a comprehensive approach to labour issues in greening the urban environment and highlights the importance of paying attention to the problems of low-income settlements in the countries of the South.

Keywords: urban Sustainability, greening urban areas, green jobs, green urban economy, labour/working conditions, decent work, urban environment.

Introduction

In order to put the role of workers in the context of environmental protection in urban areas, the introduction will first present background information on environmental issues.

The environmental impacts of urban areas have been well documented (Gallego et al., 2009; Gangolells et al., 2009; Keivani et al., 2010; Khatib, 2009; Moavenzadeh, 1994; Sarsby & Meggyes, 2010; The Environment Agency in England and Wales et al., 2011). They relate to the choice of sites for construction, to the construction process and the choice of building materials and equipment, emissions from the production processes in the different sectors of the urban economy, emissions from buildings, transportation, and waste. In specific relation to climate change, urban areas are the main sources of greenhouse gas emissions. The environmental impacts of urban areas are key contributors to the depletion of natural resources and are intrinsically linked to energy and resource consumption, through production and use of goods of the various sectors of the urban economy (UN-HABITAT, 2011).

While all the different types of environmental impact of urban areas are important and need to be addressed, there has been a preponderant worldwide attention on energy use and its impact on climate change, given the risk it implies for the survival of the planned (Werna, forthcoming-2011). Therefore, more information on this issue is provided below.

According to a newly published UN-Habitat report on cities and climate change (2011), the cumulative share of greenhouse gas emissions from urban areas could range from 40-70 percent if production-based figures are used (i.e. figures calculated by adding up GHG emissions from entities located within cities) or 60-70 percent if consumption-based method is used (i.e. figures calculated by adding up GHG emissions resulting from the production of all goods consumed by urban residents, irrespective of the geographic location of the production). In this context, buildings alone are responsible for 25 to 40 percent of global energy use, and 30 to 40 percent of global greenhouse gas emissions (UNEP, 2008). Other contributing factors could range from energy use for lighting and transportation, to industrial, commercial and household consumption to reduction in the amount of green cover in urban areas (jeopardizing a city's ability to reabsorb CO_2) to poor waste management practices. All these issues point to the necessity of making the activities related to the production and use of the goods of the sectors of the urban economy an integral part of the solution in the fight for improving the environment.

To this end, there is a substantial body of knowledge on the technical aspects of greening[2] urban areas, as by and large researchers and practitioners have already mapped out the necessary techniques to do so. However, the role of workers in greening the urban environment has received relatively little attention.

The objective of this section is to contribute to addressing this issue and stimulate discussions on the topic. The section is predominantly a product of desk research and also reflects the professional observations and experiences of the authors and mainly qualitative data gathered by the

International Labour Organization (ILO). Although a substantial amount of work has been put into the relevant literature, due to the novelty of the subject the main contribution of the section is to map out the labour issues related to the greening of urban areas, under the conceptual framework of Decent Work. Therefore, the section adds value by bringing Decent Work into the discussion of the urban environment.

The section starts with a section linking urban sustainability to labour issues and the combat against urban poverty, and presents the overall concept of Decent Work, which encompasses the different aspects of labour. It proceeds with subsequent sections analyzing each component of Decent Work one by one, explaining existing challenges in urban areas that need to be addressed in order to improve the urban environment, and presenting some suggestive actions. It also pays special attention to developing countries, which concentrate urban poverty and decent work deficits, which are necessary to be addressed in order to ensure inclusive greening of the urban environment. The section concludes with a call for adopting a comprehensive approach to labour in urban areas and recommendations for further research, while highlighting the specific need for paying attention to low-income settlements and bridging intra-urban differentials.

1. Urban Sustainability and Labour

Sustainable development, including in urban areas, is widely defined as an approach to development that focuses on integrating economic activity with environmental protection and social concerns (e.g. Perdan, 2010). Labour issues, being an integral part of the wider phenomenon of social justice, falls within the "social" pillar of sustainable development. However, there is still a gap in the literature in regard to a broad analysis of labour issues, particularly in reference to greening urban areas.

Cities and towns will not be sustainable if the livelihoods of their inhabitants are not adequately addressed. There is a need and an opportunity to invest in employment creation and greening production in order to promote urban sustainability. According to United Nations Human Settlements Programme (UN-Habitat), urban poverty is widespread, especially in the South, and is increasingly outpacing poverty in rural areas (UN-HABITAT, 2010; Werna, 2000). Poverty is not only a toll on the living conditions of large numbers of urban dwellers, but also limits the capacity of workers to fully contribute to the urban economy and the greening of the economy in particular. For example, urban development strategies such as infrastructure development, inner-city regeneration, slum upgrading, and other similar avenues which can be pursued and optimized for greening the urban environment will not be sustainable without adequately addressing livelihoods and working conditions of the urban workforce.

The ILO and other entities use the concept of Decent Work[3] to analyze and take action on the different aspects of labour issues. Poverty is related to deficits in the four components of Decent Work, namely: employment creation, workers' rights, social protection, and social dialogue.

254

Greening the urban environment provides an opportunity to address decent work deficits through creation of green jobs[4]. In order to achieve this, workers need to be well trained and have good working conditions to effectively support a green urban economy. There exists a possible win-win scenario for greening the urban environment and creating green and decent jobs at the same time—as both of them can be mutually beneficial. Ensuring appropriate labour conditions within the concept of decent work will be beneficial to making this win-win scenario possible.

The four components of decent work will be analysed below, highlighting their implications for promoting green urban areas.

2. Employment Creation

Today, half of the world's population lives in urban areas (UN-HABITAT, 2010) and poverty and unemployment in urban areas remain a pressing concern for many countries around the world. Developing and developed countries alike face unemployment challenges. While in developed countries, the scarcity of jobs may be a consequence of financial crises, in the developing world unemployment is more endemic (UN-HABITAT, 2008), although such countries are also affected by crises. The expansion of urban population is outpacing employment opportunities (especially in the developing countries) and the inability of cities and towns to absorb the influx of rural-urban migrants and generate enough quality jobs has led to rising levels of poverty and insecurity in urban areas (e.g. Lawrence & Werna, 2009). A large number of people have to resort to informal or casual employment, and many work in precarious conditions. Many workers, especially in the informal economy are working long hours for low pay without any form of representation or social assistance—often engaging in dangerous and sometimes in violent and illegal activities. Municipal government feel the impact of unemployment and underemployment in terms of decreased tax revenues, social assistance and welfare expenditures, and crime and social unrest (ILO, 2004 & 2006; Gil & Werna, 2009).

Workers who are underemployed have clear limitations to contribute to the green urban economy. And the unemployed are completely excluded. Restructuring the urban economy provides a great opportunity for addressing unemployment and underemployment. There is a great deal that governments and the private sector can do to combine green urban development and employment creation. For example, according to a recently published report by the United Nations Environment Programme, investing 0.34% of global GDP per year over 2010-2050 in the transport sector only can contribute to reducing oil-based fuel usage as much as 80% below business as usual, while increasing employment by 10% (UNEP, 2011). Similarly, according to this report, investments in improved energy efficiency

255

in buildings could generate an additional 2-3.5 million jobs in Europe and the United States alone. If the demand for new buildings (social housing, hospitals, schools, etc.) that exists in developing countries is considered, the potential is much higher.

Some of the commonly adopted urban development strategies that can lead to greening of urban areas while creating green jobs include promotion of energy efficiency in buildings, creation of denser, mixed use neighbourhoods, adoption of energy efficient transportation systems, and promotion of localized production and consumption patterns (ILO, 2011a). Greening programmes to upgrade roads (for better environmental sustainability), drainage, water and energy facilities, sewerage systems, public buildings, public transport, and waste management and recycling facilities for example could bring about immediate employment gains and have long term impact on incomes and living and working conditions (see, for instance, ILO, 2011a), for suggestions on greening such public works programmes). These initiatives often require awareness raising and skills development for enterprises and workers, while providing an opportunity to convey information and knowledge exchange about green practices. Similarly, community contracting (funds disbursed to and managed by community organizations, and usually involving local labour and expertise) can create local jobs, empower the community, and improve skills (Tournée & Esch, 2001).

Through subsidies governments can stimulate green job creation in other sectors of the urban economy—in which they are not directly involved. Supporting private entrepreneurship, especially micro and small enterprises that are responsible for a significant proportion of urban employment is a clear example in this respect (Atkinson, forthcoming-2011). Provision of support to greening of private enterprises is likely to create green jobs and help address the environmental problems faced by many of such enterprises. Investment in training and occupational safety and health is also fundamental for green employment creation (ILO & CEDEFOP , 2011-forthcoming).

3. Workers' Rights

Many urban workers still face challenges related to their rights, which have implications for their living and working conditions and productivity. Examples of issues related to workers' rights in urban areas include informality, casual work, migration, child labour, bonded labour, and discrimination against female workers (Lawrence & Werna, 2009; Lawrence, Gil, Fluckiger, Lambert, & Werna, 2008).

Informal and casual workers are particularly at risk. The relationship of workers with employers and governments is not regulated, making the situation challenging for them to demand their rights. Migrant workers who abound in urban areas are also particularly at risk, because often times they have to accept precarious working conditions in order to survive in their host countries (ibid). Child labour is an issue that also deserves special attention because of the moral imperative and because it undermines education, which would be required for the children to find decent and productive work later in life. In addition, the existence of child labour diminishes the opportunities for adult workers to find employment. Today, with rapid urbanization and rising poverty, a large number of children do not have proper care from their families and a number of children are orphaned by HIV-AIDS epidemic. This trend renders young people increasingly vulnerable to exploitation, illegal, underground, and hazardous activities (ILO, 2010 & 2011b).

Bonded labour is another issue that negatively affects workers' rights in urban areas. Additionally, there is evidence regarding deficits in the rights of female workers in urban areas which points to lack of equal treatment compared to their male counterparts and existence of harassment (Gil & Werna, 2009; ILO, 2004 & 2006).

In sum, the deficits in workers' rights undermine their working conditions and productivity, and hence their capacity to fully engage in the development of a green urban economy/environment. Conversely, improving workers' rights may lead to better productivity and preparedness of the urban workforce to effectively participate in greening of the urban environment.

There are many possible actions to address the plight of different groups of workers based on ILO's conventions, recommendations, and instruments (ILO, 2011c). ILO has instruments for each aspect of decent work including workers' rights, which can be often supplemented by specific initiatives from governments, non-governmental organizations, international organizations, and other actors. One example, among others, in this respect is the ILO's International Programme for the Elimination of child labour, which can be supported and relevant concerted efforts explored (ILO, 2011b).

Broader synergies can also be explored. There is a burgeoning discussion on "the right to the city" (**Dag Hammarskjöld Foundation,** 2011; Purcell, 2002; Right to the City, 2011; TIDES, 2011; UN-Habitat, 2010) with a focus on community and consumers rights, which was also the theme of the latest World Urban Forum held in Rio de Janeiro, 22-26 March, 2010. This can be effectively extended to include workers' rights as well.

There are embryonic examples of coalitions of urban workers (such as in Brazil[5]), and, in parallel, specific initiatives related to the rights of urban citizens to a better environment, supporting a green economy (Berg, 2011; DePhillis, 2011; Kousis, 1999; Losito, 2010; Network for Improved Policy in South Asia, 2011; Tree Media Group, 2011; UNEP, 2005). Promotion of a greener urban environment and promotion of the rights of urban workers can reinforce each other.

4. Social Protection

Lack of social protection is a major cause of poverty, especially—but not exclusively—for urban informal and casual workers (ILO, 2004). Their living and working conditions expose them to risk on a daily basis. Sickness, disability, accidents, and premature death, in addition to loss of assets are combined with lack of clean water and proper sanitation, exposure to fire and flood, use of toxic substances at work, overcrowding, and crime. Crises are standard features in the lives of the urban poor. Exposure to these multiple risks is high and the people in low-income settlements are the least protected. Numerous urban workers and self-employed entrepreneurs do not have access to an adequate system of healthcare, paid leave, protection against loss of pay when laid off, ill health, accidents or old age. Although the poor work hard to keep their heads above the water, without adequate social protection provisions the smallest of the crises can ruin their livelihoods. Should one income earner in the household be injured or fall sick, the family risks falling into absolute despair, poverty, child labour, or debt (Gil & Werna, 2009; ILO, 2004 & 2006). This situation can seriously jeopardize the potential expansion of a green urban economy.

In addition to these problems, it is important to note that the move to a green economy entails changes in the process of production, with new implications for working conditions. According to the ILO (2011a), the gradual expansion of green jobs will generate new challenges. This is caused by a change in work environments, by the introduction of new technologies, new substances and work processes, by changes in the structure of the workforce and the labour market and by new forms of employment and work organization. One example relates to occupational safety and health conditions. Green jobs include activities related to the production of new (green) products and the assembly of new equipments—such as solar panels and wind generators—which require specific provisions to protect the workers, and need to be taken into account. Reported examples include cases of accidents involving workers in activities such as assembling wind generators.

Similar to workers' rights, ILO instruments provide a sound basis for actions that are specifically related to social protection. Poor people have also at times mobilized their own resources and organized their own risk protection through mutual health protection mechanisms and community surveillance. There are also examples of partnership practices involving local governments, the private sector, and local communities. Support should be given to such initiatives in order to help facilitate greening of the urban environment. In sum, any effort devoted to greening urban areas should take into account the importance of social protection for workers and include actions and strategies to address them.

5. Social Dialogue

Social dialogue has been an important tool for governments, employers, and workers to negotiate and discuss labour related issues, and is one of the core labour rights (Kuruvilla, 2006). Successful social dialogue structures and processes have the potential to resolve social and economic issues, encourage good governance, advance social and industrial peace, and boost economic progress. Yet, a significant number of urban workers, particularly in developing countries are not adequately organized. Under such circumstances, they remain excluded from the mainstream social and economic dialogue—especially the poor who do not have the time and capacity to initiate collective action or mobilize resources on a sufficiently large scale. According to the ILO the right to organize is considered a basic workers' right and a crucial means of action to build stable, mature societies capable of curbing social tension by integrating different points of views constructively.

Some micro-entrepreneurs join trade associations for pragmatic reasons, usually related to their immediate working environment. Here and there, community based organizations, or ethnic associations attempt to fill the gap in representation. In many cities, groups of street vendors, domestic workers, micro-entrepreneurs and market women are developing and using networks to remain up to date with relevant business information and protect their interests. But the majority of these associations are weak and unsustainable as they lack appropriate legal status, and do not have diversified and stable sources of income. As a result they cannot obtain the required degree of public legitimacy and often times operate under unfavourable political, legislative, and regulatory environment.

The low level of organization among many urban workers, especially—but not exclusively—in informal sector is a cause for concern. Socially viable cities and towns cannot exist without fair representation of workers in the decision making process that affects them (Gil & Werna, 2009; van Empel & Werna, 2010). It follows from this that any efforts put into greening of cities may not be sustainable in the long run if effective social dialogue is not sufficiently ensured. Workers and employers should be involved in the discussions concerning the greening of cities and towns together with the governments, as they are the ultimate actors who will deliver the necessary goods and services required to do so.

Organization is the first step towards bringing urban workers into the mainstream of the urban economy (ILO, 2004 & 2006). There are cases of good practice of urban multi-sectoral dialogue that can be mainstreamed and proliferated. Examples include the city of Marikina (Philippines), the municipal decent work programmes in Belo Horizonte and in a number of towns in the metropolitan region of Sao Paulo (Brazil), and the organization and involvement of informal construction workers in social dialogue in Dar-es-Salaam (Tanzania) (Jason, 2008; van Empel & Werna, 2010). For the purposes of this section, one example from Hong Kong is presented in Box 2 below.

Greening of the urban economy can provide a specific focus for such type of action, so the potential of effective organization and social dialogue to this end should be sufficiently explored.

6. Conclusions

The desk research of the authors, their professional observations and experiences and qualitative data gathered by the ILO show the importance of labour in the greening the urban environment. It supports the argument that ensuring decent labour conditions and greening the urban environment can be mutually reinforcing. Cities offer vast opportunities to create effective win-win scenarios to combine greening efforts and decent work conditions. If decent work is not sufficiently addressed, greening of cities will be limited—and addressing the social dimension of sustainable development will be far from ensured. It is important that urban actors including workers, employers and governments adopt a comprehensive approach to address decent work conditions and improve the urban environment. Doing so, not only will help ensure the environmental sustainability of cities, but it will also help address the social and economic aspects of sustainable development at large.

An important issue which is of utmost relevance to the discussions put forward in this section is the importance of greening low-income neighbourhoods. With few noticeable exceptions, by and large the existing practices of greening urban areas tend to focus on higher income neighbourhoods (everywhere, but more so in developing countries). While this may be the beginning of a trend that could be extended to other neighbourhoods it is important to ensure that such scaling up takes place and low-income neighbourhoods are meaningfully considered. Otherwise, there is a risk that cities face a green-brown divide: green neighbourhoods for the rich, and non-green neighbourhoods for the poor, which could exacerbate intra-urban differentials already abound in developing countries. While greening of low-income neighbourhoods encompass many factors—such as investment trends, poverty reduction efforts, political and social circumstances—the training of workers and improvement of working conditions for them are surely an important part of the picture and a beneficial venue to greening the urban environment, creating green jobs for the poor, and addressing intra-urban differentials largely prevalent in the cities of the South.

While this section presented the broad scenario of decent work in greening the urban environment, it was beyond its scope to elaborate in detail on its multiple facets. Each issue included in the section (e.g. each element of decent work) is vast and deserves specific research. Therefore, as a follow-up to the present study, detailed research on such issues is recommended.

Bibliography

Atkinson, A. (forthcoming-2011). Cities with Jobs-An Urban Employment Policy Note. EMP/INVEST Report. Geneva: International Labour

Organization.

Berg, N. (2011). Grassroots Environmental Movement Sprouts in China. Retrieved June 24, 2011, from http://www.planetizen.com/node/30782

Dag Hammarskjöld Foundation. (2011). Another Development. Retrieved June 23, 2011, from http://www.dhf.uu.se/about/another-development/

DePhillis, L. (2011). The "Livability Movement": Successor to the Environmental Movement. Retrieved June 24, 2011, from http://www.washingtoncitypaper.com/blogs/housingcomplex/2011/01/14/the-livability-movement-successor-to-the-environmental-movement/

Gallego, E., Roca, X., Perales, J. F., & Guardino, X. (2009). Determining Indoor Air Quality and Identifying the Origin of Odour Episodes in Indoor Environments. **Journal of Environmental Sciences**, 21 (3), 333-339.

Gangolells, M., Casals, M., Gassó, S., Forcada, N., Roca, X., & Fuertes, A. (2009). A Methodology for Predicting the Severity of Environmental Impacts Related to the Construction Process of Residential Buildings. **Building and Environment: The International Journal of Building Science and its Applications**, 44 (3), 558-571.

Gil, M. P., & Werna, E. (2009). Local Authorities and the Construction Industry. In Lawrence, R. And Werna, E. (Eds.). **Labour Conditions for Construction: Building Cities, Decent Work & the Role of Local Authorities** (pp. 51-81). Oxford: Wiley-Blackwell.

ILO (International Labour Organization) (2004). Cities at Work: Employment Promotion to Fight Urban Poverty. SEED & EMP/INVEST Report. Geneva: International Labour Organization.

ILO (International Labour Organization) (2006). A Strategy for Urban Employment and Decent Work. Fact-sheet. Geneva: International Labour Organization.

ILO (International Labour Organization) (2010). Accelerating Action Against Child Labour. IPEC Report. Geneva: International Labour Organization.

ILO (International Labour Organization) (2011a). ILO Backgroung Note to "Towards a Green Economy: Pathways to Sustainable Development and Poverty Eradication". Green Jobs Programme Report. Geneva: International Labour Organization.

ILO (International Labour Organization) (2011b). Children in Hazardous Work - What We Know, What We Need to Do. IPEC Report. Geneva: International Labour Organization.

ILO (International Labour Organization) (2011c). International Labour Organization Website. Retrieved June 24, 2011, from http://www.ilo.org/global/lang--en/index.htm

ILO (International Labour Organization) and CEDEFOP (European Center for Development of Vocational Training) (2011-forthcoming). Skills for

Green Jobs: A Global View. Retrieved June 23, 2011, from http://www.ilo.org/wcmsp5/groups/public/@ed_emp/@ifp_skills/docume nts/publication/wcms_156220.pdf

Jason, A. (2008). Organizing Informal Workers in the Urban Economy: The Case of the Construction Industry in Dar es Salam, Tanzania. **Habitat International**, 32 (2), 192-202.

Keivani, R., Tah, J. H., Kurul, E., & Abanda, H. (2010). Green Jobs Creation Through Sustainable Refurbishment in the Developing Countries. Sectoral Activities Department, Working Paper 275. Geneva: International Labour Organization.

Khatib, J. M. (Ed.). (2009). **Sustainability of Construction Materials**. London: CRC Press Llc.

Kousis, M. (1999). Environmental Protest Cases: The City, The Countryside, and The Grassroots in Southern Europe. **Mobilization: An International Quarterly**, 4 (2), 223-238.

Kuruvilla, S. (2006). Social Dialogue for Decent Work. In D. Ghai (Ed.). **Decent work: Objectives and strategies** (pp. 175-215). Geneva: International Labour Organization.

Lawrence, R. J., Gil, M. P., Fluckiger, Y., Lambert, C., & Werna, E. (2008). Promoting Decent Work in the Construction Sector: the Role of Local Authorities. **Habitat International**, 32 (2), 160-171.

Lawrence, R., & Werna, E. (Eds.) (2009). **Labour Conditions for Construction: Building Cities, Decent Work, and the Role of Local Authorities**. Oxford: Wiley-Blackwell.

Losito, B. (2010). Citizenship Education in a Changing Urban Environment: Opportunities and Challenges. Retrieved June 24, 2011, from http://www.bpb.de/files/BIOAQO.pdf

Moavenzadeh, F. (1994). **Global Construction and the Environment: Strategies and Opportunities**. Oxford: Wiley.

Network for Improved Policy in South Asia. (2011). SHEHRI-Citizens for a Better Environment. Retrieved June 24, 2011, from http://www.nipsa.in/shehri-citizens-for-a-better-environment/

Perdan, S. (2010). The Concept of Sustainable Development and its Practical Implications. In Azapagic, A. and Perdan, S. (Eds.), **Sustainable Development in Practice: Case Studies for Engineers and Scientists** (Secon Edition). Chichester: John Wiley & Sons, Ltd.

Purcell, M. (2002). Excavating Lefebvre: The right to the City and its Urban Politics of the Inhabitant. **GeoJournal** , 58, pp. 99-108.

Rajendran, S., & Gambatese, J. A. (2009). Development and Initial Validation of Sustainable Construction Safety and Health Rating System. **Journal of Construction Engineering and Management**, 135 (10),

1067-1075.

Rajendran, S., Gambatese, J. A., & Behm, a. M. (2009). Impact of Green Building Design and Construction on Worker Safety and Health. **Journal of Construction Engineering and Management**, 135 (10), 1058-1066.

Right to the City. (n.d.). Right to the City. Retrieved June 23, 2011, from http://www.righttothecity.org/home.html

Sarsby, R., & Meggyes, T. (2010). **Construction for a Sustainable Environment**. London: Taylor and Francis Group.

The Environment Agency in England and Wales; SEPA in Scotland and the Northern Ireland Environment Agency (2011). How can Construction and Building Trades Affect the Environment. Retrieved January 20, 2011, from http://www.netregs.gov.uk/netregs/businesses/construction/62311.aspx/

TIDES. (2011). How We Work. Retrieved June 23, 2011, from http://www.tides.org/about/how-we-%09work/

Tournée, J., & Esch, W. v. (2001). Community Contracts in Urban Infrastructure Works: Practical Lessons from Experience. EMP/INVEST Report. Turin: International Labour Organization.

Tree Media Group. (2011). Urban Roots. Retrieved June 24, 2011, from http://www.treemedia.com/treemedia.com/Urban_Roots.html

UNEP (United Nations Environment Programme) (2005). Urban Environmental Accords. Retrieved June 24, 2011, from http://archive1.globalsolutions.org/programs/health_environment/urban_e nvironmental_accords.pdf

UNEP (United Nations Environment Programme) (2008). Green Jobs:Towards Decent Work in a Sustainable, Low-Carbon World. Nairobi: United Nations Office at Nairobi.

UNEP (United Nations Environment Programme) (2008b). UNEP Background Paper on Green Jobs. Nairobi: United Nations Office at Nairobi.

UNEP (United Nations Environment Programme) (2011). Towards a Green Economy: Pathways to Sustainable Development and Poverty Eradication: A Synthesis for Policy Makers. Retrieved June 07, 2011, from http://www.unep.org/greeneconomy/Portals/88/documents/ger/GER_synt hesis_en.pdf

UN-Habitat (United Nations Human Settlements Programme) (2008). **The State of the World's Cities 2010-2011: Bridging the Urban Divide**. London, Sterling, VA: Earthscan in the UK and USA for UN-HABITAT.

UN-Habitat (United Nations Human Settlements Programme) (2010). Taking Forward the Right to the City. Retrieved June 23, 2011, from http://www.unhabitat.org/downloads/docs/Dialogue1.pdf

UN-Habitat (United Nations Human Settlements Programme) (2011). **Cities** and Climate Change: Global Report on Human Settlements 2011. London;Washington DC: Earthscan for UN-HABITAT.

Van Empel, C. and Werna, E. (2010). Labour Oriented Participation in Municipalities: How Decentralized Social Dialogue Can Benefit the Urban Economy and its Sectors. Sectoral Activities Department, Working Paper 280. Geneva: International Labour Organization.

Werna, E. (2000). **Combatting Urban Inequalities: Challenges for Managing Cities in the Developing World**. Cheltenham, UK; Northampton, USA: Edward Elgar Publishing, Limited/Inc.

Werna, E. (2011-forthcoming). Green Jobs in Construction. In Ofori, G. (Ed.), **The Construction Industry in Developing Countries** (pp. 427-458).

[1] Dr. Edmundo Werna and Mr. Abdul Saboor Atrafi (M.Sc.) work at the Sectoral Activities Department of the International Labour Organization. Contact details: ILO, 4 route des Morillons, 1211 Geneva-22, Switzerland. Phones: + 412279960036 and +41227997165. E-mails: werna@ilo.org and g3sds@ilo.org

[2] According to Cambridge Online Dictionary greening refers to ''the process of understanding more and becoming more active about protecting and looking after the environment". This paper strives to adopt this definition and apply it to the specific context of urban development. Greening the urban environment means making urban areas more energy efficient and reducing their collective impact on the natural environment and climate change. It also refers to greening of the various sectors of the urban economy.

[3] The ILO defines Decent Work as the summing up of "the aspirations of people in their working lives." http://www.ilo.org/global/about-the-ilo/decent-work-agenda/lang--en/index.htm, 2011

[4] According to UNEP a green job is defined as one that "help(s) to protect and restore ecosystems and biodiversity, reduce energy consumption, de-carbonize the economy, and minimize or altogether avoid the generation of all forms of waste and pollution." (UNEP, 2008)

[5] For example, representatives of Brazilian workers held an event on this topic during the latest World Urban Forum (held in Rio de Janeiro, 22-26 March, 2010).

Chapter 11: Green IT, and technology jobs

11.1 Green IT.

Rakesh Kumar

Green IT has become a much used and abused term to incorporate a large number of technologies and programs over the last 2 years. Many vendors believe that by associating their products or services with this very important aspect of the emerging technology spectrum, they will sell more products. The reality, however, is that there is a lot of confusion about what the actual Green IT issues are and about which products or services actually help to tackle user concerns.

Gartner's research shows that the spectrum of Green technologies, services and legislation that users can focus on can be broken down into the immediate, mid term and long term activities. This chapter focuses on the immediate area.

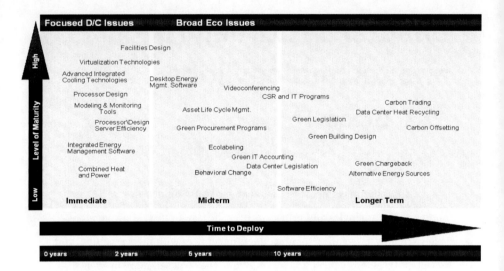

Focused D/C Issues	Broad Eco Issues	

High

Level of Maturity

Low

Facilities Design

Virtualization Technologies

Advanced Integrated Cooling Technologies

Desktop Energy Mgmt. Software

Videoconferencing

Processor Design

CSR and IT Programs

Modeling & Monitoring Tools

Asset Life Cycle Mgmt.

Carbon Trading

Data Center Heat Recycling

Processor\Design Server Efficiency

Green Legislation

Green Procurement Programs

Carbon Offsetting

Green Building Design

Integrated Energy Management Software

Ecolabeling

Green IT Accounting

Combined Heat and Power

Data Center Legislation

Behavioral Change

Green Chargeback

Alternative Energy Sources

Software Efficiency

Immediate   **Midterm**   **Longer Term**

Time to Deploy

0 years	2 years	5 years	10 years

IMMEDIATE PRIORITIES

Gartner research has shown that the immediate Green IT issues are around power, cooling and floor space problems in data centers and office environments. We believe, therefore, that user spending should focus on these areas. Over 70% of the Global 1000 will face significant data center problems over the next 4 years requiring substantial capital costs to build new facilities or refurbish existing ones. The Uptime Institute published a report in March 2008 stating that over 40% of the organizations surveyed would run out of data center power over the next 24 months. With new data centers costing at least in the tens of millions of dollars and running to hundreds of millions for high end Tier4 sites, the sums involved are very large. However, even more important than this is the fact that new generation of data centers will be very different to existing ones. They will need to flexible, modular and have an integrated software nervous system; they will need to behave like living organisms

One other key area of concern is the use of energy in offices. This covers the use of computers, printers and even the design and layout of the office. Energy use in desktops in much higher than it needs to be because of behavioral problems. People seldom switch machines off at night or at weekends.

Modern Data Center Facilities Design Concepts

Whether building a new data center or refurbishing an existing one, users need to deploy modern design caharecertstrics. There are very different from those existed as little as 5 years ago. In order to create such an entity, users need to build in a modular manner. In other words, rather than building a site that has the capacity for, say, 20 years, it is more efficient in the long run to build a module that has a capacity for 5 years worth of growth. Once this modules comes close to being fully occupied, then a 2nd module should be built. This is the best way to minimize costs, manage a rapidly changing design envelope and future proof as much as possible given the variable nature of capacity growth and changing technologies.

Users also need to design from the inside out. This means that they need to look at the thermal profile of their topology and design the energy distribution and cooling that is most appropriate to that particular hardware set up. For example, the energy and cooling needs of a mainframe system is very different to that of a rack of blades. Deigning the power distribution and cooling to the maximum specification will result in over provisioning and hence a waste of energy.

Advanced Cooling Technologies

Data Centers typically spend as much energy on cooling their IT equipment as they do on powering it. Moreover, in certain cases, such a high density and/or high performance computing environments, they could use a lot more. Traditional computer room air conditioning systems use a large amount of energy and in many cases are proving to be sub optimal at cooling different types of equipment. Gartner recommends that users apply a mixed cooling approach combining free air, air conditioning and liquid cooling. This means that outside free air should be used as much as possible given local climatic conditions. In most temperate climates, this will result in free air usage of between 3 to 6 months a year. Moreover, running data centers at around 24 degrees Celsius Rather than the 18 degrees that has been typical will also result in lower energy use. We also recommend using variable speed fans for greater granularity.

There are some emerging technologies that users should evaluate cautiously. For example the use of in server cooling techniques such as spaying a fluid onto the processor may seem attractive but is not widely used. Also, the use of CO_2 gas pumped across the rear of servers is used in a few instances around the world but carries maintenance and reliability problems.

Use of Modeling and monitoring software

One of the most important developments of Green IT in data centers is the use of infrastructure modeling and monitoring tools. These are tools from vendors like Emerson, Schneider, 1E and nlyte provide the capability to model the physical assets, energy use, available capacity and thermal characteristics of both IT components and facilities components. From a green IT perspective, they allow energy optimization and the ability to plan more carefully the energy related consequences of infrastructure changes in the data center.

Virtualization Technologies

Virtualization technologies for thex86 and RISC UNIX space can be used to great effect to improve the environmental footprint of data centers. Essentially, virtualization improves the utilization of serves. Currently most x86 servers are utilized at around the 10% mark on daily basis and the typical scenario is a new server for a new application. By increasing this to around 50 % and even higher, then multiple applications can be run on the same hardware box. This will result in fewer servers used with consequential benefits of less floor space needed, less transportation and recycling of those servers and less manufacturing energy expended. From an energy usage perspective, virtualization needs to be linked with consolidation and decommissioning. Its only be decommissioning servers that the significant energy savings are made.

Processor Design and Server efficiency

Processor and server manufactures are beginning to take a much more balanced view of new systems than ever before. In new design, the need to provide significantly improved compute performance over previous technology is still important, but is now balanced with the energy and thermal implications of the increased compute power. Moreover, organizations like HP and IBM are spending more resources in designing better server blowers and fans as well as better electrical conversion and battery technologies. The problem for users is in doing a like for like energy or indeed full life cycle green benchmark. With the introduction of SPECPoewer benchmark about 8 months, the relative energy consumption for a standard workload can be compared. The US Energy Star program will be rolled out to the server space, but it may take a few years.

Energy management for the Office Environment

Whilst data center energy usage is a significant problem because of the concentration effect of having a large number of servers in relatively small area, Gartner research has shown that over 30% of IT related CO_2 emissions come PC's and monitors. Moreover, PC's tend to be used for only a third of one day but tend to remain switched on for the whole day. This results in a considerable amount of energy being wasted in offices.

Newer systems tend to use less energy than older ones. For example, a modern desktop with a 19" LCD monitor would use about 1/3 of the energy of a 2004 system with a 17" CRT monitor. Hence upgrading to newer systems will help. Windows typically has 3 power saving modes; standby, hibernate and off which can be used. Moreover software from companies like 1E and

Verdium can be used to provide additional power saving functionality.

Perhaps the biggest problem in the office environment is to do with human behavior. Incentivising (positively or negatively) people to become more conscious of their environmental responsibility tend to work in the short term and needs constant reinforcement. The tools mentioned above do provide on screen usage gauges that can be used in this manner.

Immediate issues but low maturity of technologies

Integrated Energy management Software Environment

The ability to integrate a multitude of different energy management, modeling and workflow tools will become essential to running modern data centers in an optimized way. This will require combining building management systems, server management systems, facility management systems and enterprise consoles together to provide a single holistic view of the data center. Moreover, in the future, such software may become linked to business process engines to automate change based upon a business trigger.

Currently the tools exist in a fragmented way and sometime use different protocols. However, we recommend that any organization going through systemic data center change should develop a roadmap for this integrated software suite and start deploying the tools where possible. There are likely to be many areas of difficulties but these should be clearly documented. Users could either develop bespoke integration policies or wait for the vendors to do some of the integration at source.

Combined Heat and Power

Combined heat and power (CHP), also known as cogeneration, is the simultaneous production of electricity and heat from a single fuel source, such as: natural gas, biomass, biogas, coal, waste heat, or oil. CHP is not a single technology, but an integrated energy system that can be modified depending upon the needs of the energy end user. Using these systems in new data centers again depends on location, availability of a fuel source and expensive equipment. The technology is not widely used in data centers today but will grow in importance over the next few years. In general terms, Gartner recommends the use of alternative energy sources as a key initial design criterion for all new data centers. Users, should then eliminate technologies that are not sufficiently mature or those that are too expensive

MID TERM PRIORITIES

Gartner views the mid term issues to cover the next 2 to 4 years. Over this time a range of new innovations will emerge across the data center and the office environment. Moreover, we believe that many processes that are currently emerging will gain significance and importance and will mature to become much more mainstream. For example, Green IT procurement will become much more institutionalized within corporate procurements department by 2010. Organizations need to start prioritizing which of the many products and services in this category will affect those most and start planning for adoption. This may involve setting up small development teams, developing partnerships with industry players to gain a better understanding of the issues and solutions or simply starting to work more closely with key suppliers.

The type of technologies, services and legislation here include:

  Green IT procurement

2) Green asset lifecycle programs

3) Environmental labeling of servers and other devices

4) Video conferencing

5) Green Chargeback

6) Carbon Offsetting

7) Green building design

8) Changing people's behavior

9) Green accounting in IT. This would include concepts such as measuring the carbon footprint of an IT project (software development and implementation) where external consultants are used. Hence the total project cost would include the carbon expenditure of the external consultants.

The areas listed above cover a time frame of around the next 2 to 4 years. This means that the amount and relevance of the investment and, hence, the return on that investment is difficult to determine (especially given that most IT budgets still run annually). We therefore, advise IT users to work closely with corporate CSR and governance groups to determine which areas are going to be most important to the business. This will also ensure access to budgets that sit outside the It department.

LONG TERM PRIORITIES

These are the issues, projects and products that will span anything from 4 to 20 years and in many cases may never materialize into concrete actions. Much of the Greenwash in the industry sits in this category. Whilst there probably is no immediate pressure to implement these programs, users need to be aware of the impact on their particular industry sector. Many of these issues require long term planning and capital expenditure that may need to be amortized over many years. Moreover, they cover areas that depend upon potential legislation and also on social and political positioning. For example, the IT departments of Government organizations may come under greater pressure to use alternative energy sources than commercial organizations. The relatively high amount of uncertainty about the technologies, services and legislation in this category compared to the 2

above means that users will have to do more scenario planning and interact

more with external bodies like Government and industry groups. We suggest

that IT users see this category as part of a much broader corporate planning

program and as such they collaborate heavily with other parts of their

businesses (CSR, governance and strategic planning groups).

The type of technologies and solutions here include:

1) Green legislation. This could cover emissions from hardware or indeed
whole data centers. We don't believe that there is a foreseeable appetite for
the European Union or the US Government to introduce any form of
prescriptive legislation. Such legislation has to be equitable and carry
penalties, both of which are hard to measure, even if the will was there.
Moreover, the large IT vendors yield considerable political influence and are
currently able to stem any move in that direction. Finally, we believe in
general terms that legislation in this area could do more harm than good.

2) Carbon Offsetting and carbon trading. Carbon trading is a market based
tool to limit green house gas emissions. Using cap and trade and credits, it
allows certain industries to meet environmental targets. The market for such
trades has grown rapidly over the last few years with the Emissions Trading
Scheme in Europe leading the way. Whilst this technique works for heavy
industries that pollute the atmosphere in measurable ways, it will be difficult
to implement such a scheme for the IT industry. Measuring the level of
pollution in the IT industry will prove to be difficult. For example, hardware
products change every 2-5 years where advanced functionality such as
virtualization and dynamic workload management will mean that
applications become decoupled from the actual hardware platform.

However, commercial carbon trading mechanisms for the IT sector may

evolve as a natural market economic dynamic. Vendors may well use carbon

offsets as inducements to users to buy their particular products and users

may trade such instruments over the life of the hardware. We advise users to

keep abreast of the developments but not to expect too much too quickly.

3)   Data Center Recycling. The heat from even large data centers is not
rich with energy. Transporting this heat with minimum loss of energy is

difficult. Hence the majority of commercial data centers that are purposely built away from populated sites will struggle to do recycling in a meaningful way. We do however encourage new data center design engineers to investigate this possibility very seriously.

4)   Alternative energy sources. Using alternative energy sources for data centers or office IT environments will prove to be difficult over the next few years. In most cases, maybe a small percentage of energy could be supplied from alternative sources and one again, new builds should consider this.

5) Software efficiency. The energy efficiency of applications has seldom been a topic of conversation. Indeed, even today, the debate in the IT industry is missing the top software organizations. Companies like Microsoft, Oracle and SAP and do not view the energy or green IT issue as one of their making or one where they carry responsibility. Yet the inefficiency in application code creates inefficient compute cycles which eventually lead to wasted energy. This area needs more investigation and then a structured approach to fix. This will take many years.

11.2 Application of Green Economics in Business and Rural India: methods and tools

Dr. Natalie West Kharkongor, Assistant Professor, IIM Shillong

This chapter reflects the practical application of a new brand of economics, *Green Economics*, which is different from environmental economics and is on the way to be a remedy to our future problems. The operational mechanism of the existing economic systems clearly shows signs that the traditional economic tools and instruments are no longer effective. Hence, there is an urgent need for new economic models and derivatives in sustaining the existing resources. Relationship between mankind and environment has to be strengthened leading to innovative ways in tapping, using, and regenerating the limited natural resources. Surprisingly, we witness more of failures and crisis with the advancement in technology and knowledge. It is high time to diagnose the root causes of the problems and address them accordingly. In answering to these questions, role of Green Economics is significant. I believe It focuses on value – in – use and not primarily on value – in – exchange, and gives importance to regeneration of individuals, communities and ecosystems rather than accumulation of wealth and assets. The section will focus on green and sustainable technologies adopted by most of the corporate in the Indian business. In addition, the section will also deal with eco – friendly technologies in rural India. The section will focus at length in how to give back to the system and not just taking from it.

Introduction

With the growing emphasis on green technology, several initiatives have taken place across various industry verticals. This section will look into the four emerging sectors viz. telecommunication, IT, automobile and banking, and the various green initiatives that have been taken up in such sectors, in the world. A mention is also made in the section about carbon credit. The section will focus on the green technologies adopted by the eight companies and banks in India viz., Airtel, Vodafone, Wipro, Infosys, Hero MotoCorp, Maruti Suzuki, ICICI Bank, IndusInd Bank in the four mentioned sectors. This is followed by the implementation of such green and sustainable initiatives in rural India.

Green Technologies in Four Global Emerging Sectors

Telecommunication is an important industry and is one of the pillars of the economy. With the advancement of technology, the world is more connected now, but at a price. The BTS towers, which provide the connectivity are one of the major consumers of electricity, and have a backup provided by diesel guzzling generators. Not only this, the mobile handsets add to the e-waste and contain hazardous and toxic substances. Of late, due to increasing awareness, several measures have been incorporated to offset this. First, solar energy and other types of renewable sources of energy are being increasingly used to power the transmission towers. Secondly, advanced batteries, which consume fraction of the energy consumed earlier, are used for providing the backup. Thirdly, operators are going in for sharing of mobile towers and other resources to lessen the number of mobile towers. Fourthly, greener data centers, and more energy efficient networking and telecom equipment are being used. Additionally, efforts are being made to make the mobiles and other equipment free of hazardous and toxic substances. Moreover, systems are also being put in place for proper disposal of the e-waste generated and also for the recycling of products.

Information Technology (IT) is an important sector, which has brought about a revolution. IT is the acquisition, processing, storage and dissemination of vocal, pictorial, textual and numerical information by a microelectronics-based combination of computing and telecommunications. The increasing dominance of computers, laptops, tablets, music players, scanners, printers, servers, other networking and storage equipment, in our lives, is due to information technology only. How these products and the IT services add to the emission, is something which is not unknown. However, importantly, this is changing. A lot of research and development is taking place which has lessened the impact of the technology on the environment. The datacenters which brought the digital revolution are being made greener. They are being increasingly powered by alternative sources of energy like solar energy, wind energy etc. and natural ways of cooling are being used to reduce the energy consumption by the cooling units. The networking and storage equipment too are being made more energy efficient. This is being coupled with smart building techniques, wherein sensors are being used to detect and reduce the wastage of electricity and water. Advanced technology has also resulted in smart grid technology, which increases the energy efficiency on the electricity grid and in homes and offices. Green IT has also enabled advanced video conferencing solutions which are being adopted by the corporate to reduce the emissions and spending due to air travel. Additionally, virtualization of servers is taking place to reduce the number of servers used. Moreover, IT has also made possible development of tools to calculate the carbon footprint, to monitor and control energy usage in homes and offices, besides providing utilities like ERP tools which aid a company to optimize their financials as regards to green concerns like energy efficiency, water, and waste and greenhouse gas emissions. Furthermore, several new systems and solutions have been put in place for effective traffic management. Initiatives have also been taken to reduce the use of toxic substances in IT products and to have better e-waste management and recycling solutions.

276

Not to be left behind is the automobile industry. Automobile industry designs, develops, manufactures, markets and sells motor vehicles and is one of the world's most important economic sectors. As per statistics, a total of 77,857,705 vehicles were globally manufactured in 2010. Adding to this, the number of vehicles already on road, the amount of fuel consumed is substantial. Apart from the fuel consumption, the vehicles also contribute to the pollution. Moreover, the manufacturing process too adds onto the greenhouse gas emissions.

Efforts have been made to make the automobile industry greener and more sustainable. These measures include, design and production of hybrid vehicles, electric vehicles, alternative fuel vehicles etc. These vehicles use electric energy or biofuels to power the cars, hence decreasing the use of conventional diesel and petrol. Other measures include greening the supply chain, wherein parts and components used for manufacture are procured from vendors who themselves adopt green practices, thus reducing the carbon footprint. Additionally, the vehicles manufactured are made in compliance with strict emission norms, to reduce the pollution and emissions. Moreover, other practices like carbon offsetting are also followed, wherein, a small fee is charged from the consumer to offset the carbon emissions incurred in the manufacturing process. This money is then used to fund other green projects or to plant trees. Furthermore, the government is also doing its bit in greening this sector by providing tax sops and other incentives for such green projects.

Banking is another important sector, which surprisingly contributes to the emissions equivalently. Daily electricity consumption, fuel consumption due to air and road travel etc. adds to the emissions. Moreover the huge amounts of section used results in the felling of trees. To make this sector more greener, one of the major initiatives has been the internet and mobile banking. Now, the banking transactions are being done through internet and mobile, and this has reduced the need for people to travel to bank. Secondly, core banking solutions have been implemented, which have minimized the amount of paper used, through the use of technology. The banks have also started sending customer banking statements through mail, further reducing the use of paper. Moreover, solar powered ATM's, and incorporation of smart building techniques in the office building has reduced the electricity consumption in a big way.

Apart from the Green technology and initiatives, the carbon credit policy also helps in minimizing the impact of technology on the environment by providing an incentive to invest in and adopt green technologies. A carbon credit is a generic term to assign a value to a reduction or offset of greenhouse gas emissions. A carbon credit is usually equivalent to one tons of carbon dioxide equivalent (CO_2-e). A carbon credit can be used by a business or individual to reduce their carbon footprint by investing in an activity that has reduced or sequestered greenhouse gases at another site. Carbon credits are bought and sold in the international carbon market - much like any other commodity. Of the total number of carbon contracts signed in the world so far, India has the second largest portfolio with a market share of 12 percent, behind China which had a market share of 61percent. In India, the Delhi Metro Rail Corporation has been certified by the United Nations as the First Metro Rail and Rail based system in the world which will get carbon Credits for reducing Green House Gas Emissions as it has helped to reduce pollution levels in the city by 6.3 lakh tons every year thus helping in reducing global warming.

Green Technologies in India's Four Emerging Sectors

Telecommunication

Airtel which is one of the leading global telecommunications companies has launched a comprehensive program in saving energy. The main motive behind the entire program is to reduce energy and diesel usage leading to carbon emission reduction. One initiative of the program is the Green Towers P7 Initiative. It aims to cover 22,000 tower sites with a priority given to the rural areas. The program is for 3 years and at the end of the 3 years period it will bring down the diesel consumption of 66 million liters per year and carbon dioxide of around 1.5 lacs MT per year. The Initiative includes the following:

· Alternate energy sources: Airtel has encouraged the use of clean energy solutions. These have proved to be the strong alternative to conventional sources of energy. The deployment of such alternate sources of energy at around 1050 sites has helped the company to save around 6.9 million liters of diesel and around Rs. 280 million.

· IPMS and DCDG: the installation of Integrated Power Management System (IPMS) and the variable speed DC generators (DCDG) at around 900 sites has been able to reduce diesel consumption by 1.2 million liters and saved Rs. 47 million.

· FCU: The use of Free Cooling Units (FCU) in place of air conditioners at around 3400 sites has saved diesel consumption of around 4.1 million liters.

In addition to the Green Towers P7 initiative, Airtel has taken up other measures to reduce energy consumption such as:

· The installation of solar hot water generators at its main campus in Gurgaon for filling hot water requirement in the cafeteria.

· Lighting Energy Savers (LES) are installed across NCR region which has reduced energy consumption to the amount of 10 – 25% in the lighting system.

· The installation of Variable Frequency Drives at its campus in AHU (Air Handling Unit) has increased the efficiency of cooling system by 10%.

The above three measures have helped the company to save around 8.5 lakh units of electricity per year. The other measures taken up by Airtel are:

· The implementation of the 'Secure Print' solution which has saved about 8 MT of paper per annually. The drive of sending e- bills to the post – paid customers leads to the saving of 12,840 trees per year.

· BhartiInfratel, a subsidiary of BhartiAirtel has installed around 3 MWT of solar capacity which has generated more than 5 million units of electricity annually.

Vodafone, another leading player too has launched a series of green initiatives. It has introduced solar chargers and handsets that make extensive use of recycled plastic and have energy efficient features. They have reduced packaging material, and have introduced e-billing. They also collect handsets for reuse and recycling and have researched capacity to manage electronic waste.

IT Services

Wipro, an IT company and also a leading provider of IT services has taken up a number of initiatives leading to greener and sustainable environment. Some of the important measures are:

· *Ecological Sustainability*: This includes reduction in Green House Gases emission by:

    Ø using alternative sources of energy for lighting like the LED lights

    Ø implementing car – pool policy for employees

    Ø reducing business commute

    Ø generating wind/solar power in campuses

    Ø running air conditioning plant on solar thermal

    Ø by planting trees on unused campus land

    ·*Water Efficiency*:The use of Sewage Treatment Plans for recycling of water. The solid waste generated from treatment is converted to bio fertilizer for use in the campus garden. Approximately, 76% of waste generated is either recycled or composted.

    · *E Waste Management*: Under e waste management, Wipro has adopted e waste take back program by following WEEE (Waste Electrical and Equipment) guidelines. Under this initiative, plastic and carton boxes are reused; the metallic parts are sent to European countries for treatment.

    · *Elimination of Toxic Chemicals*: Under this initiative the Company has implemented 100% RoHS (Restriction on Hazardous Substances) compliant desktops and laptops and elimination of 21 hazardous chemicals. Additional products are free from toxic chemicals like PVC (poly vinyl chloride) and BFRs (Brominated Flame

Retardants).

· *Greener and Ethical Supply Chain*: Under this measure, the suppliers are expected to supply products and services meeting environmental standards.

Other initiatives are Clean Energy, Green IT Infrastructure, IT for green products and services.

Infosys, another IT giant too is not far behind. It has implemented database archival, and document sharing to minimize the use of paper. It has procured electricity through mini hydel plant, and has plans to install bio gas generation facility in its campus. Besides efficient building cooling solutions, smart power management tools, cloud computing solutions and greener data centers it also has effective waste management strategies in place.

Automobile

Hero MotoCorp has adopted a number of initiatives and tools in its organization to minimize the use of resources and to take care of the waste product leading to sustainable development. Some of the initiatives are:

· *Green Technology*: Hero MotoCorp has introduced a special painting process known as Acrylic Cathodic Electro Deposition (AECD) for the frame body. This new process leads to 99% paint transfer efficiency as well as minimizes effluents. The Company also used water soluble paint which is environment friendly ensuring quality and product.

· *Cleaner Processes*: Raw materials and chemicals are first tested on their impact on environment before introduced them in the process of production. Hero MotoCorp has eliminated the use of harmful substance like Hexavalent Chromium, Asbestos, and Phenolic Substances for many years now.

· *Green Roof program*: This program saves huge amount of energy by moderating temperature of roof and surrounding areas. It also helps in reducing storm water runoff volume and peak flow rate. In this way this eco – friendly method restores ecological and aesthetic value.

· *Green Supply Chain*: In the supply chain, the Company has launched two programs, The 'Green Dealer Development Program' for the front end and the 'Green Vendor Development Program' for the backend of the supply chain. In each of these programs, the partners are made aware of the importance of environmental issues as well as managing material resources, energy resource, industrial wastes, pollution and other effluents.

· *Rain Water Harvesting*: The Company has introduced Rain Water Harvesting at both its plants in Dharuhera and Gurgaon of Haryana, one of the driest states in India. In both plants, 16 rainwater harvesting catchments have been set up covering an area of 31540sqmts saving around 18 million liters of water annually.

Maruti Suzuki, another Indian automobile giant, has introduced fuel efficient engines, which gives greater mileage. They have also introduced vehicles which are factory fitted with dual fuel engines, and comply with European ELV norms, which mean that nearly 85% of the car is recyclable. They have strict adherence to BS III and BS IV emission norms and have brought reduction in landfill waste, reduction of groundwater consumption, reduction in CO_2 emission through processes like installation of solar panels, LED lights.

Banking

Reserve Bank of India acknowledges the term *green banking* in its publication, Policy Environment, 2009 – 2010. This report also provides the outlines for the implementation of Green IT in all areas of work in the financial sector. Subsequently, financial institutions are taking up a number of philanthropic activities under the CSR banner. In an emerging market such as India, projects which focus on clean production, good corporate governance, and sustainable energy are considered attractive business opportunities for the financial institutions.

The Indian financial institutions have incorporated sustainability by incorporating in their functions. They have embedded the concept of sustainability in their core business processes like decision making and risk management. Generally, in India, a separate organization or foundation is set up with the main purpose of giving back to the society. The main activities of such an organization relate to under privileged, education and social initiatives, partnering with an NGO or charity house, organizing employee engagement drives, in which employees donate part of their income, volunteer their time and share their knowledge for various community services.

Disclosure of sustainability performance helps in the ranking of financial situations based on global indices such as the Dow Jones Sustainability Index (DJSI), which tracks sustainable – driven companies worldwide on their financial performance. According to Ernst & Young Report, the steps that a financial services organization can take towards sustainability reporting are:

· develop a sustainable strategy

· identify a sustainability reporting roadmap

· develop and implement sustainability management systems

· assess sustainability relating to risk and opportunities

· obtain assurance on sustainability reports including on health and safety aspects

ICICIBank has promoted a number of green programs and technologies as part of giving back to the system. Some of these are:

- *Home Finance*: Under this program, the Bank offers reducing fees to customers who purchase homes in 'Leadership in Energy and Environmental Design' (LEED) certified buildings.

- *Vehicle Finance*: Under Vehicle Finance, the bank offers 50% waiver on processing fee on car models uses alternative mode of energy. These cars include Hyundai's Santro Eco, Maruti's LPG version of Maruti 800, Civic Hybrid of Honda, Omni and Versa, Reva Electric cars, Mahindra Logan CNG versions and Tata Indica CNG.

- *Instabanking*: This refers to Internet banking, i – Mobile banking, and IVR banking.This helps to reduce business commute.

ICICI Bank has also launched programs for employees such as follows:

- Fully utilizing power saving settings when in use and turning off lights and electronic equipments when not in use

- Use of CFLs bulbs

- Using online Webinars to save travel cost and time

- Use of car pool and public transport system

ICICI Bank has also initiated and promoted a program in making institutions, corporate, banks, and government agencies aware of environment issues like biodiversity, wildlife habitats and environment.

IndusIndBank, another local bank has initiatives like solar powered ATMs, thin computing, e-archiving, e-learning, e-waste management, paperless fax, energy conservation and also supports finance programs with incentives to go green. With the solar-powered ATM, the bank expects to save around 1,980 Kw of energy annually besides reducing carbon emissions by 1,942 kg. It also expects to save power bills of around Rs. 20,000 per year in urban areas, where it replaces diesel generators with solar panels.

Application of Green and Eco – Friendly Technologies in Rural India

India at present has promoted and facilitated a number of green and eco – friendly technologies in the rural sector. These technologies are implemented at the national level, regional level, and at the state level as given below:

At the National level:

- *SOLECKSHAW*: CMERI has developed a Solar Powered Electric three – Wheeled Vehicle, named as SOLECKSHAW. This vehicle transporting people through small distances, especially in busy streets of cities. It is an environment – friendly car since it is free from toxic emissions. The novelty of this invention is the use of Brushless Direct Current (BLDC) hub motor instead of Permanent Magnetic Direct Current (PMDC) motor. The electric drive has been separated by installing BLDC motor directly on to the front axle and the mechanical drive on the rear axle. This system has also eliminated the use of mechanical devices like spring loaded frictional plate and couplings.

- *Cabinet Dryer and Washing Unit for Ginger and Turmeric*: CMERI has developed an Improved Cabinet Dryer with higher drying rate. The availability of the sun is uncertain and hence the cabinet dryer serves as a useful device for preservation of ginger and turmeric produced by rural farmers. Likewise, CMERI has developed a continuous type washing unit where waste water is being filtered and re – circulated.

- *Cultivation of Medicinal and Aromatic Plants*: The cultivation and processing of aromatic and medicinal plants have enriched the bio – diversity of North Eastern Region as well as opening new opportunities for income generation in the rural sector. IIIM has developed and standardized cultivation and processing technologies in the case of rose, lavender, clarysage, rose geranium and others.

- *Low – Cost Oxygen Monitor*: The system is useful for measuring the oxygen percentage in the stack gas monitoring which in turn improves the combustion efficiency of the oil fired boilers used in various industries, ultimately to a cleaner and friendly environment

The successful models taken by the State Science and Technology Councils in India are as follows:

Technologies for Water Purification and Waste Management

- *Plastic and hospital waste management system*: Four plasticand hospital waste disposal demonstration plants based on indigenously developed plasma incineration technologies were set up at ecologically fragile locations having tourist influx at Goa, A&N Islands, Himachal Pradesh & Sikkim and other locations in the states of Andhra Pradesh, Haryana, Uttar Pradesh and Tripura.

With a view to provide safe drinking water, *water purification technologies* are adopted to remove contaminants from drinking water. These technologies are installed in different states in India.

- *Pilot demonstration plant* for treatment of hard/brackish water based on indigenously developed Reverse Osmosis Technology was installed at UttarlaiAirforce Station, Barmer. The project is successful and has been providing drinking water to inhabitants of air – base as well as nearby villages.

- *A sea – water desalination plant* based on 2 – Stage desalination process

283

development indigenously was installed in Nelmudar village, Tamil Nadu.

Distributed Energy Systems

In order to promote decentralized energy generation based on locally available resources, the following technologies are demonstrated at various places:

- *Bio – Diesel production plant* (100L/batch)set up at Orissa with IIT Delhi Technology.

- The Bio – Fuel Plant developed at JSS Academy of Technical Education, Bangalore has been installed at Utthan Center for Sustainable Development and Poverty Alleviation, UP & Raipur Institute of Technology, Raipur Chattisgarh.

- *Biomass Gasifier Project* using 30kg woody biomass per hour with 100% producer gas based engine has been installed at village Bagdora, Chattisgarh. The plant is operated by the Village Energy Committee (VEC). The plant is operating in the morning for commercial activity for 2 hours and in the evening for lighting purpose for 4 hours.

- *Biogas enrichment plant* to meet the electricity requirement has been installed at Rajasthan Go – SewaSangh, Jaipur, The plant has a biogas enrichment system used to get 95% Methane for power generation based on water scrubbing technology developed by IIT, Delhi.

- *Ferro Cement Roof Top Rain Water Harvesting Technology* constructed by Himachal Pradesh State Council of S&T, which was installed at Shimla.

At the Regional Level with Reference to North Eastern Region

In the North Eastern Region of India, the North – East Institute of Science & Technology which was established in the year 1961 has promoted a number of green initiatives. Some of the initiatives are as follows:

- *Agro practices of medicinal plants* like dioscorea, solaniumkhasianum, annatto, bhringaraj, kalmegh, punarnava, agechtachitrak, vedailota, and iswarmul which are used in treating diseases.

- *Bio – Organic Fertilizer*: It is an ecofriendly product of bioactive and organic compound. It enhances the soil fertility and plant growth, and it protects the soil and soil beneficial microbes. This fertilizer can be used for all types of cultivation.

- *VERMICOMPOST*: It is well recognized as an important organic manure for plant growth and development. It improves the physical conditions of soil, and helps in biodegradation of organic compounds and therefore improves the soil fertility.

- *Bacterial Culture for Crop*: It is a new formulation based on plant growth promoting rhizobacteria. It is used for all types of crops and it protects the plant from fungal diseases and enhances the microbial biodiversity. In this way, it increases crop yield.

- *Ceiling Board*: It is an environmental friendly product. The process is based on agricultural waste and by – products. Its main raw materials are agricultural wastes like paddy husk.

- *ACRYLAMIDE*: It is an environmental friendly product. It has a great demand a starting material for production of various polymers to be used as flocculating agents, stock additives and polymers for petroleum recovery.

- *Electronic Grade Potassium Silicate*: It is used for fixing TV tubes and screens. The product is an electronic grade and purity is very high. It is free from environmental hazards.

- *DEOILER*: It is used in oil industry for removal of oil from large volume of associate water effluent. It is an environmental friendly chemical and can remove as much as 90% of the oil present in the water.

- *Banana Fibers*: Fibers from banana pseudo stem can be used for manufacture of ropes and twines for packaging industry and also for manufacturing hessian clothes. It can also be utilized for making dolls, bags, table and door mats, baskets, and other products. Its process is eco - friendly with less disposal problem.

At the State Level with reference to Meghalaya

In the state of Meghalaya, the State Council of Science, Technology & Environment has adopted a number of green and eco – friendly technologies. The innovative technologies are:

- Improved Chula
- Water Filtration
- Solar LED Lighting
- Stabilized Mud Block
- Fire Retardant & Life Extended Thatch Roof
- Low – Cost Sanitation
- Rain Water Harvesting
- Organic Chapter 10Composting
- Pedal Pump
- Hydraulic Ram Pump
- Low – Cost Oven
- Low – Cost Cold Storage
- Leaf Plate Making
- Paper Re-cycling

There is no denying the fact that India has done a lot of work in saving resources, environment preservation and in giving back to the system, but there is a lot more for India to achieve in this regard. At present, there are no strict regulations that mandate sustainability reporting. However, certain measures are taken up by Government of India to make Indian corporations environmentally and socially responsible. One of such measures is a policy that will cause all PSUs, companies and financial institutions to invest 50% of their CSR funds in afforestation initiatives. Secondly, the Confederation of Indian Industry (CII) is coming up with a *green rating system* for the companies. Thirdly, the Institute of Chartered Accountants of India is working on a new set of rules on CSR. The urgency to adopt sustainability has been intensified with the launch of Sustainable Development Funds and Indices in India such as CRISIL, S&P ESG Index.

The paper concludes by seeking suggestions from the other learned international speakers to address crucial issues of India like the recycle of huge amount of waste resource and empowering the law enforcement authority which at present is weak.

References:

1. Annual Report 2009-10, Department of Scientific and Industrial Research, Ministry of Science and Technology, Government of India.

2. State Science and Technology Program (SSTP), 2010, Ministry of Science and Technology, Government of India, New Delhi.

3. Annual Report, 2010, North Eastern Institute of Science and Technology, Jorhat, Assam.

4. Annual Report, 2006, RRL Jorhat Technologies, Assam.

5. Newsletter, September 2010, State Council of Science, Technology & Environment,
                    Meghalaya.

6.Maruti Suzuki Sustainability Report 2009-10

7. Infosys Sustainability Report 2009-10.

8. Finesse, Financial Service Newsletter, Nov 2010-Feb 2011, Ernst and Young.

9. http://en.wikipedia.org/wiki/Automotive_industry

10. http://www.oica.net/category/production-statistics/

11. http://en.wikipedia.org/wiki/Information_technology

12.http://www.airtel.in/wps/wcm/connect/About%20Bharti %20Airtel/bharti+airtel/media+centre/bharti+airtel+news/corporate/pg-statement-from-bharti-airtel-green-initiatives

13. http://ibnlive.in.com/news/icici-goes-green-makes-offices-ecofriendly/86140-7.html

14. http://business-standard.com/india/news/for-banks-green-isnew-black/395561/

15. http://www.icicibank.com/go-green/Index.html

16.http://www.wiprogreentech.com/recycled_plastic_content.html

17. http://www.businessstandard.in/india/news/indusind-bank-launches-first-solar-powered-atm/81456/on

18. http://www.indusind.com/indusind/wcms/en/home/top-links/investors-relation/analyst-meet/QIPInvestorPresentationAugust2010.avsFiles/PDF/QIP%20Investor%20Presentation.pdf

19. http://www.epa.vic.gov.au/climate-change/glossary.asp#CAM

20. http://climatechange.worldbank.org/node/3828

21. http://www.delhimetrorail.com/whatnew_details.aspx?id=LrHUclpDo3glld&rdct=d

22.http://www.vodafone.com/content/dam/vodafone/about/sustainability/reports/vodafone_sustainability_report.pdf

Chapter 12: Biodiversity

12. Introduction: The importance of the physical aspects of Green Economics

Miriam Kennet

When I conceived the academic discipline of green economics, I imagined that we need to consider the social aspects -the economics and the physical aspects which I thought about as being the earth sciences. At the time this was considered bordering on the crazy. However events have proven that a wider scope of economics is actually " correct " as volcanic activity for example imposed huge costs on European aviation and the climate rapidly changing to very hot or very cold and extreme events starts to impose massive costs and limits on the economy and trade.

My idea was that economics theory should now expand to include all people everywhere, nature, other species, the planet and its systems.

Such systems included climate but also seismic activity which has begun to be affected by human activity and needs to costed in as a background to many economics activities.

12.1 Human vs. Nature: Finding the controversial balance between economic survival and ecological preservation on the Galapagos Islands

Grit Silberstein

The Galapagos Islands are one of the few last paradises on our planet. Known as the place where nature is shown at its first stage and reflecting the living example of Charles Darwin's evolution theory, Galapagos offers a natural treasure not existing anywhere else. But in a world of consumption and luxury not even this paradise has been spared from the influence of mankind and is now suffering the consequences of this.

Despite the fact that 97.3% of the archipelago has been declared a national reserve by the Ecuadorian Government and that the National Park Administration and the Ingala (Instituto Nacional Galapagos) are constantly monitoring all activity on the islands, the problems that mankind has introduced are now irreversible. Introduced fauna and flora are only a small part of the problems destroying the balance of the ecosystem.

The main issue that affects the Galapagos is the local population that has been living there for many years. For many generations the so called "Galapaguenios" have learned to respect the fragile ecosystem which humans have intruded upon and have realized that the only way of surviving on the islands is to become part of nature and not to exploit and destroy it. Galapaguenios have lived from fishery and tourism for many years. But in a world with constant economic growth, globalisation and demand for luxury and living in a country that has had an unstable economy for the last 60 years, the Galapagos have become subject to international corporations trying to exploit the islands with tourism and over-fishery of its unique underwater wildlife, as well as a growing population that due to the influences of the external world has seen itself in a situation where economic survival goes before their appreciation of nature.

As the Galapagos Islands are appreciated worldwide as one of the last few natural paradises untouched by mankind, this situation has increased the concern about the destruction of this fragile ecosystem. This chapter will discuss the ecological problems that the islands are currently facing and the balance between human and nature that the Galapagos Park Administration and the Ecuadorian Government are trying so hard to find.

The battle human versus nature started a long time ago, when the Spanish conquerors first sailed out to the Pacific Ocean in the 15th century and found the untouched Archipelago. In the years to come the Islands remained forgotten by civilisation and were used by British pirates to hide and store their captured goods (Ingala, 2010). Pirates and whalers were for a long time the only permanent visitors to the Islands and took advantage of the natural richness of its fauna. Tortoises were used as living food rich in fat and meat and easy to store for long journeys. Even being an almost untouched Archipelago and without having the tools mankind has today, these people were unfortunately able to reduce the tortoise population and even eliminate complete species. It was not until 1832 that the Islands were officially declared part of the Ecuadorian territory.

The man who had the greatest influence on the Islands was probably Charles Darwin, who, as a young student sailed to the Galapagos as the first person to carry out a scientific study there. Thanks to the five weeks of study he spent on four of the Islands, he found a base for the evolution theory, which today is world known and has had great influence in the world of science and religion (Ingala, 2010). The Ecuadorian Government first utilized the Islands for convicts and criminals, who were the first permanent inhabitants on four of the biggest Islands (Epler, 2007, 7)

During World War II, Galapagos was used as a base for the US-Military, who used the Island of Baltra as naval base. Today Baltra remains the island with the smallest percentage of protected area, serves as the main airport to the Islands and still has remaining pieces of the former US-base distributed all over the island.

A research station was built on the main island of Sta. Cruz and Ecuador established the Archipelago as protected National Park. Since the 1960's the National Park Administration has regulated the annual number of visitors, being only 1000 back then and increasing to 60000 annually in 1991 (Ingala, 2010). In 1978 the UNESCO recognized the Islands as World Natural Heritage, being extended to the marine reserve in 2001.

The inhabitants of the Islands had been living mainly from agriculture and fishery until the Ecuadorian Government realized that tourism would probably be the biggest and most sustainable long term income source for the islands. According to MacFarland (2001), the Charles Darwin Station "felt strongly that nature tourism represented the economic activity that was by far the most compatible with conservation of the archipelago's biological diversity, evolutionary and ecological processes, and environment"(Epler, 2007, 7).

In 1968 the first steps towards today's tourism industry were made, by introducing cruise tours around the islands and regular flights from the Ecuadorian mainland twice a week. It was not until the late 1970's when tourism started to expand and clearly proved to be the holding ground for the emerging economy on the islands. Being mainly controlled and owned by the Galapaguenios at the beginning of the tourism boom, large international companies soon started investing in the islands, expecting high returns to take to their home countries. The oil boom that the government was experiencing in the early 1980s helped to invest more public funding into the province of Galapagos. The National Institute of Galapagos (INGALA) was created to help the National Park Administration to combine economic growth and development projects with the big task of conservation of the

Islands (Epler, 2007, 8).

Galapagos turned from the feared home of convicts to the most prosperous province of Ecuador, offering a very low unemployment rate and higher salaries than the mainland. This attracted many Ecuadorians to move to the Islands.

Over the years, the number of tourists has increased drastically. For this reason not only Ecuadorians from the mainland left their homes to live on the Enchanted Islands, but also many foreigners and even agriculturists from the Islands itself saw the opportunity that the tourism market was offering and decided to invest into it.

With an increasing tourism market, the National Park saw the danger that uncontrolled tourism could be for the Islands and decided to take action and create a tourism management system to regulate it as much as possible. Several restrictions were introduced that have been kept until today.

One of the main restrictions has been to control the vessel movements on the Archipelago, allowing each vessel only to sail a certain route and visit certain Islands only. The control and monitoring of this restriction is much regulated and is punished severely if violated by the vessel-owners. Together with this restriction the National Park has categorized the Archipelago into three different sections, restricted areas (no tourism allowed at all), intensive areas (only monitored visits) and recreational areas (Direction del Parque Nacional Galapagos, 2010). A second regulation in 1993 was to introduce high entrance fees to the National Park that cannot be avoided by tourists under any circumstances and have to be paid directly by entering the airport.

The formation of SICGAL, the inspection and quarantine program, in 1999, was one important step which benefits the conservation of flora and fauna on the Islands. This program is in charge of dealing with the problem of introduced species on the Islands that have been interrupting the ecosystem since men first put foot on the Archipelago.

"In 1535 the Galapagos Islands were discovered. From that moment and with the onset of human activities, began its process of degradation, due in particular to the effect that introduced species had in an environment where indigenous species evolved without the presence of large predators" (National Park Galapagos, 2010)

Rats, goats, dogs and cats are only some of the species that endanger the Islands. Also plants like the blackberry and guayaba have devastating effects on the Islands. It is estimated that 36 species of introduced vertebrate and 543 invertebrate animals are currently living on the Islands and have already caused the extinction of several native species, such as the Galapagos rat. One way of controlling introduced species has been through the detailed control of any merchandise that is sent to the Islands. For the matter SICGAL has trained 32 specialized inspectors working on the Islands and on the Ecuadorian mainland controlling every single item that is being sent. On the other hand there have been several projects of eradication of species already existing on the Islands (National Park Galapagos, 2010).

The National Park Administration is currently putting great emphasis on the sustainable development of the Islands. The main aim of this is to find a solution to the dilemma man vs. nature on the Islands and to create a sustainable environment in which the economic aims of the population and the conservation of the Islands can be assured.

One main project is the environmental management of populated areas. Although the populated areas of the Galapagos are only 3% of the whole Archipelago, it is vital to manage the environment, and not only in the natural and marine reserve (National Park, 2010). One of the biggest disasters on the Galapagos caused by mankind was indisputably the accident of the oil-tanker Jessica in 2001, which split more than 800,000 gallons of oil into the waters surrounding the Islands. Only a miracle was able to prevent the worst and the oil was drawn into open sea (Diario El Hoy, 2001). The rapid population growth on the Islands which in 1974 was only at roughly 4000 inhabitants and in 2006 already at over 14.000 inhabitants (National Institute of Statistics and Census) also increases the demand of basic needs, such as water, electricity and food, which has to be provided by the Government. Population growth is one of the main issues that put pressure on the natural capital that the Islands have preserved for so many years. A detailed management plan is therefore required that delivers solutions to the increasing demands of the population and is capable of preventing catastrophes, such as the Jessica accident in 2001. The National Park is aware of these risks and is constantly working on new ideas for a sustainable living on the Islands, such as renewable energy, land usage planning and waste management (National Park Galapagos, 2010).

One important issue on the Galapagos not discussed in this chapter so far is fishery. Fishery is one of the two most traditional productive activities on the Galapagos. But it is also a goldmine for the international fishery industry due to its unique location between the cold Humboldt Current and the warm current from the north, which provides a wide range and number of fish. Since the 1950s Galapagos has been subject to the international fish trade, but it was only in the 1970s when fish cutters with on-board freezers were introduced, that the fish market on the Islands was exploited. In these years up to 186 annual tons of cod were exported from the Islands to the rest of the world (Oxford P., Watkins G., 2009). Lobster and sea-cucumber are also high-demand goods on the international market. The National Park Galapagos has elaborated a special regulation plan called "Special Fishing Regulations in the Galapagos" developed especially with the idea of a sustainable marine reserve and conservation priorities. Additionally to this the Park regulates fishing through fishing permits and does only allow the so called artisanal fishing. Fishery permits and allowed amounts of fish are constantly adapted to the conditions of the marine reserve. The fishery of sea-cucumber for example had been restricted for several years in the past. Due to a high demand on the Asian market and its high value, fishermen have demanded to open the fishery for this exotic animal. The Ecuadorian government released the restriction and now allows the fishery under very strong monitoring in order to guarantee sustainable fishing (National Park Galapagos, 2010).

It is now clear how close the natural preservation of the Enchanted Islands is to the economic necessities of its inhabitants and the Ecuadorian government itself. Tourism is one of the major sources of income in Ecuador which is mainly due to the attractiveness of the Galapagos Islands. As the fact is that the Islands will never be without human influence again, it is the task of the Ecuadorian government and its population to assure a sustainable development in which the Islands can keep their untouched nature as far as possible and the paradise can be preserved intact. Surprisingly the Ecuadorian government has shown that its interest has always been to achieve this goal and has worked since the very early stage of human settlement on the Islands to find a harmonic coexistence between mankind and nature on the Archipelago. The influence of government has increased along the years introducing more restrictions and raising awareness among the population, but the task of teaching mankind to respect its nature regardless of the benefit that could be obtained through its exploitation is very hard to achieve and it is clear that in order to accomplish this there are many more milestones to reach and many obstacles to overcome. But it is not only the task of the Ecuadorian government, but also from every single on of us to open our eyes and save the probably last remaining untouched paradise on our planet.

The ideas in this chapter were first published in the Proceedings of the 5th Annual Green Economics Institute Conference at Oxford University, July 2010, and published by the Green Economics Institute.

12.2 How do you conserve elephants in an area which is already suffering from poverty and resource degradation?

Susan Canney

Under conventional top-down "management approaches" (Homer-Dixon,2006), it is an impossibility, because the area is vast (40,000km2) and because the government does not have the resources in money or personnel. Here, a more fine-grained "green economics" approach (Kennet and Heinemann, 2006) is taken that focuses on what we wish to achieve, and then finds the means to deliver in a way that is equitable, participatory,inclusive and consensual to ensure long-term sustainability. The desired results are: the peaceful coexistence of elephants and humans; the rehabilitation of the ecosystem; an improvement in local livelihoods, and our means to achieve them was to bring together the diverse sectors of the community and empower them to find solutions.

This area lies south of the bend in the Niger River where an internationally important population of around 550 "desert elephants" makes the longest migration in Africa. Data from GPS elephant collars collected by Save the Elephants was used in conjunction with satellite imagery and GIS data to understand how they have survived in this harsh environment where others on a similar latitude have disappeared (Canney et al.,2007).

The way elephants use space is critical: dry-season water is available only in the north of their range, good quality forage is found in the south, and they avoid human activity wherever possible. They move rapidly along migration corridors between areas where they linger. These contain key resources required at particular times of the year. One of these, for example, contains the only accessible water at the end of the dry season, Lake Banzena. In the south, a powerful pastoralist chief has prevented an area of rich wet season forage from clearance by agriculturalists. In another, Burkina Faso's protected areas along the international boundary are a legacy of the 1980s border-war. Meetings and workshops with community leaders (both traditional and elected), government administration and technical services, NGOs and projects operating in the area, helped to understand attitudes towards the elephants and links to the wider socio-environmental context. Pastoral livelihoods in this area have historically depended on negotiated, non-exclusive access to water and reciprocal land-use agreements between pastoralists and agriculturalists. This was a flexible system that could respond rapidly to changing environmental conditions, but during the wet years of the 50s and 60s, a focus on modern, technocratic solutions to development resulted in the over-extension of agriculture, the northward expansion of cropl land into marginal areas, increases in stocking and subsequent resource degradation.

When rainfall decreased again in the 70s and 80s, famine and death of humans and livestock ensued, accompanied by great societal disruption (Dong et al., 2011). Today, the north of the elephant range is predominantly a pastoral area, while much of the south between stabilized sand-dunes is agricultural and agro-pastoral. Threats to the elephants are the same as the threats to the livelihoods of the local population and the resilience of the ecosystem to cope with environmental change, namely:

* Pressure from the south, as people search for new land to farm, and dispossessed herders try shifting agriculture that ultimately results in soil erosion and loss.
* The legacy of well- intentioned development interventions e.g. financial incentives to develop market gardens around water holes attracting agriculturalists from elsewhere.
* Livestock pressure from the river towns where middle classes amass huge "prestige" herds that need to travel further and further afield to find pasture
* Urban commercial interests cutting trees and gathering non-timber forest products.
* The disinclination to respect the resource management systems of another ethnicity.

Our aim is to combat the current anarchic use of natural resources by bringing the diverse clans, ethnicities and interests together so that local communities can sustainably manage their water, pasture, trees and wildlife. We began at Lake Banzena, the lynch-pin of the elephant migration where competition for resources between a recently resident population, commercial interests, "prestige" herds, and the elephants is most severe. Household visits and community meetings enabled us to tease out the dimensions of the problem and canvas opinions. Surprise findings were that 96% of the cattle using the lake belonged to "prestige herds" and that over 50% of the population suffered from water-borne disease.

We helped the community to (i) agree on the problems and their drivers, (ii) find inclusive and equitable solutions that all subscribed to, (iii) draft the text of formal conventions. The resulting plan was to relocate to a currently waterless area outside the elephant range
with abundant pasture by providing three wells, and establishing structures that placed the resources of the area under the control of the local community:

* A management committee, that determines the rules of resource management to allow use limitation if necessary, charge others for access to

resources, and protect the migration route
* Brigades of young men to patrol and work with government foresters to deal with infringements
 * A council of elders who determine the penalties for offenders
The management committee's first action was to designate a 40,000 hectare sylvo-pastoral reserve to ensure that there is pasture through the dry season. This was spontaneously added to by adjacent communes to make a total of 923,800 hectares. Every year much of the area burns but supporting the community construction of fire-breaks meant that this area was the only part of the northern range not to lose its pasture in bush fires. Other communities are now asking to join the process.

While it acts in the spirit of Mali's decentralization legislation, it is a new approach and following visits by the Minister and top levels of the civil service, national government has provided two of the three water-points and helped enshrine these systems in national law,
supporting its extension throughout the elephant range.

This adaptive, learning approach has revealed solutions that would be invisible to sectoral perspectives, and created synergy between existing assets and structures to respond to local needs, roots initiatives locally, and enhance long-term sustainability.

References
Canney, S., K. Lindsey, E. Hema, V. Martin, I.Douglas-Hamilton. The Mali elephant initiative: a synthesis of knowledge, research
and recommendations concerning the population, its range and the threats to the elephants of the Gourma. Wild Foundation—Save the Elephants—Environment and Development Group, Oxford,
2007.
Dong, S., L. Wen, S. Liu, X. Zhang, J. P.Lassoie, S. Yi, X. Li, J. Li, and Y. Li. 2011. Vulnerability of worldwide pastoralism to global changes and interdisciplinary strategies for sustainable pastoralism.
Ecology and Society 16(2): 10. [online] URL:
http://www.ecologyandsociety.org/vol16/iss2/art10/
Homer-Dixon, T. The Upside of Down: Catastrophe, Creativity and the Renewal of Civilization. Random House Canada, Toronto, 2006.
Kennet, M. and V. Heinemann. 2006. Green Economics: setting the scene. International Journal of GreenEconomics 1 (1/2) 68-102.Inderscience Publishers

12.3 EU Fisheries Policy and Estonia

Maret Merisaar MP

If we learn that someone has dealt with illegal felling of trees or find a clearing area with too high stumps, then we used to be very indignant. In Estonia, most of the people have helped to plant new trees under the supervision of a local forestry board or at least they agree, that a proper forest management means that the clearing areas need to be reforested. But economic activities under the water surface that do not respect the ecological reproductivity requirements (read: overfishing) do not catch our eye in normal everyday life and the wider public does not consider this problem which touches them very closely. Thus even the chair of the fisheries commissioner in the European Commission and the appointment of a freshly elected MEP into the relevant EP working committee are said to be the least popular choices. At least this is what the author of the present article was told at a seminar on EU Common Fisheries' Policy Reform held in Poland recently. It is small to wonder that the main goal of the CFP has been the possibly best supply of fish products to the European citizens' dinner table. Until now, the efforts of the scientists and ecologists to knock on the consiousness of the politicians and remind them about the reproductivity capacities of the fish stocks has not been successful.

The same can be said about the work at the Baltic Sea Fisheries Commission, that was located in Poland, Gdansk, where in the distribution of fishing quotas, the voice of the industrial fishing companies was always stronger than that of the experts. One of the international meetings of that Commission has been held in Estonia, Tallinn, a number of years ago, and the Estonian young environmental activists organised a street action with fish-shaped leaflets and real fishing nets that caught a lot of media attention. The leaflets were demanding a temporary total ban on cod fisheries and on the harmful fishing gear: nets with too small a mesh size used for fishing sprats and small herring.

Green winds

Today the fishing rights in the Baltic Sea are supervised by the Regional Advisory Committee located in Copenhagen where the European Commission has a very strong mandate and where one third of the delegates represent different non-governmental organisations of fishermen. Although the so called industrial fishermen have a stronger voice, now once again the anglers ' organisations from all countries around the Baltic Sea can have hope to see a ray of light from the current reform of the CFP; that is supposed to be based on ecosystem philosophy in the future.

Green principles are very slow to enter the the EU agricultural and fisheries policies but this time the expectations of the ecologists and nature protection activists are quite high. It should be said that the positions of the government of Estonia on the discussion document called Green Book on CFP were almost one to one (ecept those on access rights) are in fact the same as those of the greenest environmentalists.

The European Commission started its public discussions on CFP reform in April 2009 and by December of the same year, they collected the opinions of different organisations on the shortcomings of the existing policy. Without willing to burden the reader with too specific details, one of the questions for example was about granting the fishing quota either to each fishing vessel separately or to each country as a whole. In the latter case, if the quota of salmon for example is exhausted by October according to the reports, none of the vessels can continue to fish it until next year. The other problems discussed included cases where tonnes of herring have been poured back to the sea to make room for catches of some more worthy species. Or how to stop landing of undersize salmon (17 cm) under the name of trout in the terminals.

On the CFP seminar mentioned above, the representatives of the Estonian, Latvian, and Lithuanian Anglers' Associations said, that in the Baltics the fishing requirements are usually strictly respected. But when the local coastal fishermen who have waited until the fish (sprat, small herring) has grown to the necessary size arrives to the harvesting site in its national territorial waters, the stocks have already been taken by some industrial fishing company under a foreign flag. To ensure the better representation of the coastal fishermen of the Baltic Sea states among the big fishing policy, an umbrella organisation for the national anglers associations was created on the same seminar. The author of the present article had the honour to supervise the signing of the oversea association contract and statute as an observer. The festive *venttook* place on the board of a former Danish fishing boat „Anton" that today serves as an environmental awareness rising campaing boat. (see photo)

Some facts about the Common Fisheries'Policy

The Common policy adopted in 1983 (even in spite of its previous reform in 2002) has not been able to avoid overfishing and, in fact that the EU level fisheries has reached a crisis. European Auditors' Court found in 2007, that the failure of the CFP to manage fish resources in a sustainable way is mainly caused by the lack of political will. Although about a half of the fishing vessels are double the size than is necessary for fishing within the permitted quota, no limists to the vessel size and capacity have been applied. The quota agreed upon ecxeed the relevant values advised by the scientists for 48% on the average. In many countries the costs for administration in the fisheries sector are twice as high as the value of the catches. So it can be said that we pay twice for our fish dishes: once in the shop and the second time as a taxpayer. As for the EU financial subsidiums for the sector, one can say that the latter are directed for increasing the existing capacities of the fishing gear instead of elaborating more sustainable methods and equipment or recreation of stocks.

According to the scientific estimations already 88% of the world's stocks are overfished and for one third of the species the critical limit has exceeded so that these populations are unable to restore themselves in natural way.

In the autumn 2010 the EU Fisheries Commissioner MariaN Damanaki received a petition with more than 28 500 signatures from the citizens that had been up on the internet since the European Fish Week heldi n spring.

The petition asks for selecting the greener choices and solutions for the final new CFP documrent that will be adopted in spring 2012. The lobbying and negotiating process has not been finalised yet and all national fisheries interest groups can still lobby their authorities who attend the negotiations to stick to as green choices as possible. The goal should be kept clearly ahead despite of the possibility that for example the French cod fishing vesels can send out various protest signals that will be widely reflected in the big media. The decision makers of te Baltic countries – at least Estonia, Latvia and Lithuania - should consider the public opinion of our coastal fishermen (who make up a condiderable part of the fisheries community) as more important than the pressure from the industrial fishermen from abroad.

In addition to the umbrella network of anglers' associations, another channel of the public opinion expressing the views of the non goernmental enviropnment protection organisations of the countries arund the Baltic Sea ids Coalition Clean Baltic, (Estonian Green Movement and Estonian Society of Nature Conservaton belong there from Estonia).Pressure on the governmental sector is expressed via various conferences and international declarations

Fisheries Policy was also discussed on the European Green Parties Council Meeting that was held in Talinn, Estonia in October 2010, where a Position paper was signedas a result of a fringe meeting dedicated to the Baltic Sea region cooperation. Political parties can also contribute to the public awareness rising on important international environmental issues.

According to the EU Marine Strategy Framework Directive all seas of the union must be in good ecological status in 2020. Another policy document, Integrated Maritime Policy is aiming at the most efficient economic usage of marine resources. Coalition Clean Baltic was actively participating in the public consultations prior to both of these two documents, replying to the questionnaires via nternet. A substantial support to CCB in the work with the maritime policy was given by the Hamburg City Green councillors.

The Common Fisheries Policy stands as a separate policy document from the Integrated Maritime policy and CCB is taking part in the relevant consultations in the frame of an even bigger network called OCEN2012.

The demands of the international fisheries lobbyists for the CFP reform:

• Environment – The new CFP must enshrine environmental sustainability as the overarching principle without which economic and social sustainability is unobtainable. The precautionary and ecosystem-based approaches to fisheries management must form the fundamental basis.

• Decision-making – A governance framework that ensures policy is decided and implemented at the most appropriate levels and in a transparent way, with the meaningful participation of the stakeholders is needed in order to achieve the desired objectives. Long-term strategic decisions should be the business of Council and Parliament, whereas operational decisions should be taken at a more local/regional level.

• Access – The marine environment is a common good, and so it is in the public interest that activities impacting on the state of its fish stocks, and the larger ecosystem are carefully managed. Under the reformed CFP, those who fish in the most sustainable way should therefore be given priority access to

fishing grounds, within and outside of EU waters. Examples of these criteria are as follows:
- o Selectivity
- o Environmental impact
- o Energy consumption
- o Employment and working conditions
- o Quality of product
- o History of compliance
- Overcapacity – The reformed CFP must reduce fishing power to match available resources. Measure to reduce capacity must ensure that the remaining fleet is sustainable in size and characteristics.
- Subsidies – Public aid needs to support the recovery of fish stocks and facilitate the transition towards sustainable fisheries and provide value to society, while subsidies that sustain overcapacity are to be phased out.
- Transparency – sufficient information for the public, including
- Publishing data on all landings (like in USA and Norway)
- Data on the Vessel Monitoring System are available for the scientists (like in the USA and Norway)
- Data on the vessels acting in the territorial waters of the third countries are available for the latter
- Impact assessmets of FPAs (Partneship contracts in fisheries) are available for the public.

Estonian Ministers of Agriculture and Environment who share responsibilities in Fisheries management and protection , agreed with most of the above-mentioned statements except the ones on acces criteria.

Access to Fisheries in Estonia

General characterization of the fisheries sector

The main aspects characterising the fisheries sector in Estonia in 2010:

There are 1416 licencies for fishing issued, including 2 enterprices dealing with remote fishing, 30 enterprices dealing with trawling in the Baltic Sea, 1119 enterprices (including single physical persons having the status of an enterpreneur) dealing with coastal fisheries in the Baltic Sea and 265 enterprices (including single physical persons with enterpreneur status) dealing with fishing in the inland waters.

The largest enterprices are AS Reyktal that is fishing shrimps on the Northern Atlantic , AS Hiiu Kalur trrawling sprat and small herring in the Baltic Sea and OÜ Peipsi Grupp Holding fishing on the Lake Peipus.

In the coastal fishing sector the licences have been distributed eavenly and there is no cause to bring out single licence owners.

At the same time the simple structure of the licence holders is not enough to characterise the enterpreneurship in the fisheries sector. For example most of the 30 trawling vessels in the Baltic Sea have grouped under three producers' organisations, that coordinate their fishing and exporting activities.

In 2010 the members of these producers' organisations own 95% of Estonian sprat quota, 86% of the small herring quota and 48% of the cod quota. With the support from the European Fisheries Foundation, the producers' organisations have made some common investments (central freezing and logistical storages), that has significantly increased their competitiveness on foreign markets.

The European Agricultural and Fisheries Council gives quota for four fish species on the Baltic Sea: sprat, small herring, cod and salmon. In addition, all fished species in the Lake Peipus (and its connected neighbour Lake Lämmijärv) are annually given quotas by the Estonian-Russian intergovernmental commission.

There are no quota for the species fished in the Baltic coastal waters (pike-perch, perch, sparling (smelt)) but the fishing is regulated by technical fishing limitations. Quota are not used on the Lake Võrtsjärv either.

A more specified overview of the fishing enterprices' structure can be obtained after the Ministry of Agriculture will publish the results of professional fishing of the first quarter of the year 2011 for each enterprice on the bases of the recently changed Fishing Law.

Fishing licences

All professionally fished species are regulated either by fishing quota (maximum allowed catch) or fishing efforts in Estonia. Quota are used mainly for the fish species that are regulated on international and EU level (shrimp, sprat, small herring, salmon and cod but also for the Lake Peipus species pike-perch, perch, bream and other species of industrial importance). In the coastal fisheries of the Baltic Sea fishing efforts are applied (number of allowed fishing devices, periods when fishing is not allowed). For obtaining a more detailed overview, including the regulations for the fishing fleet, each fishing region should be charaterised separately, as there are several specifications in the relevant regulations.

According to the Fishing Law Paragraph 131 and paragraph 132 the fishing licences for the fishing fleet and the fishermen's licences for the enterpreneurs who are registered in the business register are issued by the Ministry of Agriculture. The order of issuing these licences is specified in the Regulation by the Government of the Republic of Estonia No 412. List of documents to be presented when applying for a professional fishing licence, the order of abolishing or stopping the validity of a fishing licence and the forms of the licence.

Each year, the fishing possibilities for each marine fishing area, county, inland waterbody and/or small island with permanent residents are established by the Government of the Republic (Fishing Law paragraph 134(3)).

According to the paragraph 134 of the Fishing Law, the licence for professional fishing is issued for a certain period not longer than one calendar year stating the the limits of annual fishing quota, number of fishing days, number of fishing devices or number of fishing fleet (in the following text called fishing possibilities). When calculating the fishing possibilities, the historical fishing rights of the certain enterpreneur (fishing possibilities used during the last three years) is taken for the basis.

Although the fishing licence is given for one calendar year, it can be terminated earlier. The bases for the latter occasion are listed in the Fishing Law paragraph 161 and include, for example, the exhausting of the particular fishing possibility, the fact that the person who received the licence is not meeting the necessary requirements any more or the person, who got the licence, or the fisherman, who has been noted on the licence, has violated the fishing demands that are listed in the paragraph 202 of the Fishing Law.

In the bases of the paragraph 11 of the Law on Environmental Charges the Minister of Environment is establishing the charges for fishing for each calendar year, taking into account the peculiarities of the fishing area, the kind of the fishing gear and its capacities or the fishing possibilities that are distributed with an international contract.

Management

A rights based management is applied in Estonia and as in one of the few EU member states, individual transferrable fishing rights are used in the whole proffessional fishing sector:

- through individual transferrable quota (ITQ) in both remote fishing and in Open Baltic trawling and
- through individual transferrable effort (ITE) in coastal fishing, inland waterbodies and partially in remote fishing.

The whole Estonian fishing fleet is involved in this system. In addition the fish resources are protected by various technical means, like certain periods or areas, when and where fishing is not allowed, especially during the spawning periods.

In addition a small number of regional limits for the fleet is applied, for example

- the trawling must not be carried out below the 20 m depth line and
- on the Livonian Bay, the trawling vessel can have up to 221 KW main vechicle.

The detailed list of regional and other limitations is published in the fishing regulation by the Government of the Republic of Estonia No 144 (from May 9, 2003).

Separate fishing possibilities are applied for the small islands like Kihnu, Manilaid, Ruhnu and Vormsi and these possibilities can only be used by the permanent residents of the particular islands.

For coastal fishing, the quota shares of the fish species, regulated on the EU level, are allocated for sprat (30% from the total Estonian sprat quota) and for cod (1% of the total Estonian cod quota)

Future plans related to the Common Fisheries Policy reform

The Government of Estonia has approved these positions on its meeting held on December 3, 2009, and the main principle running through is, that although the principal questions on fisheries policy should be solved on the level of the European Commission and European Parliament, the practical issues like system of the fishing regulation etc should remain in the competence of an individual member state, so that it would be possible to take into account local biological, social and economic circumstances.

At the same time, the European Union should share the best practices on the fishing right systems. For certain, Estonia with its individual quota is a good example of a local solution.

Translated from the Estonian by Maret Merisaar

12.4 Subspecific Variation – Biological and Economic Implications for the Conservation of Biodiversity

Russel Seymour

A Discussion of priority setting in conservation biology.

The "Principles" section provides some useful background material and is followed by four "Case Studies" where different problems are presented.

Principles

Systematic biology is the science that orders and classifies biodiversity. It informs all other areas of biological sciences, including conservation biology. Animals and plants are grouped and separated according to similarities and differences. The resulting classifications provide a logical structure that provides information on the evolutionary relatedness of different species and describes a hierarchy that links all known life.

Many species have widespread distributions spanning different environmental conditions and different habitats. Such wide ranging species typically include variation in both the appearance (the "phenotype") and genetic make-up (the "genotype"). The fact that species vary across their range is a logical result of Darwinian evolution by natural selection; different areas of the range will have different conditions and so will have different evolutionary forces acting. The 'survival of the fittest' means that those individuals most suited to their local environment will reproduce most effectively and so will pass on their genes to the next generation, bestowing desirable, inheritable traits to their offspring. This variation may demonstrate evolution in action and so is of great interest to evolutionary biologists. Organisms are also affected by their environment during their development (an effect known as phenotypic plasticity). The preservation of all geographically structured patterns of variation should also be important to conservation biologists. Identifiable geographically discrete variants may be recognised as subspecies and assigned a taxonomic name. The subspecies may, therefore act to define 'units' of biodiversity at a fine level within the species.

Much international legislation provides *de facto* recognition of the importance of within species diversity. For example, the Convention on Biological Diversity (the Rio Convention) and CITES recognise "diversity within species" and "subspecies or geographically separate population thereof" respectively. The IUCN also recognise and assess subspecies in their Red Data List of conservation threat levels.

However, 'units of biodiversity' may not, necessarily, be the same as 'units for conservation'. Units of biodiversity are determined by biologists and defined and described taxonomically. A 'unit for conservation' is a social construct determined by policy makers, administrators and politicians. While these people should take notice of the advice provided by the biologists, conservation policy may be set by taking in to account social, aesthetic, economic, ecological, religious, political, spiritual and other factors.

Conservation policy often requires legislation for its implementation. It should be remembered that biological inference derives from observation, typically from a set of specimens, to make generalisations about a population. It includes measurements and observations and must account for inherent error and variation. In contrast legislation requires definitive and unambiguous interpretation.

Four case studies are presented, briefly, below. These consider black rhino, impala (a small African antelope), ostrich and giraffe; each of these is considered to be a 'good' species and each has a widespread distribution.

Examples

"Fortress Conservation" - Black rhino (*Diceros bicornis*)

Black rhino numbers were severely depleted through the 1970s and 1980s. Numbering 65,000 in the mid-1960s numbers dropped by more than 95% leaving fewer than 3,000 individuals by the 1990s. Since then numbers have improved. The rhinos were killed for their horn which was used in traditional Chinese medicine and in making traditional carved dagger handles, particularly in Yemen.

Poaching pressure lead to serious declines in East African countries and gradually moved south as numbers declined. At one point the poaching pressure was so severe that a suggestion was made to capture and translocate as many black rhino as possible from all over the continent to a single (or a few) locations in southern Africa that could then be heavily guarded by military-style game rangers thus securing the future of the species.

Genetic Introgression (hybridisation) - Black faced impala (*Aepyceros melampus petersi*)

The black-faced impala is a small, distinct population of impala found in northern Namibia. As the name suggests this group has a unique black 'mask' from the forehead down the muzzle making it distinct from other members of the species, which is found over much of sub-Saharan Africa. The black faced impala has been variously described as a full species (*Aepyceros petersi*) or as a subspecies of the common impala (*Aepyceros melampus petersi*). The black faced impala population is relatively small (a few thousands of individuals) and lives almost entirely within protected areas.

In recent years farmers in areas surrounding these protected areas have

304

realised that there is more money to be made from tourists than from producing crops and have broadened their businesses into game ranches. To attract tourists they must first have facilities in which to house the tourists but, most importantly, they must have the animals that the tourists want to see. Many farms have few animals and it would take too long for the animals to recolonise naturally so the farmers have been buying in animals of various species from all over Africa. Where these new 'safari reserves' border on to protected areas the 'alien' impala have strayed into the protected areas and have begun to mate with the black faced impala, 'diluting' the genetic stock and reducing the incidence of the diagnostic black face.

Reintroducing 'lost' species – Ostrich (*Struthio camelus*)

Ostrich had been extinct in the Arabian peninsular for many years, most likely extirpated by man's activities including hunting, when a decision was made to reintroduce the species in an attempt to recreate the former ecosystem. The question that had to be asked was where should the ostriches come from to repopulate the Arabian peninsular?

There were museum specimens and pictures of Arabian ostriches. Eventually, based on morphological and habitat similarities as well as being the most geographically proximate population, ostriches were taken from east Africa for introduction. Subsequent genetic analysis showed that the extinct Arabian ostriches were more closely related to the ostriches found in north Africa.

High species numbers, low population numbers – Giraffe (*Giraffa camelopardalis*)

The giraffe is a species well known around the world. Almost everyone would recognise the unique long neck and long legs of the giraffe. However, few people realise that there are at least six types (subspecies) of giraffe. The IUCN considers the giraffe, as a species, to be "Low Risk – conservation dependent". This means that, so long as minimal effort is paid to looking after populations (for example those already inside protected areas) there is little risk of the giraffe, as a species, going extinct. It is true that numbers are healthy for the species (around 110,000), but there are a few subspecies where numbers have declined drastically in recent years and numbers are very low at present. The Rothschild's giraffe (*G. c. rothschildi*) has reduced to around 445. The western giraffe (*G. c. peralta*) is now down to only 70 individuals in Niger.

Questions

1. What should be the aim of conservation? Think in terms of patterns versus processes or species conservation versus ecosystem function. Are these mutually exclusive? [Hint: consider the rhino and ostrich examples]

2. How do you 'value' species, subspecies, populations or individuals? That is, how do you turn "units of biodiversity" into "units for conservation"? [Hint: consider the impala and giraffe examples]

3. What is the 'cost' of species conservation versus subspecies conservation? Don't just think in financial terms but in social, aesthetic, economic, ecological, religious, political and spiritual terms. What might the evolutionary cost be? [Hint: consider the rhino and impala examples]

12.5 Strengthening the forest cultural ecology environment protection education in China

Zhang Ying
Song Weiming

Forests have economic, ecological, social and cultural functions. Though there is substantial progress in China's forest ecological protection in recent years, there also exist the problems of insufficient attention to the forest cultural ecology environment protection education. This also includes the insufficient reinforcement of the social and cultural functions of the forests. This chapter observes that China's socio-economic development has come to a phase of maturity and consumption, so that forest cultural ecology environment preservation education is becoming the key to the future development of forestry; especially, with the higher level of urbanization, urban forest is the focus of the cultural ecology environment protection. Finally, the study suggests that forest cultural ecology environment protection education should be taken into forest legislation and management, so that with forestry development planning, the physical and spiritual wealth can be integrated, and the forest cultural ecology environment preservation education and green culture development can be promoted in China.

Introduction

Culture preservation is an issue arising in recent years. It mainly refers to the planning and protection of urban spaces, in order to realize comprehensively the civilized environment of the city or the so-called "built environment". Any city will be incomplete and lack internal value if it does not preserve its cultural ecology well, such as its history, humanities, arts, and science, though it may have good ecological environment and order.

Forests have economic, ecological, social and cultural functions. In recent years, the utilization and protection of forests' economic and ecological functions have advanced substantially, while the social and cultural functions have lagged. Preservation of forest ecology is the foundation for the development of forestry, whereas preserving the socio-cultural aspect of the forest, i.e. the forest cultural ecology, is the key and soul of future forestry. Therefore, forest cultural ecology environment preservation education is very urgent in China.

Necessity of the preservation education of forest cultural ecology environment

The current situation of China's forest ecology environment preservation education

Forest ecology preservation is concerned by every society in the world, as an important part of the global environment protection. Especially, with the popularity of the concept of sustainable development and the important role played by the forest in reducing the emission as the goal of the Kyoto Protocol, forestry is bestowed with ever more imprimaturs. While the traditional mode of forest management is being replaced by the more sustainable ones, in each country, forest ecology preservation has been enhanced to an unprecedented level and becoming one of the central strategic issues of national developments.

China has made great progress in forest ecology preservation (Cao, S., 2010). Firstly, the natural forest protection project has been implemented and deforestation has been prohibited. Till the end of year 2010, the natural forest under practical protection has reached 0.101 billion hectares nation-wide, accounting for 84.17% of the overall coverage of natural forestry. Secondly, the shelter forest system has been built up. Since 1950s, China has set up "three-north shelterbelt", coastal and Yangzi River shelterbelt subsequently, which has gradually improved the ecology status. Thirdly, the grain for green project has been implemented. As a result of which, 20.7902 million hectares of new forest is created, accounting for 2.83% of the total area of the project (State Forestry Administration, P. R. China, 2010). National compensation has also been arranged for the grain for forest project, to ensure the resumption and reconstruction of the forests institutionally. Fourthly, barren mountain and wasteland afforestation including overall resumption of vegetation coverage. The government will provide seedling for free and administer the policy of whoever owns the forest and whoever takes care of the forest benefits. Felling is subject to the constraints of national law and regulations. Fifth, is the construction of methane generation pits in the countryside, to stop burning woods for energy. "Gas for wood" has corrected the wantoneed for felling of trees to some extent and pushed ecology preservation forward. The current forest ecology preservation in China, however, cannot fully adapt to the demands of the society, economy and sustainable development, particularly the protection education of forest cultural ecology environment is far from enough, not even cultural ecology environment conservation awareness of forestry.

Existing problems in forest ecology environment preservation education

First, in contrast with the ever enlarging scale of forest ecology preservation, the cultural and social functions of forest education are not stressed accordingly. Many people simply equalize forest ecology preservation to afforestation, setting up natural reserve zone or forest park, and/or developing forestry tourism (State Statistical Bureau, P. R. China, 2010), leaving its socio-cultural functions largely disembodied. Some local governments only pay their attention to simple afforestation, tourism and economic benefits, ignoring spiritual, educational, cultural or entertainment activities; poor diversity in afforestation, and ecology tourism is also under-developed. Some other local governments have actually damaged the original natural scenery by putting in too much artificial scenery in natural reserve zones to solely enlarge tourism.

Secondly, forestry legislation has not yet emphasized from a holistic perspective that forest is integral to the whole ecological system, still withholding the resource economy mentality. China's Forestry Law is intended to protect the environment and provide forest products to meet the demands of economic development and people's livelihood, while dispensing with the resource economy mentality, is insufficient for reiterating forest resource development from the higher standpoint of ecological system protection. As a result, the current Forestry Law somehow weakens the social and cultural functions of forest resources, similarly, the forest ecology environment preservation education is ignored though it stresses the economic function of forest resources.

Thirdly, the shortcomings in forest management are hampering ecological system protection and forest cultural ecology environment education development. The backward management of China's forest resources and the insufficient investment is restricting the sustainable development of the forest resource. It is already held worldwide that as a social welfare enterprise, forest resource fostering needs policy support and capital provision from the government to improve ecological environment. The long term planned economy in China has still its influence in management of forest resources, including the separation of the owner and the user of national forest, the heavy forest taxation, and the lack of funding for forest construction. Although felling quota has been implemented to restrict felling activities in recent years, the overall insufficient investment has affected the ecological system preservation and forest cultural ecology environment education development.

Forest cultural ecology environment preservation education is the key and soul for future forestry development

With GDP per capita reaching 4000 dollars, China's social and cultural development has come to a stage of maturity and consumption. The next stage will be the pursuit of life quality. According to Marslow's Demands Hierarchy, after the lower physiological, security and emotion demands are satisfied, people's ascend to higher demands such as respect and self-realization (Zhang, C. & Luo J., 2007). Marslow and some other behavior psychologists stated that, the demands level that most of the people of a country are at in the hierarchy is in direct correlation with the development level of that country's economy, science and culture as well as people's education level. In under-developed countries, physiological and safety demands predominate, and the more advanced demands are restricted only to a minority of people. The contrary is true in the developed nations. Despite the big gap between the rich and the poor, with the increase in GDP per capita year on year, the pursuit for the quality of life and environment is becoming the theme of China's socioeconomic development. The improvement on the quality of life and environment needs the support of desirable cultural ecology and a healthy ecological system. In consequence, we need to protect and develop forest cultural ecology now, to make early planning and arrangement, in order to make forests meet the higher demands beyond resource economy. Consequently, in the future forest development, economic development is the core, forest ecology protection is the foundation, education first, and forest cultural ecology environment education is the key and soul.

Urban forest cultural ecology environment preservation education as the key

Forest industry has passed the stage of satisfying the demands for wood and forest products, multi-functional utilization of forest resources and forest ecology system management, and is taking forest cultural ecology preservation and development as the new direction for advancement. Following urbanization, urban forest becomes the key for cultural ecology protection. According to the statistics, China's urbanization rate has reached 46.59%, still leaving a great gap from the average 70% urbanization rate in world's developed countries (Zhang, Y., 2010). In accordance with the implicatures of cultural ecology preservation, alongside the protection and construction of historic, architectural neighborhood and green cultures, city view should also be emphasized, therefore, the cultural ecology environment preservation education is necessary.

Urban forest is an important part of urban infrastructure. Urban forest has the following roles to play in the urban cultural ecology preservation and development: firstly, bearing rich historical, cultural and social messages that has a significant impact on people's personality, quality and characteristics, or even the traits and spirituality of a nation. "Ten years to bring up a tree and ten years to bring up a person." Any city with deep rooted culture possesses ancient woods and famous trees, which are witnesses of transitions and historic events; the protection of which is the duties and responsibilities of city planners. Secondly, architectures are stone history books, which directly reflect the features of a city. Urban forest is the carrier of spirituality, liable to exhibit culture and upgrade functions of the city. Urban forest is the lifeline of a city, closely related to the life of the dwellers. Thirdly, urban forest is the carrier and proponent of green culture. Green color is an important constituent of a city's landscape and is also the major carrier of urban public arts. Many cities impress the tourists with their characteristic native breeds of trees and flowers. Green culture is an advanced culture, indicating the values of a city's material wealth production and the direction of a city's spiritual advancement, aiming to bring about the harmony between man and nature, among people, as well as within people themselves. The construction of city landscape can push the city with incessant momentum only when it carries green culture throughout. In the construction of city parks and public green lands, besides distributing sculptures, artifacts, road markers and trash bins that bear the city's humanity messages into the green, the cultivation of local breeds of tree is also important for keeping the culture. In the meantime, urban construction should reserve green land, water body, and wet land, balancing the relationship between construction and environmental protection hence creating good city and cultural ecology. With the speeding up of urbanization in China, the environmental preservation education of forest cultural ecology should play the central role, since it keeps the city life, exhibits the city's history and culture, develops green culture, and also supports the intrinsic spirit of the city.

Forest cultural ecology environment protection education should be included in forest legislation and management

It has become a universal consensus to protect ecological environment, forbid public hazard, and prevent pollution. However, ecological environment protection is not equal to cultural ecology protection. Therefore, it is necessary to first acknowledge the importance of cultural ecology protection and then legislate. Forestry Law can be based on ecology or cultural ecology, as well as on resource economy. The protection and construction of forest cultural ecology should begin with education, revision of Forestry Laws and solving the problems in setting the forest ecology and cultural ecology protection as the standard.

In management, education planning should be stressed to profile the organic integration of material and spiritual wealth, pursuing the harmony between man and nature, people and people, as well as people and themselves. At present, many cities have overlooked the functions of local breeds of trees and flowers in preservation education and development of cultural ecology, instead, transplanted southern breeds to the north or grown large areas of expensive foreign lawn turfs. All these represent violations of the rules of cultural ecology preservation, also damages the cultural ecology environment protection education. American architect Sharin once observed, "A city is an open book, from which you can see its aspirations. Let me see your city, and then I can tell what the inhabitants there are pursuing culturally". On the other hand, forests lacking cultural ecology protection and management are fragile forests without internal supporting spirits, grounding and soul, indicating an incomplete understanding of the management of forest ecological system, these will take some education.

Finally, strengthen the management of forest resources and promote the development of green culture. The overall management of forest resources does not only include expanding the area, but also include increasing the variety and quality. To solve the problem of supply and demand of wood and to meet the requirements of national economic development for forest products, it is necessary to improve forests' age structure, breed structure, productivity and utilization rate. Currently, many scholars are studying "ecology culture", "ecology civilization", and "green culture", etc., these are another important part of forest resource management and forest ecology preservation. Whatever the title, the core here is the integration of forest physical and spiritual production. This is the direction and momentum of forest resource production and management. In consequence, reinforcing forest resource management and propelling forest cultural ecology protection as well as green culture development are the direction of future forest resource management and the major content of perfecting forest ecological system regulation, forest cultural ecology environment protection education is an important step, and is the basic work.

Discussion

Forests have economic, ecological, social, and cultural functions. In recent years, the utilization and protection of forests' economic and ecological functions has advanced substantially, while the social and cultural functions are less developed in China, in particular, the forest cultural ecology environment protection education has not yet been under taken. Forest ecological preservation is considered by every society in the world as an important part of global environment protection, and the cultural ecology environment protection education is also part of environment protection. More recently, the importance of forestry has increased with the popularity of the concept of sustainable development and the important role played by the forest in carrying out the emission reduction goal of the Kyoto Protocol. Sustainable development also includes cultural sustainability and cultural sustainable development. In this context, we propose forest cultural ecology environment protection education to promote sustainable development of cultural environment, hoping that the proposal can be applied to other countries and regions. It may become a subject - the forest cultural ecology protection education, that in future we can make further worthy discussions and study.

Conclusions

To summarize with regard to future forest industry, the economic development is the core, ecology protection is the foundation, and the cultural ecology preservation is the key and soul, where forest cultural ecology environment protection education must be foremost. The socioeconomic development of China has entered a stage of maturity and consumption, therefore, the next stage is pursuing quality of life. This specific juncture requires forest cultural ecology to play a significant role, consequently, how to better preserve forest cultural ecology by means of legislation, planning and regulation are important projects ahead of us. The forest cultural ecology environment protection education should also be included on this agenda.

China has made substantial advancement in the management of forest resource and ecology. Forest cultural ecology protection and regulation related to "ecological culture "and "green culture" contribute a great deal to the improvement of residents' life quality as well as happiness index. Forest ecology needs to be protected, even more so are the preservation education and regulation of the cultural ecology of forests.

Acknowledgements

This research is funded by State Forestry Administration (Nos.200904003) and Ministry of Education (Nos. 09YJA910001), P. R. China. We thank Dr. Lloyd C. Irland at the School of F&ES, Yale University for editing an early version of this chapter, and Haron Jeremich for editing some parts of this chapter.

References

Cao, S. Socioeconomic road in ecological restoration in China. Environ. *Sci. Technol.*2010, 44,
5328-5329.
State Forestry Administration, P. R. China. *Yearbook of China's Forestry Statistics* (2009); China
Forestry Publishing House: Beijing, 2010.
State Statistical Bureau, P. R. China. *Yearbook of China Statistics* (2010); China Statistical
Publishing House: Beijing, 2010.
Zhang, C. & Luo J. The sustainable development of forest ecology preservation in the western
region. *Agricultural Economy* 2007, 10, 38-40.
Zhang, Y. *An Evaluation of the Environmental Benefits of China's Urban Forest*; China Forestry
Publishing House: Beijing, 2010.

12.6 Towards the development of a Green Economics Model (GEM) that benefits Africa's people and natural environment

Isayvani Naicker

Introduction: Green Economics and Africa

Current neoliberal economic approaches to economics, also commonly referred to as neoclassical, mainstream or orthodox, have seen the discipline change from political economy, formerly part of a moral philosophy critically involved with social issues, to a specialised scientific discipline fascinated by mathematical-deductivist modelling and increasingly removed from social concerns (Peet, 1999, Lawson 2003). New approaches too are returning to social issues, and also including concerns about ecological sustainability, social justice and distributional equity, in economics. Ecological and Green Economics approaches, are but two examples, where the aim is to bring back the social, and introduce environmental issues into the theory and practice of economics. Ecological economics is an example of such an approach that looks at the role of natural capital in achieving sustainable development and requires that the issue of sustainability versus efficiency be broadened, to include the goals of distributional equity (Lawn, 2007).

Green Economics provides an enlightened response to the shortcomings of current neoliberal economic approaches. It shifts away from the principle that stimulating economic growth will lead to human development, poverty alleviation and social upliftment. Current experience of growth centric neoclassical economic approaches, for example, those that promote the extraction of natural resources for the benefit of multi-national corporations, are failing Africa's people and environment. The aftermath of the global financial crisis is being felt by economies across the globe and part of the problem has been the pursuit of growth at the expense of safeguarding savings, while building social and maintaining natural capital. Green Economics is a new approach to economics that seeks to 'examine reality by means of multidisciplinary, complex, holistic, and very long term methods as well as to take into account the political and social aspects' (Kennet and Heinemann, 2007). It is an approach being developed by researchers at the Green Economics Institute in the United Kingdom in partnership with colleagues from around the world (including from the developing world). Green Economics approaches choose a focus on equity alongside growth, and propose a more 'holistic approach' that requires 'economics focuses on environmental and social equity. A Green Economics approach offers

314

considerable benefits for the sustainable use of Africa's natural wealth for the benefit of its people.

While at the national level African governments and people face the challenge of eradicating poverty experienced by a large proportion of African people, at the international level they face a concomitant challenge to conserve the wealth of biodiversity that is contained within Africa's natural environment, for the benefit of all future generations of people. The Millennium Ecosystem Assessment conveyed the message starkly, when it noted in its 2005 report, that many people have benefited over the last century from the conversion of natural ecosystems to human-dominated ecosystems and from the exploitation of biodiversity. However, at the same time, these gains have been achieved at growing costs in the form of losses in biodiversity, degradation of many ecosystem services, and the exacerbations of poverty for other groups of people (MEA, 2005). The need for development in Africa is unquestionable. But instead of following, Africa has the opportunity to lead by embracing alternative approaches to economic development that prioritises people and nature. Green Economics, as a proposed alternative approach to development, is the focus of this paper.

1 The need for alternative approaches to development in Africa

In "Development as Freedom" Sen (2000) conceptualised development as the expansion of human capabilities that places human well being at the centre of economics and development. To reorient development towards human wellbeing there is a need to reclaim development. In "reclaiming development" there is a need to consider economic approaches and policy alternatives that challenge the existing "neoliberal orthodoxy" which has dominated discussions of development policy during the last quarter of a century(Chang and IGabrel, 2004; Soludu et al 2004)). The intellectual crisis facing neoliberal economics is captured in the hopeful and critical works 'Reorienting Economics" (Lawson, 2003) 'Economics for the Future' (Kiston, 2005) and the impatient and rebellious 'Death of Economics' (Omerod, 1994). These works provide insights into the shortcomings and failures of the current neoliberal economic model and presents thinking to stimulate, and ideas to develop, in alternate approaches to development following more heterodox economic traditions, for example, post Keynesianism, feminist economics, new institutionalism (Ostrom), Marxian economics and social economics amongst others.

In developing these ideas the individual experiences of different African countires on their path to development need to be considered. They incorporate a broad range of cultural, natural, political and economic diversity in over fifty countries and five regional economic communities spanning Africa. This paper does not attempt to summarily characterise, or generalise their experiences, or make national comparisons and overviews of country experiences. The common feature in most countries in Africa is that they are faced with balancing green (conservation and use of biodiversity, genetic resources, ecosystems services, natural resources) and brown (access to sanitation, water, health, education, jobs) issues in their development agenda. There are many case studies, books and research papers that focus on different aspects of Africa, continentally, regionally and by country. These include its changing geography (Chapman and Baker, 1992), politics of economic recovery (Sandbrook, 1993); democracy (Diamond et al 1998), politics of trade and industrial policy (Charles Soludu et al ,2004); economic change, governance and natural resource wealth (Reed, 2001); greening (Harrison, 1987) and management of sustainable development (Patrick Fitzgerald et al,1995) and others. These are a small selection amongst the many books that offer African and regional and country analysis and overviews. A range of multilateral donor agency websites contains issues and strategy papers and case study reports focusing on regions and individual countries in Africa. These include the UNDP (Human Development Reports), the World Banks Poverty Reduction and Strategy papers, and the UNICEF and UNDP African Environmental Outlook, the Convention on Biological Diversities National Biodiversity Strategy and Action Plans (NBSAPs), amongst others.

In balancing green and brown issues in the development of countries in Africa, Green Economics offers a welcome alternative perspective. It is recognised that the diversity of socio-economic and environmental and political situations and the specificity of issues in different countries do entail future development of Green Economics and other approaches that are appropriate and relevant to the particular situation in the different country and regions of Africa. These require country specific case studies looking at social, environmental and economic issues and how Green Economics approaches, in contrast to neoclassical approaches to economics, will realise benefits for biodiversity and people of the particular African country. This is future work that needs to be done for Green Economics to demonstrate how it is a holistic approach' that ensures 'economics focuses on environmental and social equity'. Necessary future work will include developing appropriate Green Economics methodology and tools, applying them in specific case studies and analysing the impacts of this alternate approach. This paper recognises the need for alternate approaches like Green Economics, which focus on both social and environmental equity as necessary for development, as well suited to the special needs of Africa. The aim, therefore, is to present the case for Green Economics in Africa, take a look at some practical cases studies that can benefit from Green Economics Approaches, and suggest alternative development models to guide Green Economics research in Africa. The development of a more comprehensive Green Economics research agenda, and practical case study applications and evaluations in Africa need to be developed as part of future collaborative projects and programmes with scientists and researchers from the continent.

2. The paradox of natural wealth and human poverty is Africa

The five regions of the African continent are divided into fifty-three countries with a varied distribution of natural resources, socio-economic development and gross domestic product. The Southern, Central, East, West and North of Africa are recognised as regional economic and political communities within Africa (NEPAD, 2001; Chapman and Baker, 1992, Africa Environmental Outlook, 2006). International reports refer to the four regions, minus predominantly Arabic North Africa, as Sub-Saharan Africa (SSA). Table 1 outlines the estimate and projection of change in population size, over four decades between 1980 to 2020 across the five regions of Africa. In terms of population size the largest is West Africa and the smallest is Central Africa. The impact of HIV/AIDS may be the largest contributing factor to the decrease in population size in Southern Africa from fourteen percent of total population in 2000 to thirteen percent in 2020. The World Conference on Environment and Development noted that in Africa, every year the number of people increases, but the amount of natural resources with which to sustain this population, to improve the quality of lives and to eliminate poverty remain finite (WCED, 1987). Three decades later, the Millennium Ecosystem Assessment found that sixty percent of global ecosystem services are used unsustainably and concluded that "any progress achieved in addressing the goals of poverty and hunger eradication, improved health, and environmental protection is unlikely to be sustained if most of the ecosystem services on which humanity relies continue to be degraded" (MEA, 2005). There is a cumulative relationship between population growth and poverty and between ecosystem degradation and poverty in Africa.

Table 1 Population changes in Africa (millions)

Sub-Region	1980	1990	2000	2010	2020
North Africa	109	140	170	209	239
East Africa	104	141	182	230	269
Southern Africa	70	90	113	129	150
Central Africa	54	74	98	127	164
West Africa	132	178	234	278	344
Total Africa	469	623	797	973	1 166

Source: FAO 2003. [Data from World Bank 2002; Africa Development Bank, 2000]

3. Green Economics Approaches : Towards conserving Natural Resource Wealth and alleviating Poverty

Green Economics approaches are being positioned to 'reclaim economics' for the benefit of people and nature and in the process allow nature and people to be better positioned as the central focus of economic models and methodologies, to come up with win-win solutions. The ecological/economic and moral problems identified and addressed in Green Economics (see Table 4) are a good starting point towards which development in Africa can reorient itself. Green Economics offers Africa a way of looking at economic development that puts long-term human development and nature conservation before short-term company profits. Sustainable development that balances ecological, economic and social goals is vital for Africa. In the developing countries of Africa the Millennium Development Goals serve as a framework for continued human development (Table 3). In the developed world the Conventions of Biological Diversity and other Multilateral and National Environmental Agreement serve as the framework for containing a myriad of environmental impacts resulting from decades of unconstrained economic development.

Some environmental costs of rapid industrialisation in the developed North include increased carbon dioxide emissions threatening all planetary systems through global warming, large-scale biodiversity loss and species extinction. For the countries of Africa, and other developing and least developing countries (economies) in the global South, development and the task of meeting the human dimensions of the MDG's, is constrained by the need to meet the goal of environmental sustainability. It is important to emphasise that environmental sustainability was notably lacking as a goal when human and economic development of the current developed nations, notably the group of eight most developed countries (G8), was at its peak. The paradox is that it is up to underdeveloped and developing countries in Africa to undertake the especially challenging tasks required to maintain biodiversity and ensure environmental sustainability, reduce poverty and ensure human development.

The latest reports on Africa's progress towards the MDGS, including the environmental sustainability goal, show that the rich natural resource base is being depleted. The continent is losing its natural resources at a relatively faster pace than other regions. Its wildlife population of rich and unique species of animals and plants is coming under increasing pressure. Forests are being depleted at a rate of about 1.3 million hectares every year. An estimated 500 million hectares of land, including about 65 per cent of agricultural land, has been affected by soil erosion since 1950. The coral reefs and mangroves on the Western Indian Ocean, wetlands and other sensitive natural systems share similar losses and pressure. On the positive side, Africa's share of global carbon dioxide emission into the atmosphere is only 3.5 percent (ECA, 2005). The natural resource wealth of African countries is being put under pressure while very little impact is being made in the continent's record in moving towards the Millennium Development Goals. This is evidence that the current economic model is failing Africa's natural environment and its people.

3. The biodiversity and poverty trap

The poverty trap that characterises Africa and the structural conditions and history that are responsible for this experience are elaborated by Jeffery Sachs (2004). He stresses that Africa needs development (economic and social) and key investments and development assistance could enable Africa to meet the MDGs (see Table 3), and to extricate Africa from its current development crisis. The unique insights offered by Green

318

Economics to the ecological and economic and the moral problems and issues that face humanity and how to address them (Kennet and Heinemann, 2007), outlined in Table 4, are relevant for African development needs. They offer a 'rethinking', and 'reorienting' of the way we do science and economics, so that science and development achieves development goals for the benefit of people in social systems, while conserving natural resources in ecological systems. Ecological and economic insights that highlight people and biosphere as beneficiaries and not outputs, diversity of economic policies, focus and education and value of all people and moral insights that focus in development as freedom and social and environmental justice, are emphasised.

The promise of Green Economics is that it focuses on ecological and economic problem as operating on the principle that the needs of people and natural systems must be simultaneously satisfied. There is a need, therefore, to redefine progress in economics to mean that both these requirements are met. The 2010 biodiversity target of a substantial reduction in the rate of loss of biological diversity can be seen is a moral commitment. There is also moral commitment to eradicate poverty for the one-fifth of the earth's 6.3 billion people that are trapped in life threatening poverty (Sachs, 2005) through the achievement of the United Nations Millennium Development Goals (Table 3) by 2015.

The challenge for researcher, politicians and practitioners is to develop, adopt and apply alternative economic models. In many cases, areas of high poverty and biodiversity cluster together. Poor regions of the world, including many countries in Africa, now face the double burden of preventing species extinction and biodiversity loss; and alleviating poverty and achieving the MDG's. Economic development to address human needs in an era of increased focus on conservation and protection of the environment is a daunting task. It requires new approaches that value social and environmental equity, are holistic and multidisciplinary, and put people and nature first. Green Economics is describing itself as bringing together approaches that embrace these characteristics. Development, adoption and analysis of Green Economics methodologies to specific case study problems and issues in countries in Africa are needed. This case study experience will help to evolve a distinctive Green Economics methodology and basic concepts for the African situation.

Table 4 Green Economics distinctive methodology and basic concepts

	Ecological/Economic	Moral
Problem/Issue	Resources of the planet being depleted. Carrying capacity of the earth compromised. Species extinction.	World Poverty. Inadequate markets, corruption and crime. Non-beneficial trade rules and trade. Achievement of the Millennium development goals.
Green Economics Methodology	Limits to Growth Ecology and Nature Emphasis on appropriate size of scale of production	Regional and locally diverse and democratic solutions. Analysis of power relations and institutions. Local wealth creation. Local economic development. Economic growth and development.
Green Economics Unique insights	Change in behaviour, appropriate consumption. Focus on education and value of all people. Needs, rights and equity met for all people. Access to economic opportunities and choice. Diversity of economic policies. Lack of dogma and domination by structures, ideologies and institutions. Growth equals abundance as in nature. See people and biosphere as beneficiaries not outputs. Inclusive of people, planet, biosphere.	Priority given to ending poverty and enabling equity rather than through same patterns of industrialisation and development or conventional growth. Reform of global institutions to reflect specific local conditions, requirements and individual choices by people and communities. Social and environmental justice. Development as freedom,

Adapted from Kennet and Heinemann (2007)

4. Some Practical Cases for Green Economics Approaches

The challenge facing African countries is to embrace economic development to fulfil the basic needs and alleviate the poverty of people while conserving the wealth of natural resources and biodiversity. Economic growth as a panacea for achieving human development is failing. The current global financial crisis highlights the failure of neoclassical economic approaches in achieving financial development and security of the countries economic wealth system. The dismal record in achieving the MDG's in many countries' records the failure of economic approaches in achieving human development and social upliftment. The dire state of ecosystems and their services as highlighted by the MEA (2005) is a result of the failure of these economic systems in ensuring environmental sustainability and inter generational equity. There is little in Africa's current dynamics that promotes an escape from poverty according to Sachs (2005). Caught in a poverty trap and with very low domestic savings and low rate of market based foreign capital inflows, to a significant extent, Africa is living off of its natural capital but counting the resource depletion as income (Sachs et al, 2004). The need for a new dynamic in Africa, that encourage the sustainable use of natural capital and promotes an escape from poverty, will require alternatives to the current economic approaches. Specific case study areas show that alternatives, like Green Economics approaches, can be applied and include areas such as agriculture and food security, climate change and global warming, biodiversity management and species extinction. The interdependence of these issues, where global warming is leading to food insecurity and to biodiversity loss, is suited to Green Economics interdisciplinary approaches.

Green Economics distinctive methodology, basic concepts

	Ecological/Economy	Moral
Problem/Issue	Resources of the planet being depleted. Carrying capacity of the earth compromised. Species extinction.	World Poverty. Inadequate markets, corruption and crime. Non-beneficial trade rules and trade. Achievement of the Millennium development goals.
Green Economics Methodology	Limits to Growth Ecology and Nature Emphasis on appropriate size of scale of production	Regional and locally diverse and democratic solutions. Analysis of power relations and institutions. Local wealth creation. Local economic development. Economic growth and development.
Green Economics Unique insights See people and biosphere as beneficiaries not outputs. Inclusive of people, planet, biosphere.	Change in behaviour, appropriate consumption. Focus on education and value of all people. Needs, rights and equity met for all people. Access to economic opportunities and choice. Diversity of economic policies. Lack of dogma and domination by structures, ideologies and institutions. Growth equals abundance as in nature.	Priority given to ending poverty and enabling equity rather than through same patterns of industrialisation and development or conventional growth. Reform of global institutions to reflect specific local conditions, requirements and individual choices by people and communities. Social and environmental justice. Development as freedom,

Adapted from Kennet and Heinemann (2007)

322

4. Climate Change

The impact of global warming, according to the Third Assessment Report of the IPCC and other studies, is being felt most by the world's poorest people, particularly those in Africa (IPCC, 2001). Africa contains about 20% of all known species of plants, mammals, and birds in the world, as well as one-sixth of amphibians and reptiles, all of which are contained in several centres of endemism (Siegfried 1989). Biodiversity in Africa is under threat from multiple stresses, which alongside climate change, include increasing land-use conversion and subsequent destruction of habitat; pollution; the introduction of exotic (non-native) species, land-use conversion from wild habitat to agricultural, grazing and logging uses, all of which leads to habitat loss and fragmentation (Nyong, 2005). The increasing impact of climate change may exacerbate the existing stress on environmental systems beyond recovery (Desanker, 2003). The heavy direct dependence on natural resources in Africa, make many poor communities vulnerable to the biodiversity loss that could result from climate change. The impact of climate change will be catastrophic for countries in Africa, even though they contribute the least to total carbon dioxide emissions per year. Figure 2 shows the emissions of carbon dioxide in Africa, compared to selected OECD countries. It indicates that Africa represents only a small fraction, 3.6%, out of the total carbon dioxide (CO_2) emissions per year, yet 14% of the population of the world lives on the continent. Within Africa the emissions per inhabitant in Libya, the Seychelles and South Africa are on the level of the lowest among OECD countries, with the other African countries trailing lower behind them. In the region, emissions (both per capita and in total) are at their highest in North Africa and in the country of South Africa.

Natural ecosystems are an important resource for African people. Their uses are consumptive (food, fiber, fuel, shelter, medicine, wildlife trade) and non-consumptive (ecosystem services and the economically important tourism industry) (Desanker, 2003). Loss of biodiversity results in serious reductions in the goods (such as food, medicine and raw materials) and services (such as clean water and nutrient cycling) that the earth's ecosystems can provide and that make human survival and economic prosperity possible (IPCC, 2001). Poor people, the majority of whom are in Africa, are often directly dependent on goods and services from ecosystems, either as a primary or supplementary source of food, fodder, building materials, and fuel. As a result of this dependency, any impact that climate change has on natural systems threatens the livelihoods, food intake and health of poor people (Reid, 2004).

Climate change will mean that many semi-arid parts of Africa may become even hotter and drier, with even less predictable rainfall. Climate-induced changes to crop yields, ecosystem boundaries and species' ranges will dramatically affect livelihoods of the predominantly poor in sub-Saharan Africa. This is because they live in areas more prone to extreme climatic events, such as flooding, cyclones, and droughts, and because they have little individual capacity and minimal state support to adapt to such shocks. This makes them highly vulnerable to ecosystem degradation, which further reinforces their poverty (IPCC, 2001; Gitay et al., 2002).

323

Studying the impacts of climate change on ecosystem productivity in Lake Tanganyika, East Africa ,O'Reilly et al (2003) present compelling evidence that climate warming is diminishing productivity in Lake Tanganyika. Lake Tanganyika is one of the world's great freshwater ecosystems. It is the second deepest lake and second largest by volume (after Lake Baikal), the second largest tropical lake by surface area (after Lake Victoria), and holds the second greatest biological diversity (after Lake Baikal). They outline that the lake has historically supported a highly productive pelagic fishery that currently provides 25–40% of the animal protein supply for the populations of the surrounding countries. Carbon isotope records in sediment cores suggest that primary productivity may have decreased by about 20%, implying a roughly 30% decrease in fish yields. The evidence O'Reilly et al (2003) shows that the impact of regional effects of global climate change on aquatic ecosystem functions and services in Lake Tanganyika can be larger than that of local anthropogenic activity or over-fishing.

5. Development Models for African Green Economics

Green Economics approaches address four categories of ecological/economic, intellectual, political and moral problems and represent the diverse issues that Africa has to address simultaneously. The traditional view is that Africa needs economic growth. Sen (2002) suggests that to focus on income growth as a measure of wealth is limited, and calls for a focus on what he calls capabilities, which are substantive human freedoms. He argues for a broad view of freedom, that encompasses both processes and opportunities, and for recognition of "the heterogeneity of distinct components of freedom". This broad view of development is sought in order to focus the evaluative scrutiny on things that "really matter" and in particular, to avoid the neglect of crucially important subjects. The natural wealth and human poverty of Africa really matters, and requires this broad view of development that focuses evaluative scrutiny on people and nature. A measure of wealth, where the endowments of nature and capabilities of people are measures towards progress, and not the merely increase gross income of individuals and gross domestic product of countries, is urgently needed in Africa.

African and other countries in the global South are following an industrialized countries model of development, focusing on economic growth as a panacea to poverty eradication and human development. They are subscribing to the myth that the 'neoliberal American model of capitalism represents the ideal that all developing countries should seek to replicate'. This is one of the six myths and realities that reclaiming development lays bare (Chang and Grabel, 2004). Holistic and alternative approaches, such as Development (Chang and Grabel, 2004) and Green (Kennet and Heineman, 2006) Economics are taking what Sen (2002) calls an "an adequately broad view of development" by addressing itself to the four main categories of environmental problems, the ecological/economic, intellectual, political and moral problems. These alternative   approaches are part of another development and the shaping of a new economics framework.

Table 5   **Research questions and themes for Green Economics in Africa**

Key knowledge gaps which need to be tackled:
- **Where the poor live** – in relation to environmental assets and problems
- **Wealth accounts** – environmental assets / damage; household use
- **Biodiversity benefits** (resilience) – and who benefits
- **Resource rights** – for different environmental assets – and why some common property regimes work and adapt better
- **Subsidies** – environmental effects of subsidies for water, fisheries etc, and their distribution

Conclusion

Approaches to economics and conservation of biodiversity, as if people matter, (Schumacher, 1973; Madhav. 1992) are important both in Africa, and globally. The immediate need on the African continent is economic development to break out of the cycle of poverty and underdevelopment. Biological diversity and environmental assets are important, as the sustainable use of these assets are crucial to the livelihoods of current and future generations of African people. Therefore, conserving biological diversity as a resource for future and present generations is an important part of Africa's development.

Radical new approaches to economics and development are required to steer the African continent on a path of sustainable growth and development and to protect the natural resource endowment that is the wealth of the people. A Green Economics approach that 'reclaims economics and development', encourages scientific innovation and intellectual advancement, has political commitment and takes forward the development of people, is such a radical new approach.

To advance approaches that tackle these demanding multidisciplinary goals, the involvement and collaboration of African economists and scientists in the emerging discipline of Green Economics, will enable 'innovative, holistic and long term' win-win solutions to be developed and tested to move Africa from wealth and poverty to wealth and wealth.

The success of the Green Economics project in Africa will also depend on its delivery of the many promises it makes and remaining committed to the ecological and economic, political, intellectual and moral issues it raises, the development of the methodologies and concepts to address them and advancing and operationalising some of the unique insights.

Photos
Upper: The Economics of peace and tranquility:
Our favourite part of Brussels
Lower: Grit Silberstein, Green Economics Institute
Economist, Galapagos and Germany.

Miriam Kennet 2010